PRACTICAL PROJECT MANAGEMENT:

RESTORING QUALITY TO DP PROJECTS AND SYSTEMS

PRACTICAL PROJECT MANAGEMENT:

RESTORING QUALITY TO DP PROJECTS AND SYSTEMS

MEILIR PAGE-JONES
FOREWORD BY ROB THOMSETT

Dorset House Publishing, 353 W. 12th St., New York, N.Y. 10014

Library of Congress Cataloging in Publication Data

Page-Jones, Meilir.
  Practical project management.

  Bibliography: p.
  Includes index.
  1. Electronic data processing departments—Management.
I. Title.
HF5548.2.P252   1985   004'.068   85-71101
ISBN 0-932633-00-5 (pbk.)

Printed in the United States of America

Library of Congress Catalog Number 85-71101

ISBN: 0-932633-00-5

Other Titles Available
from Dorset House Publishing Co.

Preface

For most of the history of the data processing industry, we have been beset by technical problems. For example, we have continually underestimated the difficulties involved in developing sophisticated software systems. At last, however, we have now begun to win the war against the worst of our technical difficulties.

But as our technical problems have waned in importance, the significance of other problems has become painfully obvious. Chief among these problems is that of poor management: A single incompetent manager can quickly nullify the productivity of a dozen technical virtuosos.

As a DP consultant, I've visited dozens of commercial shops, both good and bad, and I've observed scores of data processing managers, again, both good and bad. Too often, I've watched in horror as these managers futilely struggled through nightmarish projects, squirmed under impossible deadlines, or delivered systems that outraged their users and went on to devour huge chunks of maintenance time.

Think about your own shop. How many times have upper managers applauded themselves for economizing and, in the process, deprived your department of vital resources (just as a person wanting to lose weight might cut off his right arm)? How many times have users ordered projects that bore no relation to the company's true needs, or to one another? How many times have you seen solid, long-term benefits sacrificed on the altar of immediate gratification? How often have your fellow managers, bending to political pressure, succumbed to truth decay and modified project status reports, timesheets, and reviews so as to soothe the nerves of upper managers? Has the importance of looking good replaced doing a good job as the primary criterion of excellence and reward in your shop? If your answers are "frequently" to the first questions and "yes" to the last one, you work in a shop where superficial considerations gain precedence over solid worth.

Our industry is an industry within all industries. The quality of a company's DP department affects the quality of the entire company, no matter what business that company is in. If indeed the shop's thin, superficial coating wears through to expose the base interior, no longer can cosmetics protect the deteriorating foundation. It is time for serious repair work to prevent the fragile state of the data processing department from damaging the whole company.

Practical Project Management is not an abstract or theoretical book, nor is it an attempt to sell another newfangled software technique. It is partly an indictment of everyday practices in many data processing departments, and it is partly a call to arms—a call to fight for management quality and to win that war, just as we are winning the war for improved technical quality.

Sometimes, it is easy to despair as you see ineffective methods of management handed down from manager to weary manager, with the attitude, "We've always done things this way (and so we always will)." I recall what the manager of a large shop once said: "What you say about quality makes sense, but I'm afraid we don't have time for quality here, because we have to spend too much time maintaining garbage systems from ten years ago." When I hear a statement like this, I feel that working toward management quality is like trying to swim while being tied to a jukebox. Yet, if data processing is to reach a healthy maturity, we must continue our battle for more effective management at all levels.

About the book

Practical Project Management contains three sections. Section I sets forth the true business of the data processing department: to serve the corporation as a whole. It examines the necessity of using the finite resources of the DP shop in the most cost-effective way and the importance of uniting the efforts of data processing and corporate management to improve the corporation's business through an integrated series of well-merited DP projects.

Section II delves into the turmoil of the project itself, exploring the problems that arise from poor project management, unrealistic and almighty project deadlines, absence of project standards, worthless reporting methods, unproductive meetings, and meaningless project reviews. Although each of these faults can seem harmless enough, together they spell the project's doom and eventually relegate the shop to the realm of mediocrity.

Section III addresses the ailments of staff management in a data processing department. It discusses ways in which to increase the effectiveness of employees by establishing good hiring and training policies and by eliminating pernicious dismissals and intolerable working conditions. This section concludes with the important issue of maintaining a constructive attitude toward your job and your colleagues in order to build a better future.

Although I believe that we can all do more to improve the standard of management, I'm not so naive as to believe in the attainment of perfection. After all, the world in general and our own mercurial industry in particular is never standing still. Problems change, problems go away—only to be replaced by new problems; old problems return; solutions to problems turn out themselves to be problems. Through it all, the unpredictability of human nature will always upset our most carefully devised plans. As Disraeli said, "No sooner has Mr. Gladstone understood the Irish question, than the Irish change the question."

Good management requires constant vigilance over an ever-shifting topography of obstacles. Nevertheless, I do believe in the pursuit of perfection as both a laudable and realistic aim for a manager. Indeed, there can be no other aim; for the alternative leads to an emaciation of quality and finally to a complete withering away of achievement.

Do not dismiss the quest for high-quality service to your users and to your company's business as being too idealistic. That is defeatist talk, which is the first and last step in the capitulation to the forces of mediocrity. Instead, grasp every opportunity to rout the enemies of quality. Go for it!

April 1985   M.P.J.
Federal Way, Washington

Foreword

Project management has rarely received the attention it deserves, and particularly within the computing profession, it has been overshadowed by the battles within the technological arena: Manufacturer versus manufacturer, development language versus development language, mainframe versus micro, operating system versus operating system are the stuff from which great legends are born and great leaders emerge as role models.

Pity the humble project manager who manages to bring the general ledger system in on time, within budget, and working to the users' satisfaction. Where is his or her day of glory in the business and trade press?

At last, there is a book to treat the topic properly. Meilir Page-Jones's *Practical Project Management* is about those managers and about a problem that has been around from the first days of computing. That problem is the management of software development and of the people who, at least for the near future, undertake the increasingly complex technical tasks involved in software development.

Perhaps one reason that project management has been such a lasting and critical problem is that the answers are so simple to articulate and understand, yet so complex to implement and effect. Let's face it: All we need for successful project management are some plans, some objectives, some consensus, a few good people, and some time; but somehow, it never is that easy when you get to a real project. Indeed, I wonder if, in our genetic makeup, the rational planning genes were left out to make our lives as project managers more exciting as our projects lurch from disaster to disaster.

I am sure that you agree that what really is exciting is the professional satisfaction of a successful project. It is the achievement of that goal for which this book is written. *Practical Project Management* contains many simple truths that will assist project managers in their professional roles. More importantly, it also contains many complex insights into the more challenging issues of applying those truths in a highly competitive and changing business world.

What *Practical Project Management* has to say will be as relevant regardless of the manufacturer or operating system that emerges the victor.

It is the simple truth.

April 1985
Sydney, Australia

Rob Thomsett

Acknowledgments

I have been influenced and inspired by so many people in my data processing career that to try to list everyone who has shaped my ideas would be to invite invidious errors and omissions. Nevertheless, there are three people who deserve my special thanks: first, Suzanne Page-Jones, for encouraging me through numerous setbacks, for suggesting many improvements to the manuscript, and for generally putting up with me for so long.

Second, Bill Stark, the "consultant's consultant," for helping me to harden some of my ideas by subjecting them to the fierce heat of his intellect. Third, Dr. Phiroze Kapadia, my former physics tutor, whose wisdom, love for humanity, and appreciation of the universe I shall remember always.

I also thank Jacob Lasky and Susan Moran for their work on previous incarnations of this book and, of course, the staff of Dorset House Publishing for wading through my manuscript with a fine-tooth comb in order to ferret out mixed metaphors and sundry other infelicities. I particularly sympathize with Janice Wormington, who at times found herself up to her neck in allegories, arcane allusions, and alarming alliteration. Thank you all.

Contents

PRACTICAL PROJECT MANAGEMENT:

RESTORING QUALITY TO DP PROJECTS AND SYSTEMS

SECTION I

Data Processing Serving the Corporation

Users. The very word is guaranteed to send a chill of animosity through many data processing managers and analysts and a shiver of apathy down the spines of most designers and programmers. Yet, it is the users—or, rather, the business of the users' corporation—that keep the DP department in business. Why are the relations between user departments and DP departments so fragile? Why have DP projects, even the so-called successful ones, failed to provide adequate service to the corporation as a whole?

The four chapters that follow address this dichotomy between the service desired and the service provided. In Chapter 1, the qualities of a truly successful project are defined and criteria are offered for establishing a project's priorities and for determining the most crucial sections of a project when time or money are in short supply. Chapter 2 explores the techniques and difficulties of making three essential estimates: those of resources, costs, and benefits.

Chapter 3 discusses how even successful projects, if considered only in isolation from one another, will lead in the long term to a paralysis of continuing DP service to the corporation's business. In the final chapter of this section, a four-step strategy is proposed for initiating projects as a way both to serve the corporation's business and to avoid the gradual encroachment of chaos.

1

Achieving Cost-Effective Projects

Let me begin this book with a startling statement: A project may be doomed to failure even before it begins. How can this be? The answer lies in my definition of *failure:* A data processing project is a failure if it does not result in a tangible, cost-effective improvement to the users' business.

In *The Politics of Projects,* Block made almost this same point when he said, "Users don't want projects; they want systems." [Block, 1983]. Fair enough, but why not take this observation to its logical conclusion: Users don't want systems; they want cost-effective business solutions. In this chapter, I examine precisely what it means for a project to be cost-effective.

1.1 Three measures of a project's success

Many companies initiate DP projects in highly unscientific ways and for the most unsatisfactory reasons. For example, a project may be initiated when unbridled enthusiasm carries the day ("Wouldn't it be great if we automated our intercompany charge-back procedures!"). Or, perhaps the squeaky wheel reason is used: "Okay, Jerry, this is the ninety-third time you've asked if we can do the NUDZH project. I guess this time I have to say yes just to get rid of you." A third less-than-satisfactory reason may be more political than anything else: "I met with the VP of production and some of her staff, who are really up for a production planning system project. I'm meeting with Pendergast Snodwhistle tomorrow to get his final okay." (It seems that this project is being established more for someone's political aggrandizement than for sound business reasons.)

In contrast, I know of several projects that were initiated for fairly sound reasons but that turned out to be losers. I don't mean that the projects collapsed spectacularly; I mean that the projects upon completion produced less than they cost. The reason for such a negative return on project investment is usually a failure at the start to make three important estimates: the cost of the project, the benefit to be yielded by the project, and the resources available to carry out the project. I mentally picture these three as a triangle (see Figure 1.1). In order for a project to be cost-effective and feasible, the project must yield benefits that exceed its costs and must not entail costs that exceed available resources.

Thus, each side of the triangle—benefits versus costs, resources versus costs, and benefits versus resources—must be analyzed before you delve seriously into a project. Since these measurements are crucial to a project's success, I discuss them in some detail in the sections below.

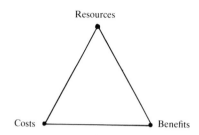

Figure 1.1. The costs-benefits-resources triangle.

1.1.1 Benefits versus costs

The following barroom hustle illustrates the relationship between benefits and costs: Walk up to someone who's drinking a martini. Place a bowl over his glass (an empty pretzel bowl or a clean ashtray will do). Then, bet the martini drinker a quarter that you can drink the martini without moving the bowl or even touching it in any way. After some pondering, most people will accept this bet.

Calmly remove the bowl, drink the martini, announce that you were mistaken, and hand over a quarter. It's not every day that you drink a 25-cent martini. (Of course, you *may* also be violently ejected from the bar.)

The error that your pigeon invariably makes is that he fails to do a cost-benefit analysis of the bet.[1] If he loses the bet, he will be out 25 cents. If he wins it, he will be ahead 25 cents but down one martini. His best bet in this heads-you-win, tails-he-loses kind of wager is not to accept the bet at all.[2]

Similarly, calculating the ratio of the benefit of your project to its cost is extremely important. If the benefit doesn't significantly exceed the cost, your users would be better off putting their money into another project (or into the local bank, for that matter). Although this concept is eminently reasonable, I am surprised at how often DP project managers and users alike almost entirely ignore benefits in their obsession with costs. But who can blame them? Most of the literature on DP project estimation dwells on costs. The traditional wrangle between DP project managers and users is over costs. No wonder that users become impatient with these managers, because all the users hear about are costs: analysis costs, hardware costs, operations costs, cost overruns, and on and on. Before long, the users may believe that a project entails only costs and no benefits. (In this aspect, at least, data processing challenges the claim of economics to be the dismal science.)

A more balanced approach is to include consideration of potential project benefits so they can be compared to project costs. How is this done? Project benefits are measured by assessing improvements to the users' business, either through the removal of a business problem or the exploitation of a business opportunity. Project benefits fall into four broad categories: first, increasing revenue (for example, by selling imperfect goods that would otherwise be scrapped to customers who will pay less for lower-quality merchandise); second, reducing business costs (say, by establishing an electronic communication system that enables a company to relocate its offices

---

[1]Throughout the book, the pronoun "he" means "he" or "she."

[2]However, he might not have been a dupe at all, reasoning that despite what he lost, he would nevertheless gain some invaluable barroom education. At least, that's how I rationalized my gullibility when I was fooled by this trick.

to lower-rent areas); third, improving customer service (for instance, by providing every bank customer with round-the-clock access to withdrawals and balance information on his account); and, fourth, satisfying inflexible requirements (by meeting a government banking regulation to report every cash deposit over a certain amount made by nonresident aliens, for instance).

In sum, then, a true benefit to the users' business results in an increase in the users' competitiveness in some way. Quantifying the increase in dollar amounts, of course, is difficult to do (as I discuss in Chapter 2). However, rather than continually harping on costs, you as the DP project manager should defy tradition and collaborate with your users in working out firm figures. At the very least, list each benefit in as much detail as possible and add the figures later to come up with a total amount of benefit.

1.1.2 Resources versus costs

The second side of the triangle to consider is the resources versus costs side. No matter how great the promise of a project is, if your users can't afford the project, they shouldn't approve the project. Also, if there is no one to do the project, the users must either go elsewhere or forgo the opportunity.

Of course, real life is rather more complex than this. Users typically have some money in their budget and can often get more money if they prove a valid need for it. You as a DP manager typically have some people available and usually can hire more people if you show a true need. Proving the need depends upon the triangle's third side, benefits versus resources.

1.1.3 Benefits versus resources

Almost everyone is faced with having more opportunities to spend money than having money to spend. Users are no different from everyone else in that respect; they have a finite amount of capital and limited opportunities to make capital improvements to their business.

Since a company's resources are not infinite, they must be carefully apportioned among projects to realize the greatest overall benefit over cost. Initiate a project only if it represents a good capital investment of the company's resources.

Table 1.1
Comparison of Benefits and Costs for Five Projects

	Project Name				
	A	B	C	D	E
Benefits (in millions)	$10	$35	$20	$30	$150
Costs (in millions)	$12	$15	$10	$12	$ 50

A simple example of how costs, benefits, and resources can work together will illustrate this point. Suppose that you have analyzed the benefits and costs of five potential projects, as shown in Table 1.1. Which ones would you initiate? First, without even considering your resources, you can eliminate project A, because it's not cost-effective. Clearly, if you had just $10 million, you could do only project C. What if you had $15 million? Project B would yield an absolute surplus benefit of $20 million (compared to project D's $18 million), but project D would yield a gross return on investment (ROI) of 2.5 to 1 (as opposed to B's 2.3 to 1). To choose between B and D ideally requires a decision by the company's accountants, financial strategists, and upper management.

What about project E, the tastiest looking project of all, with a benefit of $100 million and a gross ROI of 3 to 1? Project E would be splendid if the users could afford it. Even if they couldn't, they may well be able to break it into smaller, more affordable portions, possibly even using the benefit of one portion to finance other portions. Breaking a project into pieces that are independent in terms of the benefits offered to the company's business is called *itemization*. It is the subject of the remainder of the chapter. (In Chapter 2, I return to the topic of the relationships between various potential projects in terms of the users' overall business.)

1.2 Itemization of costs, benefits, and resources

So far, the discussion has considered projects as a whole, each with a single cost and a single benefit. If every project addressed a single user problem, this would be valid, but in reality, most medium to large projects attempt to solve many business problems. For example, a project's charter in a manufacturing and sales business might be to increase the speed of order taking, to anticipate production needs, and to better match existing inventory with customer orders.

Each part of the project, each problem to be addressed, yields its own benefits, entails its own costs, and requires its own resources. Studying these costs, benefits, and resources individually and in as much detail as possible is necessary for four reasons. First is to aid in deciding which, if any, of the parts of the project to carry out; and second is to help determine what order to implement the project's parts (if you're using a development technique that permits incremental implementation).[3] A third reason is to aid in deciding what to postpone or cancel should the project run short of resources; and finally, to aid in estimating the overall costs and benefits of the project.

To understand these four reasons, let's look at the itemized benefits and costs of a project to introduce an automated system into a manufacturing and sales company. The system comprises five major subsystems: production planning, order entry, inventory allocation, management information, and billing. Each subsystem being developed consumes its own portion of the total development costs (see Figure 1.2). Certain costs, such as problem definition costs and full analysis costs, apply to the project as a whole and are not easily attributable to a particular subsystem. So, canceling or postponing development of a given subsystem will not affect the costs marked P.[4]

The benefit rate that each subsystem provides over its lifetime varies with time. For example, the rates in Figure 1.3 assume that over the first five years of operation, business will increase in volume and interest rates will steadily fall. Thus, curves 1, 2, and 4 increase with increasing business. Curve 3 has an initial, one-time benefit, as existing inventory is reduced, for example, by matching inventory to customer orders with less stringent requirements. Later, curve 3 increases once more with increasing business.

Curve 5 also has an initial, one-time benefit during the first year from the improved management and recovery of uncollected debts. Curve 5 then falls with (the assumed) declining interest rates, only to rise again gradually under the influence of increased business. Curve 4 represents the huge benefit to be gained after a thorough study of the three years' worth of statistics that will be gathered by the system. These statistics might help management, for instance, plan a

---

[3]Incremental implementation is the implementation of a system in stages.

[4]Conservative development requires analysis to be completed before design or programming can begin. Radical development encourages the commencement of design before analysis is complete. Note that the percentage of P is greater for a conservative development approach than for a radical development approach, because in the conservative approach, a full analysis and design is completed regardless of which, if any, subsystem is implemented. Conservative and radical development are discussed in Chapters 6, 7, and 8.

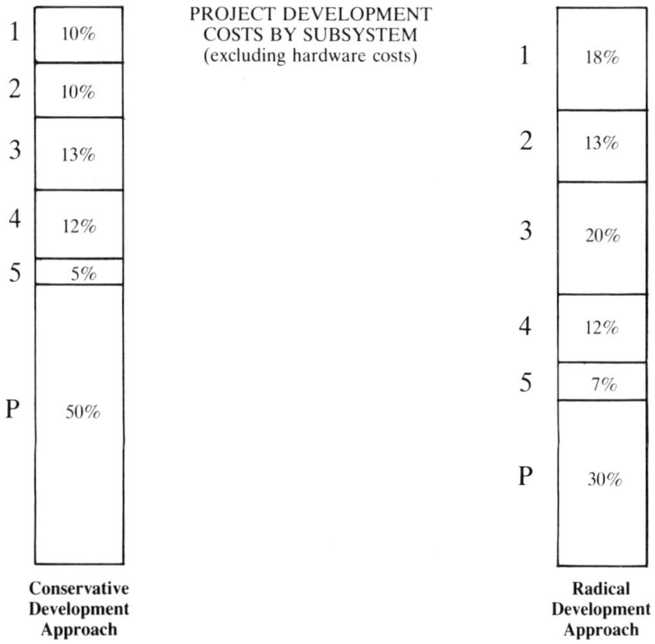

PROJECT DEVELOPMENT
COSTS BY SUBSYSTEM
(excluding hardware costs)

Conservative Development Approach:

1	10%
2	10%
3	13%
4	12%
5	5%
P	50%

**Conservative
Development
Approach**

Radical Development Approach:

1	18%
2	13%
3	20%
4	12%
5	7%
P	30%

**Radical
Development
Approach**

Key

1	Production planning subsystem
2	Order entry subsystem
3	Inventory allocation subsystem
4	Management information subsystem
5	Billing subsystem
P	Overall, unattributable project costs

Figure 1.2. System costs.

more effective marketing strategy, including tapping new markets and improving service to existing customers. Using the above example, let's look at each of the four reasons for detailed itemization.

1.2.1 Deciding which parts of a project to do

Simply because a project as a whole is expected to yield benefits that exceed its costs, it does not necessarily follow that every part of the project exhibits this happy characteristic. The sections of a project that do not offer substantial benefits are obvious candidates for cancellation, or at least indefinite postponement. Other possible candidates are those parts of a project that offer benefits approximately equal to their costs but that make prodigious demands on scarce resources. Their being brought to fruition should perhaps await days of more plentiful resources.

For instance, the current manual billing system may be so simple and debt management so minimal that carrying out project 5 in Figures 1.2 and 1.3 may not be worthwhile. Indeed, it may even cost more than it yields. Note that you cannot normally carry out these itemizations and make the decisions at the very start of the project, but you must wait until some of the analysis is done when you will have a clearer picture of the project's anatomy. Chapters 2 and 3 deal further with this point.

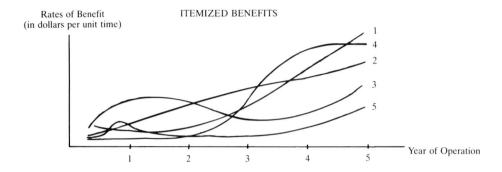

Figure 1.3. System benefit rates.

There are three cases when you do not want to cancel a portion of a project, regardless of that portion's ratio of costs versus benefits or the resources available. The first is political, the second technical, and the third strategic. In the first case, for example, the nephew of the Chairman of the Board demands that his tennis ladder program (a wonder of his own design) be implemented as part of an employee skills inventory subsystem. I wouldn't even bother estimating costs and benefits on this one, but of course if such political games are allowed to prevail, all pretense to professionalism within the shop disappears.

As an example of the second case, the inventory allocation subsystem requires a massive conversion from manual records to database ones before it can be brought on line. Itemizing the conversion section of the project reveals some small benefits (such as revealing errors in the old records), but it has mainly costs. However, since the benefits of the subsystem cannot be realized without the conversion, it is impractical to consider carrying out the rest of the project without the conversion.

The third case involves corporate strategy. For instance, you may decide to implement all of the accounting subsystems in one go, although some of them are less beneficial than, say, some of the manufacturing subsystems. By making this decision at the start, you can construct an integrated plan of attack to make full use of your accounting talents while you have them available, and avoid leaving the accounting department with a motley quilt of old and new systems. (Chapter 4 discusses strategic planning at the upper levels of the users' business.)

1.2.2 Determining system implementation order

In our example, which subsystems should we implement first, if we choose to use incremental implementation? From Figure 1.3, we might decide that the inventory allocation subsystem would be best, since it yields early, large benefits. However, there is a vital technical snag in that plan: How can we allocate inventory if we have no data in the system about which orders to allocate it to? Therefore, to gain the benefits of subsystem 3, we first must implement at least a part of subsystem 2. (Remember, too, subsystem 3 entails a large data conversion effort before it can really do anything.)

With incremental implementation, you have a bewilderingly large number of sequences in which to install system components. Unfortunately (or perhaps fortunately), many of them make little practical sense, as we saw above. The best way to choose an incremental implementation plan that does make sense is to itemize costs, benefits, and resources, and to select parts of the overall system that satisfy three criteria: They yield substantial benefits over costs, they have costs within the currently available resources, and they fit together technically. To help you analyze the third criterion, use a graphic technique such as structured analysis to identify the relationships between various parts of each subsystem.[5] With the itemization and the graphic document, you can choose an implementation strategy that yields maximum benefits early and that is also technically feasible.

For example, in Figure 1.2, you might eventually decide to implement the production planning subsystem first, together with a piece of the management information subsystem, which presumably would also deal in some way with production. Then, you would implement perhaps a part of subsystem 2, most of 3,and another piece of 4, and so on.

1.2.3 Deciding what to do should resources run short

Companies sometimes begin projects believing that their coffers are overflowing with milk and honey, only to find halfway through the project that their true situation is not quite so mellifluous. The normal reaction of upper management is to panic. Managers rush about, not so much axing projects as strangling them to death in a blind frenzy.

When during such a budget crisis you feel the lean hand of economics clutching at your throat, do not panic. Instead, revise your itemized list of resources to reflect this new age of austerity, and decide which pieces of the project can be postponed until better times. Typically, you will find, assuming as always that technical considerations permit their postponement, that the following types of subsystem are candidates for deferment:

- costly subsystems (for example, subsystem 3 in Figure 1.2), although they are often the ones that yield the greatest benefit. However, in bad times, belts must be tightened and benefits forgone.

- subsystems with small benefit (such as subsystem 5, which is a likely candidate for cutting even after the analysis stage).

- subsystems that won't produce immediate benefit (so long as postponing the subsystem's implementation won't significantly delay its benefit further). For example, postponing subsystem 1 will not have much effect for a while. However, postponing any statistical data gathering in subsystems 2, 3, 4, or even 5 might delay the benefit that subsystem 1 will eventually provide, since management decisions require several years' history of data.

- subsystems whose values don't drop sharply at an early date.

These subsystems also are typical candidates for postponement:

- reporting subsystems rather than data-capturing ones, since you can always capture data without generating reports, but you cannot generate reports without having the data.

- procedural rather than informational pieces of the system (that is, code rather than database). Procedural pieces tend to be less intercoupled than informational system pieces and are hence more easily added to the system later.

- informational entities with few relationships, rather than those with many. It is awkward to use a system that continually refers to customers, say, by an internal

---

[5]Of necessity, I cannot go into detail about these development techniques, so for additional information on incremental implementation, see [Yourdon and Constantine, 1978]. See also [DeMarco, 1978; Gane and Sarson, 1977; and McMenamin and Palmer, 1984] for excellent discussions of structured analysis.

ID, but in which all real customer data is contained on manual file cards sorted by this artificial ID.

Remember, however, that postponing or mothballing subsystems brings its own costs. For example, the documentation of a mothballed portion of a project must be made even more rigorous and explicit than usual, because the original project team may no longer be around when that piece of the project is eventually restored.

1.2.4 Estimation of the overall costs and benefits

The fourth reason for itemization is that it promotes greater precision in making estimates of costs and benefits. This is part of the larger topic of estimating resources, costs, and benefits, which I deal with in Chapter 2.

1.3 Summary

For a data processing project to be a success, the resulting system must not only be of high technical quality, but it also must yield some cost-effective improvement to the users' business. To be cost-effective and feasible, the project must supply benefits that exceed its costs and must not entail costs that exceed available resources.

A project yields benefits either by solving a business problem or by exploiting a business opportunity. Benefits fall into four classes: increasing business revenue, reducing business costs, improving customer service, and satisfying an inflexible business requirement. In short, a benefit is an improvement to the competitiveness of the company.

In order to evaluate a project's cost-effectiveness, users need to itemize costs, benefits, and resources for each part of a project. This procedure is necessary for four reasons: to decide which parts of a project to carry out; to decide in what order to implement parts of the system by means of incremental implementation; to decide which parts of the project to postpone or cancel should resources run unexpectedly low; and to make better estimates.

Chapter 1: Exercises

1.   Imagine that you have a fairly old car that continually breaks down, thus causing you great inconvenience and incurring high maintenance costs. Your project is to identify ways to improve your personal transport by either increasing revenue, reducing costs, improving service, or fulfilling inflexible requirements. Assume that you use this car for your business.

     In doing this exercise, consider the differences between how people tend to view spending their own money for personal transport and how they view devoting the company's resources for computers. What are the reasons for these differences?

2.   Make a list of the existing systems in your shop. For each system, write down the following:

     ■ the benefits to the users' business that the system was intended to yield
     ■ the benefits that you think it actually yielded
     ■ whether you think it was a success, and if not,
     ■ whether it was a failure even before it began. (Look out particularly for systems that replace the work of four clerks by five computer staffers, for example.)

2

Estimating Resources, Costs, and Benefits

The current state of what masquerades under the name of estimating in the data processing industry is abject. Figure 2.1 shows where I believe so-called DP project estimating falls along the spectrum of accuracy.

Now, I'm certainly not suggesting that project estimating should be moved all the way to the left side of the spectrum; if it were, then it couldn't be called estimation. But it certainly needs to be moved much closer to the center than where it is now, somewhere between guesswork and random number generation.

Since whole books have been written on the subject of estimation, I shall not attempt to cover it in depth here. Nevertheless, in this chapter, I give a brief overview of estimating as it applies to data processing, with references to sources that explain techniques for estimating your own projects. I begin with the easiest quantities to estimate (resources) and end with the hardest (benefits). In the middle, therefore, are costs.

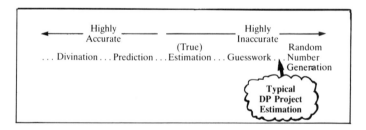

Figure 2.1. Range of estimating's accuracy.

2.1 Estimating resources

Estimating resources would appear to be extremely straightforward. "After all," a manager might reason, "I know what my project budget is; I know what staff I'll have; I know what access to the users we'll have. Thus, I know what all my resources are fairly accurately."

"But," I would retort, "will they come when you do call for them?"

The problem implied here is that predicting the present is easy. Predicting the future is what's difficult. As the project proceeds, your available resources may diverge considerably from what you first expected. By the time you arrive at database design, for instance, the hotshot database designer on whom you were counting may have gone to lusher pastures. You would then have to ask the database group's staff manager for a replacement. His willingness to oblige you may in turn depend upon a designer's being released from another project, either full-time or part-time.

So as you can see, even estimating resources as far as the project's horizon has its pitfalls. Always consider the possibility of losing one or more resources. Ask yourself, What if another project ran late and denied this resource to me on time? What if the budget were cut by twenty percent, what parts of the project could be truncated?

2.2 Estimating costs

DP project cost estimating is like predicting the weather: Everybody talks about it but nobody does anything about it. Indeed, when I was a seminar instructor, questions about cost estimating would always pop up at the end of each seminar, no matter whether the seminar was on analysis, design, programming, or management. In response, I would trot out an algorithm that I hoped sounded erudite, along the lines of, "Look at the structure charts of your system, consider the complexity of each module, and multiply it by the alpha factor. Then, look at the complexity of each interface and multiply it by the beta factor. Add all the numbers, multiply the result by 1.25, and add a week for luck."

Before the seminar attendees could ask me what the alpha and beta factors were, I would mutter something about an airplane, grab my belongings, and flee the room. I left each attendee with an expression on his face of one who has hitchhiked to Delphi to find the answer to the Ultimate Question of Estimating, only to discover that the Priestess of the Oracle was out to lunch.

Why is it that realistic DP project cost estimating is so intractable? Why does the mere mention of the subject reduce perfectly normal managers to gibbering wrecks and put otherwise fearless seminar instructors to flight? There are two reasons. The first is a failure to identify all tasks of the project—a sin of omission. The second is the inaccurate estimation of the tasks that are identified for lack of correct historical data—a sin of commission. Below I elaborate on these two reasons.

2.2.1 Failure to identify all tasks

How do you make an estimate of the total cost of a project when all you know is its acronym? You cannot. Yet, some DP managers do attempt to make such preliminary estimates on huge monolithic projects by means of various hocus-pocus techniques. Here's one popular technique: Mention a large sum of money to the users. After gauging the decibel level of their reaction, mention progressively smaller amounts. The estimate of the project's cost is the first sum mentioned at which the users' screams fall below eighty decibels. I call this the Maximum-Acceptable-Sum-of-Cash-Having-Indicated-Sonic-Threshold estimation technique. (Unfortunately, it usually leads to unrealistically low cost estimates and consequently high amounts of unpaid overtime for project team members.)

In order to get a good handle on estimating costs, you must divide the project into its component tasks. The chief benefit of this subdivision is identifying tasks that you might otherwise miss. This raises a logical question: How can you know at the beginning of the project what tasks lie ahead? As one manager recently exclaimed, "Trying to make a firm estimate at that stage sounds like asking for the check at a restaurant before you have even ordered the meal."

That manager was exactly right. Before beginning the analysis stage of the project, you cannot be absolutely certain which of the users' business problems you will be solving or which of their business opportunities you will be exploiting, and you certainly cannot know how you will solve these problems and exploit these opportunities.

Therefore, at the start of a project, any estimate is likely to have zero percent accuracy. But, on the other hand, your users won't wait until the end of the project for a (presumably) one hundred percent accurate estimate. I suggest a compromise: First, do a preliminary mini-analysis that consumes about two person-months and produces a provisional breakdown of the likely tasks required to execute the project based on the facts and assumptions at that time. The resulting cost estimates from this mini-analysis are crude, but they can at least serve as a basis of comparison with budgeted resources. That is, the estimates can indicate whether the project appears likely to consume too many resources or whether the benefits appear to be less than or dangerously close to its costs.

If the mini-analysis estimates are encouraging, then proceed with the full analysis and derive a second set of estimates. These estimates will be more accurate, since your knowledge following the analysis stage is more complete. If there are multiple options for implementing solutions to the users' problems, itemize the tasks and other costs for each option. If the estimates from the mini-analysis are not encouraging, you may wish to change the terms of the project and try a new mini-analysis. Or you may opt to abandon the project entirely.

Remember that a good estimate requires time, effort, and attention to detail, and consequently expense. But for any serious DP project, a free estimate is worth exactly what you pay for it—nothing!

2.2.2 Inaccurate estimation of identified tasks

However finely you manage to subdivide a project into tasks and however few tasks you overlook in doing so, all is for naught if you cannot attach some realistic cost figures to each identified task. The best way to assign a cost to a given task is to identify the cost for an identical task performed earlier in your shop. Unfortunately, few project managers have the opportunity to do that. Even though similar file updating programs may have been written twenty-two times within the shop, estimating the cost of the twenty-third file updating program is as hard as estimating the cost of the first one, simply because no data about the other twenty-two times was ever recorded. To paraphrase George Santayana, shops that do not study the history of their previous projects are condemned to repeat their history of poor estimates and cost overruns.

There seem to be six reasons for this extraordinary lack of data about projects in a large majority of shops. In the words of some hypothetical managers, they might be expressed thus:

"I'm worried that my project will fail and the last thing I want around if it does is hard data that I can get nailed with."

This statement betrays a poor political atmosphere in this manager's company, a topic that I discuss in Chapter 15.

"Everybody knows that time reporting is a joke around here. How you report your time depends on which budget is the fattest one this week."

I address this problem of timesheet corruption in Chapter 9.

"I don't see the sense in recording project data. After all, every project is different."

Every project *is* different, but if you subdivide projects into detailed tasks—and having a record of previous projects actually helps you to do that—you will see that most DP projects are composed of almost identical types of tasks.

"I've never seen any manager using data from previous projects, so why bother to collect it?"

This circular argument reminds me of a story from Weinberg's *Rethinking Systems Analysis and Design:* A train company received a petition from a small town's residents asking that the express train stop at 2:30 each afternoon at their local station. The company replied, "Since we've never seen anyone waiting at the station for a 2:30 p.m. train, we conclude there's no demand for it. Request denied." [Weinberg, 1982].

"My people have no time to collect project data." And, "Nobody in this shop has the statistical skills to apply the collected data meaningfully."

These two very reasonable statements are best answered by an idea from DeMarco's *Controlling Software Projects,* whose central theme is that poor estimation stems from the lack of data.[1] DeMarco proposes the establishment of a metrics group, whose members would have these basic characteristics:

- They would be specialists in measurement and estimating and would develop their skills over many projects.

- They would be independent from the project manager and the project developers.

- They would not be subject to political pressure or bias; their charter would be to predict what will be, not what should be.

- They would be both estimators of incipient projects and measurers of current ones. The beauty of this idea is that in a sense they would be their own "users"; they would learn firsthand what to measure by discovering what they need to measure in order to make estimates.

Such a metrics group with statistically formulated estimating techniques would circumvent many of the difficulties that undermine traditional estimating, but it would also create new difficulties. Obviously, a metrics group is not without cost; neither would it produce instant results. Also, DeMarco is not altogether clear about how to deal with some of the problems attending this innovation, for example, how to satisfactorily apportion work between the project manager and the metrics group, or how best to divide authority between the metrics group manager and the project manager. However, a staff/line matrix structure, such as the one I discuss in Chapter 5, has mechanisms already in place for handling these problems. The metrics group would be a staff group, and the project team, as usual, would be a line group.

Despite the difficulties in establishing and running a metrics group, the drawbacks are minimal when compared to the chronic bloodletting that currently attends DP projects endemically out of control for lack of solid estimates and measurements. And that doesn't even include those projects that should have been drowned at birth because their costs, if only anyone had any notion of them, would either greatly exceed their benefits or would strain resources to the breaking point.

When you begin to study the empirical science of project management and cost estimation in your own shop, you will be in for some occasionally unpleasant surprises. But your choice is either a revelation now or an apocalypse later.

2.3 Estimating benefits

As I indicated at the start of this chapter, trying to estimate the benefits that a project will bring to your users' business is most difficult, because not only does benefits estimation have the

---

[1][DeMarco, 1982] also contains many other suggestions on controlling projects. Not only is it an excellent book for DP project managers, but it also contains eye-opening material for users. I suggest that you supply your company's upper managers and users with copies of this book. Another good book, on a specific technique of DP project cost estimating, is [Boehm, 1981].

same difficulties as resource and cost estimation, but it also has other unique challenges.[2] These are detailed in the paragraphs below.

Because benefits analysis is highly specific to the users' business, no DP project manager should attempt to estimate benefits to the users' business without the active cooperation of experienced users. In order to be an expert benefits estimator in a business, you first must thoroughly understand that business (more on this in Chapters 3 and 4). Understanding the opportunities for the steel industry, say, is very different from understanding those for insurance companies.

A second obstacle to estimating benefits derives from the many unpredictable external factors at work. In Figure 1.3, I showed the benefit rate of the billing subsystem. This rate was determined from assumptions about future changes in interest rates—entities that are notoriously even more difficult to estimate than DP projects. In general, then, the expected benefits from a project depend upon the vicissitudes of your company's business. If you could predict those accurately over a period of years, you would become even more famous (and certainly more wealthy) than Nostradamus.

A third difficulty in estimating benefits is that benefits to be gained from different parts of a project may affect one another. The separation of benefits by subsystem (or even problems to be solved) is often artificial. For instance, in Figure 1.3, if you assume that one of the benefits of the management information subsystem is increased business, that benefit in turn augments the benefits of the order entry subsystem. But despite such interactions, your goal is to estimate the relative benefits of each subsystem and to derive a reasonable idea of its absolute benefit. Also, as with every estimate, record your assumptions on which your estimates are based, so that you can later change your estimates when your assumptions change.

A final challenge in estimating benefits is that benefits to be gained from innovation cannot be predicted from existing data. Who knows what will happen when new technology is introduced into a business? The following example illustrates the bizarre and unpredictable problems following a gross underestimation of the improvement to customer service that a project yielded.

Several years ago, a bank decided to improve its service to customers by being the first in the neighborhood to install twenty-four hour banking machines. These machines allowed customers to carry out simple transactions (such as withdrawing money or making mortgage payments) at any time. The machines did indeed improve service—so much so that the bank was inundated by new customers. As a result, many of the bank's manual systems virtually collapsed, and the service provided by the Customer Assistance Department, for one, deteriorated markedly. Another problem was the potential for violent crime, as customers were sometimes mugged by enterprising robbers who lay in wait.

The increase in the number of customers also created problems for the system itself. On weekends, long lines of impatient, grumbling people formed at the machines, and the customers' composure was not improved by the prolonged response times common for the machines by this time. Consequently, new projects were required to deal with these problems, including the installation of additional banking machines, security systems, and CPUs, and the expansion of several departments. (When the bank's Chairman of the Board learned of these additional requirements, he is reported to have cried all the way to the bank.)

As this story illustrates, all solutions bring new problems, and all new systems perturb the systems around them. In this case, the problems and perturbations were much greater than anyone expected, because of the failure to anticipate how to deal with the consequences of the original project's benefits.

---

[2]A good introductory text to this subject is [Mishan, 1982]. For a superbly detailed account of costs and benefits of computer systems, see [Gotlieb, 1985].

2.4 Summary

Estimating is difficult because it requires predicting the future. However, the estimation of resources available to a project is easier than the estimation of project costs, which in turn is easier than the estimation of project benefits. The reason is that the resources available to a project are usually known fairly accurately at the start of the project and diverge from the expected only with time. One of the chief reasons for the difficulty in estimating project costs is that in most shops, little if any data is kept on previous projects' itemized costs.

Project benefits are influenced by many factors that are almost impossible to determine at the outset of a project, so that estimating benefits is somewhat of an art. Nevertheless, even if benefits estimates are tentative and riddled with assumptions, making such estimates and collecting data on them are imperative. Without estimates of project benefits, a crucial side of the costs-benefits-resources triangle is missing, and you and your users risk being swayed into dubious subjective judgments by beguiling hopes and the false glamour of a new computer system.

Chapter 2: Exercise

1.   Costs and benefits of a project cannot be estimated precisely; they can be estimated only as a range, as shown in the examples below. (For simplicity, I'm assuming that the project is addressing only one problem.)

In Example 1, the project is likely to bring high return, since the benefits greatly outweigh the costs. However, there's a small but real risk that the benefits will actually be less than its costs.

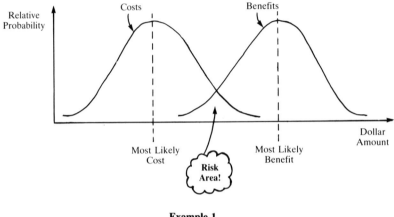

Example 1

In Example 2, the return is less but the risk of losing money is almost nil. Of the two, which project should your company attempt? (Note that there is no absolutely right answer, but in your answer, try to relate these ranges of estimates to the financial strategy of your company.)

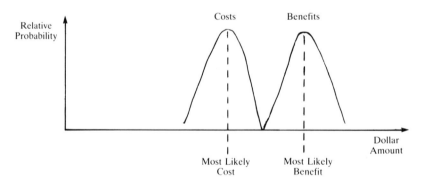

Example 2

3

Combining Successful Projects into Successful Systems

Even when the costs of, resources for, and benefits of data processing projects are carefully estimated, there remain two fundamental faults in the way DP projects are typically initiated: First, projects are considered in isolation from one another. As a result, there is a lack of technical coherence between developed systems. Also, it is difficult to compare projects' estimated costs and benefits in order to best apportion resources among projects.

The second basic problem is that projects are often initiated to address local operating problems of the business and are not based upon a comprehensive understanding of the business or of upper management's business strategy. This leads to an unevenness in applying data processing to the business; an application of data processing that is in conflict (or, at best, irrelevant) to the basic business strategy; an emphasis upon increasing operating efficiency rather than making fundamental and imaginative changes to the ways of doing business; and a failure to provide informational support for upper management of the company.

This chapter explores the consequences of projects' traditional faults, while Chapter 4 examines how these faults can be overcome by the establishment of a special group to foster a thorough understanding of a company's business operations and strategy. For further reading on the subjects of this and the next chapter, see [Nolan, 1979] and [Cortada, 1984].

3.1 Lack of technical coherence

When DP projects are considered as separate entities rather than as part of the whole organization, the systems that result from the projects may be technically incompatible. For example, different systems may use incompatible hardware devices or employ many different software techniques, making software maintenance confusing and arduous. They may also use incompatible database techniques, so that sharing data between systems or integrating local databases is difficult, if not impossible; or they may duplicate data or procedural code across several systems. Sad to say, these inconsistencies are the rule rather than the exception in many DP shops. In fact, many shops don't truly have *systems*. What they have is a miscellany of ill-fitting programs and files that appeared one after the other throughout the 1960s and 1970s as answers to a variety of unrelated needs for computerization. Such "systems" were never planned, but, like Topsy, they just "growed." Today, many shops have to live with a hodgepodge of hardware and software with radically different design and programming techniques, documentation styles, programming languages, file structures, and operation methods. In addition, years of arbitrary maintenance have bestowed hideous rococo embellishments upon these gothic mansions of disorder.

Obviously, coping with such conglomerations of hardware and software isn't easy for DP departments, and they often become utterly thwarted when they try to make significant improvements in their service to the company's business. Let me present a small sample of the difficulties experienced by an actual shop.

The Wizard Pinball and Games Machines Co. had three systems: The Customer Order System (COS), the Customer Service System (CSS), and the Transportation System (TS). The first two had been converted from batch systems to online (but not database) systems in the mid-1970s. The TS (which was a fairly complex system handling van scheduling, loading, routing, maintenance, and so on) was a batch system developed in the late 1960s, but had recently acquired an online front end for data collection.

One problem with the CSS, COS, and TS, taken as a group, was that they all needed the same data about customers (for example, name, addresses, and phone numbers). Thus, certain customer data was triply redundant, as shown in Figure 3.1. An attempt was made to partially correct the problem by merging customer data between the CSS and COS, as shown in Figure 3.2.

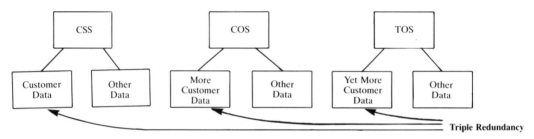

Figure 3.1. Triply redundant customer data.

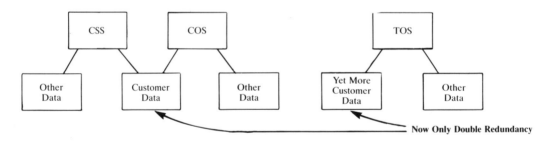

Figure 3.2. Doubly redundant customer data.

But because of problems with updates to customer data occasionally vanishing mysteriously or becoming garbled, no further attempts to reduce redundancy were made. (A cursory investigation revealed that the problems were due to a lack of file interlocks and some program bugs.) So, redundancy was accepted surprisingly cheerfully, as was a certain amount of inconsistency. For instance, a customer's telephone number in the CSS/COS might well be different from that entered in the TS. ("How do you know which one is correct?" I asked. "We call the customer and ask him," came the straight-faced reply.)

However, a much larger problem than the redundancy of data was the DP shop's inability to create useful interrelationships among the systems. For example, the users continually requested (and were repeatedly denied) an enhancement to enable them, upon taking an order, to quote the customer a reasonable delivery date. Unfortunately, up-to-date van schedules were not readily available to them through the COS, nor was order information available to the TS in order to project van requirements.

DP management decided to modernize the TS by making it fully online but otherwise unchanged in function. In order to appease the users while DP staff members were making those changes, they added rudimentary mechanisms to transfer data between the TS and COS, as shown in Figure 3.3. These mechanisms were a file in the TS to hold some order data, a file in the COS to hold some transportation data, a job (Job X) run nightly to move data from the COS to the TS, and a more frequently run job (Job Y) to move data from the TS to the COS.

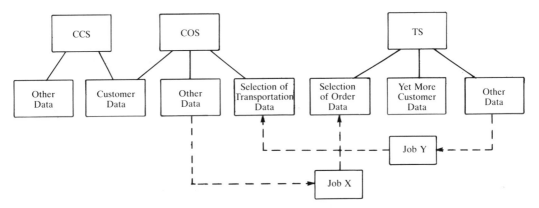

Figure 3.3. Data transfer between two systems.

Although the users were pacified by this solution, I was not impressed. The new software added redundancy and complexity to the systems, but still did not provide timely transportation data to the COS. As the shop's consultant, I recommended that it no longer change systems in superficial ways but do a complete informational analysis of the whole company and then develop some integrated software around one or more databases. Those who received my report were aghast. "We can't afford to do that!" they protested.

"You can't afford not to," I countered. "Every person-year you spend on a new system or program in your shop is a person-year backward—one more person-year of software that you'll eventually have to replace."

The DP department manager finally accepted my views, and the company's top managers, after resisting initially, approved a provisional general analysis of their company's information needs. One of the startling preliminary results of this analysis is that it would be cheaper in one or two cases to scrap the computer system, with its inflexibility and huge maintenance costs, and replace it with a manual system!

3.2 Difficulty in comparing separate projects' estimates

Potential projects are normally considered one at a time over a period of years. How, then, can the return on investment for a potential project today be compared with one three or four years hence? Clearly, without some idea of what future projects are likely to be needed, we cannot make such a comparison, and so we may lack sufficient resources when a better project perversely reveals itself later. Moreover, as Chapter 2 pointed out, you cannot make a valid estimate of the project's costs and benefits until at least part of the project's analysis phase has been performed. So, how can we possibly compare several projects' estimated costs and benefits to determine which projects to initiate unless we initiate them all simultaneously?

The answer is to be found in achieving a global understanding of the company's business, rather than narrowly focusing on an individual project. Such a global perspective means understanding the company's operations, upper management's strategy for the company's business, and management's needs for information. Equipped with this understanding, you would pursue analysis simultaneously in several areas of the business. In those areas bearing little promise, you could cease this exploratory analysis early. In other areas, you would drill deeper into the problems and opportunities of the business, in order to gain better estimates of the costs and benefits of the various ways to improve the business. Finally, you would use the company's resources to initiate cost-effective projects to tap those benefits that you identified.

There is a further benefit in having a general understanding of the company's business as a solid frame of reference for projects: handling changes in available resources. Budget cuts should not create pandemonium, for when DP managers know the business's priorities, they can sensibly redistribute resources among projects. This is especially valuable to reduce confusion in matrix-structured shops when projects must compete for suddenly scarce resources. Deriving a global understanding of a business is the topic of Chapter 4.

3.3 Unevenness in applying DP to the business

In almost every company, the basic mechanism for bringing a potential project to the attention of the data processing department is the so-called user request. This is usually in the form of a statement from a manager (typically in a finance or operations department) about a problem that he believes can be solved, or about an opportunity that can be exploited, through computerization. Ideally, this user request is then evaluated by upper management or their delegates, first comparing the expected costs and benefits of the candidate project, then comparing them with those of other candidate projects on request, and finally comparing the costs and benefits of all projects with the resources of the company.

Although user requests appear to be a sound method for discovering viable projects, a project can be initiated only if a user submits a request for it. So, if there is no user request, there is no project, regardless of its potential value to the company. A user may be reluctant or unable to point out possible golden projects for many reasons, including apathy, lack of imagination, previous bad experiences with the DP department, fear of losing control of his job or department, or hatred of computers.

Even apparently worthwhile user requests may miss their mark in providing substantial benefits to a business. The following extract from Wigander and others provides an excellent example of how a DP project initiated in isolation and with narrow aims failed to address the true problems of a business [Wigander et al., 1984]:

> A large organization experienced such an increase in the number of orders it was handling that its order-processing system exhausted its capacity. Having completed an ordinary feasibility study, the organization expended over 40,000 worker-hours to increase its capacity through a new information system. While that new system was being implemented, a separate study of the company's delivery times was undertaken. The study revealed that an average of seventy days elapsed between the time packing slips were prepared and the time of delivery. A partial delivery procedure with separate invoicing was pacifying customers to some extent, but most of the apparent increase in the number of orders was actually back orders which had to be filled, invoiced, and delivered separately. The new information system and increased computer capacity could do nothing to solve the real problems in the functional area—problems which resulted from a badly coordinated material flow throughout the operation.

> In this case, a feasibility study which reviewed only a part of the business resulted in large expenditures without solving the major business problem. The system which was developed treated only a symptom and left the root of the problem untouched.

On the other hand, some users are fanatical in their desire for projects to be initiated in their departments and submit a disproportionately large number of user requests. Such users may have a great enthusiasm for modern technology, or they may see the initiation of projects as a way to gain visibility in the company or to defend and expand their organizational empires. While such project requests may not be frivolous, they are likely to speak eloquently only for their authors' vested interests. What thus emerges from a collection of these user project requests is hardly a coordinated picture of the informational needs of the company. Instead, they are a raggle-taggle bag of bids for narrow—and sometimes conflicting—palliatives for the fast, temporary relief of minor, nagging irritations. Faced with such requests, the head of a DP department often throws his hands in the air and initiates projects carelessly, tossing new projects to slavering users, like bones to dogs.

Unevenness in project identification and initiation, with some departments being awarded too few projects and others being awarded too many or the wrong ones, results from the lack of an integrated data processing strategy based on the needs of the business as a whole. User requests for projects are often excellent in revealing otherwise overlooked opportunities to improve the company's business, but by themselves, they produce only a fragmented data processing policy. They cannot replace a total understanding of the whole business, its problems, and its opportunities.

3.3.1 Lack of DP applications to support corporate strategy

Ideally, data processing projects help a company to accomplish its business goals. At the very least, projects should provide information to management on how well its business strategy is working. Nevertheless, I know of one company whose avowed aim was to increase its market share but which had neither computer systems to help directly in that aim nor even systems that gave management immediately useful information on progress toward that goal.

DP personnel are often blamed for this lack of effective systems to support a company's basic business strategy. They are blamed and criticized for not understanding the company's true business requirements. However, not only are many DP people ignorant of the company's business needs, but so also are many of the users. There are two closely related reasons for this. The first is users' lack of perspective; the second is poor communication between upper management and the operations departments.

Although most users are expert at *how* they perform their jobs, some users either don't know or no longer remember *what* they're supposed to accomplish. And few indeed pause to question *why* they're doing it—that is, to understand to what business goals their work contributes. But no one can blame users completely for this failure. They're far too busy actually doing the work to have time for such questions. And perhaps if they were to think too much about their work, they might start to trip over themselves like introspective centipedes.

Secondly, in many companies, upper managers do not explain their business strategy to operations managers. This can lead to such absurdities as a manager committing to a project that streamlines his department in a splendidly cost-effective way, only to learn a year later that his department is being abolished and that he is being reassigned.

3.3.2 Emphasis on projects that do not yield true business benefits

Since current information processing technology affords the opportunity to depart from traditional methods of doing business, every company needs to consider carefully how modern computer systems can improve its business. In order to avoid overlooking precious opportunities to make qualitative rather than merely quantitative improvements to its business, a company's members need a broad understanding of the total services to customers before plunging further into computerization.

To illustrate my point, I recall a trivial but revealing tale of a significant missed opportunity by a major health company. My medical insurance premium was $82.60, but by mistake I mailed the insurance company a check for $82.40. I ignored the subsequent demand for payment, since my check was on its way. But I then became annoyed when a form letter arrived notifying me that my health insurance coverage was to be terminated. When I called the company, a representative assured me they hadn't made an error—I simply hadn't paid.

Resignedly, I stopped payment on the first check and mailed another check, this time for $82.60, with a covering letter, as I no longer had the premium-invoice stub to enclose with my payment. I needn't have bothered to pay the $5.00 to stop payment on the first check: The next day, I received from the insurance company the check for the incorrect amount, which had ''Insufficient Premium'' stamped all over it. Believing that the situation had reached its denouement, I wrote off the $5.00, a postage stamp, and an hour of wasted time to the cost of living in modern times. But I was wrong. Although the company cashed my second check, it went ahead with canceling my policy, notifying me the following week that I was no longer covered by them.

Time to call the insurance company again! After numerous attempts to straighten out the problem, I finally learned what had happened: Because my second check had not been accompanied by the standard return stub, it had been shunted to the Exceptions area. Although the check had been cashed, it would take about a week before the amount would be posted to my account. The person in the Query Department who was handling my phone call assured me, however, that she would personally see that my policy was reinstated.

Once she reinstated me, I entered an eerie, although not altogether bad, situation. Part of the insurance company's system thought that I was insured and would pay me benefits, but another part believed the opposite and would never bill me for a premium. Although I don't know whether I want to continue being an exception for the rest of my life, I dread to think of what I'll have to go through to become a normal customer again.

Incidents like this used to generate great hilarity in the popular press as computer snafus, but such fiascoes often have little direct connection with computers. Instead, they're the result of manual operations established decades ago. The computer represents only a missed opportunity to reappraise the business in the light of modern technology.

Consider the typical organization of manual work in, say, an insurance company. The company offers several lines of insurance, including homeowners', automobile, personal liability, disability, and health. Each line is handled by its own department. Furthermore, each transaction in a given line is processed by a separate group of clerks, with one group handling new accounts, another one billing, another claims, and so on. Each clerk's job comprises the same small set of actions (such as checking that a form is complete), carried out day after day with mind-numbing repetition. Since most clerks are not allowed to exercise any intelligence, exceptions are handed over to a special exceptions area. Figure 3.4 diagrams this organization.

The effects of this assembly line organization of work are twofold. From the company's viewpoint, the result is an efficient, though demeaning, use of human labor. From my point of view as the insured customer, the effect is poor service. No one in the insurance company knows me and no one can see me as a single entity, a human being, with my own insurance needs and problems. Instead, each member of the insurance company's staff sees a minute part of me (for example, my car insurance payments) along with the same piece of the company's other customers.

The bad effects are further compounded by the company's multiple types of insurance. Unfortunately, each department sees me, the client, as a different person, and consequently I receive five different premium bills; I may as well deal with five different companies and choose the cheapest rate offered in each line. As far as the insurance departments are concerned, they may

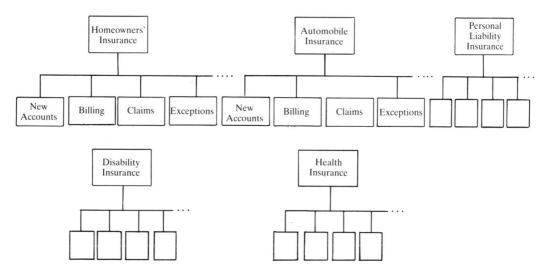

Figure 3.4. A typical insurance company's organization.

as well be dealing with five separate people. Figure 3.5 shows this company's fragmented view of customers.

Figure 3.6, on the other hand, represents *my* view of my insurance services. At the top of the diagram, not being particularly schizophrenic, I see myself (or, rather, my account) as a single entity. Below that, my insurance needs split into more and more detail.

This company squandered the opportunity to profoundly improve its customer service sometime during the transition from its old manual operations to its new computerized ones, because it failed to see its business holistically. The company's old manual system was certainly too unwieldy to provide a view of the customer as an integral person and to exploit the efficiency of the assembly line. But a computer system can process transactions sorted by type in an assembly line fashion and also provide a profile of an individual customer by means of database technology. Although databases may not have been practical during the original computerization, now there is no such excuse.

Regrettably, however, few corporations are taking advantage of the computer's flexibility in order to improve the operation of their business. Such improvements may favor not only the customer but also the employees of the company. For example, instead of having ten clerks, each handling the same transaction for a thousand customers, the company could arrange one clerk to handle all the transactions of, say, twenty customers. In this way, the clerks would have more interesting and complex jobs and would have the chance to develop an understanding of the total needs of people.[1]

---

[1]Of course, I don't intend you to take these numbers or this precise organization literally. A realistic organization following this principle would be far more complex and would require much preliminary research from many perspectives before it could be established. In the example, I describe a transformation from a specialist style of working (with its efficiency, but great need for communications) to a generalist style of working (which is more satisfying, but demands greater expertise from each worker). I cover this topic further in Chapter 5.

Key

NA	New Accounts
B	Billing
C	Claims
E	Exceptions
ME	Me
J	My neighbor Julie
P	My neighbor Pete

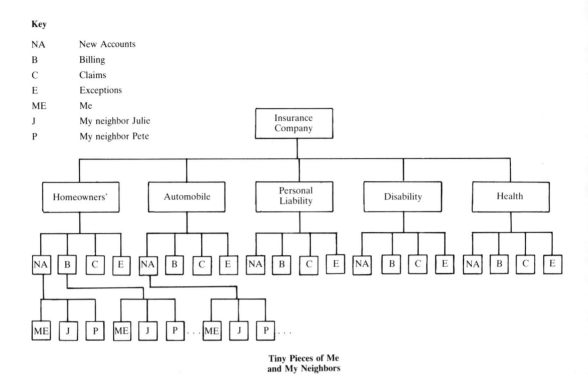

**Tiny Pieces of Me
and My Neighbors**

Figure 3.5. How the insurance company sees me and my neighbors.

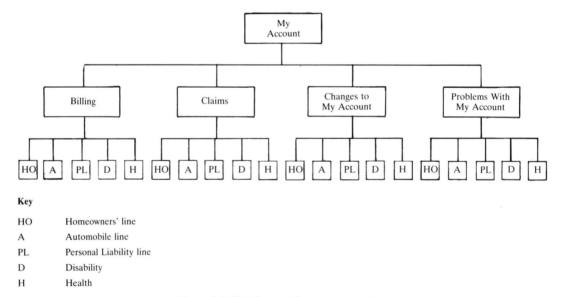

Key

HO	Homeowners' line
A	Automobile line
PL	Personal Liability line
D	Disability
H	Health

Figure 3.6. How I see my insurance account.

3.3.3 Failure to provide support for upper management

A company (excluding its DP department) has two basic areas: strategic (upper management) and operations (executors of the company's day-to-day business). Figure 3.7 shows the interactions with each other and with the DP department.

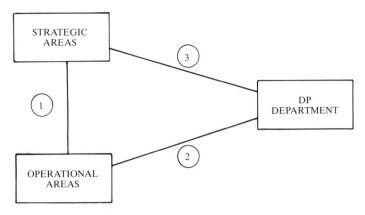

Figure 3.7. A company's departmental interactions.

The first line of communication—between the strategic and operational areas—is fairly strong in most companies, although admittedly in *some* companies, upper management neglects to communicate its business strategies to anyone. The second line of communication is the traditional one between DP and the users. Historically weak, this link has recently strengthened considerably, since most DP departments now take better care of their users than in the past because of the use of more enlightened analysis and systems development techniques and because of increased awareness of the need to keep users informed.

But what about communication between the company's strategic managers and the DP department, the line marked 3? In most companies, this line is nonexistent; even the head of the DP department usually reports to someone in the operational area of the company, probably a financial officer. The DP personnel in many companies regard their top managers to be unapproachable, while top managers rank data processing people somewhere beneath the creatures that crawl over the face of the earth upon their bellies.

Such feelings do not make for a good working relationship between the strategic apex of a company and its DP department. In that poor relationship, it is the upper managers who are the bigger losers, because they lose vital support for their business strategies. Strategic planning in the modern business world calls for analyzing large amounts of information and answering such difficult questions as, How large a market share do we have? How often do we turn over our inventory? What are the seasonal/geographical variations in our sales/profit? What are our best products? Who are our best customers? How do we compare with our competitors? From the answers to these questions come other questions about strategy, such as, Should we grow by increasing our market size or our market penetration? In which sections of our business should we introduce new products? Is our priority to increase revenues or to decrease costs?

Who better to provide the information needed for strategic decisions than the data processing department? Unfortunately, in a remarkably large number of companies, corporate management muddles on interminably, never making use of the huge well of data in the DP databases for planning and executing sound business strategies.

3.4 Summary

A group of successful data processing projects does not necessarily amount to a successful group of data processing projects. Traditionally, DP projects are considered in random sequence, uncoordinated with one another, and based on no more than certain individuals' narrow understanding of the company's business. This has led to the following problems and missed opportunities: Systems lack technical coherence, projects' costs and benefits are difficult to compare, data processing and computerization are applied unevenly or irrelevantly to the business, operating efficiency is emphasized to the detriment of real business changes, and sufficient support is rarely provided for upper management of the company.

To avoid these difficulties, you need a broad understanding of the company's business *as a whole* before you can consider any projects to improve that business. How such an understanding can be achieved is the subject of the next chapter.

Chapter 3: Exercises

1. Look at the systems in your shop, together with the projects currently under way. Which systems will probably need to be integrated sometime in the future? What difficulties would this integration entail?

2. Does your shop record the same data more than once? If so, does that cause any problems?

3. Do some areas of your company receive more data processing support than others? Is that justifiable? If not, what reasons can you find for the variation?

4. Categorize your company's DP systems as much as possible into those that increased operating efficiency, those that made fundamental changes to the company's way of doing business, and those that offer real support to upper management. Are the last two categories well represented? If not, what business opportunities have been missed?

4

Integrating Data Processing
Applications
with Business Strategy

As we saw in Chapter 3, carrying out a series of disjointed data processing projects without an overall plan eventually leads to chaos and unachieved business objectives. How do you develop such a plan based on your company's business? In this chapter, I propose a four-step method for developing and executing a coordinated, company-wide DP strategy:

- establish a business understanding and strategy group
- through this group, develop an understanding of the company's business, and particularly its informational needs, from three major viewpoints: the external, strategic, and operational points of view
- devise a technologically based strategy for improving the company's business
- formulate and carry out projects to accomplish the strategy

By following these four steps, projects can be made to serve the business and can transform a mediocre data processing project into a stunning business triumph.

4.1 Establish a business understanding and strategy group

The charter of the business understanding and strategy (BUS) group is to form a global picture of the company's business and to formulate ways in which the business strategy of the company can be aided through information technology. The BUS group is composed ideally of representatives from both the DP group (for their analytical and informational skills) and the users' area (for their expert business knowledge). This mix is good for political reasons as well, since you need to promote dialogue, mutual respect, and cordiality between DP personnel and the rest of the company. More important than a BUS member's expertise is his ability to blend many diverse perceptions into an understanding of the total business.

A good workable number for the BUS group membership is six people, with the initial composition shown in Table 4.1. The original group members carry out the overall, general study of the company, as described in the following section. Thereafter, as specific sections of the

Table 4.1
Composition of the BUS Group

Users	Data Processing
a senior manager	an upper manager
a middle manager	a senior analyst
a worker	a junior analyst
	(or possibly a consultant,
	for an objective viewpoint)

company are analyzed, mini-BUS groups are formed to carry out the more detailed work as required.

4.2 Develop an understanding of the company's business

To analyze the company's business, the BUS group uses different techniques for exploring each of the three major areas—external, strategic, and operational. However, because the three areas overlap to a degree and share certain activities, some of the same techniques can be used throughout. Figure 4.1 shows the three areas to be studied and where they are placed relative to the organization. Below I consider each in turn.

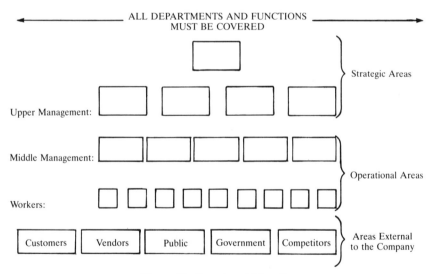

Figure 4.1. Departmental functions.

4.2.1 External viewpoint

The external viewpoint is that of entities outside the company, for example, the company's customers, distributors, and vendors. By studying the company from the outside, especially from the customers' viewpoint, the BUS group learns a great deal more about the company's business than simply what the company's products are. As the adage states, A well-run company behaves as if it knows where its money comes from.

Obtaining the external view of a company isn't simple, because a live customer cannot always be captured for close scrutiny. The BUS group nevertheless must figure out what goes through a customer's mind as he decides to purchase a product from the company, rather than another product and/or another company. Customers are the ultimate judges of the company, and so understanding them is necessary for upper management to create an effective business strategy. Studying the external viewpoint may reveal unpenetrated markets, for example, or a competitor's imminent attack on the marketplace. Most profoundly of all, it may reveal what the company's true business is.

What, for instance, is the business of a record company? records? If that were so, a record company's goal could be to produce the best and cheapest records in the world. But then, just as it congratulates itself on its high quality, the company might go bankrupt through a sudden popularity of video games. An analysis of the company's customers might show that eighty percent of its business is for teenagers' entertainment. With this information, the company then could watch for any competition that diverted teenagers' discretionary spending away from record purchases. For example, it might develop an intelligent laser disk home video game, so that the viewer could affect the outcome of an adventure through skillful play, and thus it could compete effectively for the teenager's dollar.

To gain the external viewpoint, you can either rely on sales and marketing information gathered from inside the company or simulate a customer in some other way. The best method is for the BUS group to become a customer: to buy the company's paint; to stay in the company's hotels; to rent the company's cars; to open a bank account with the company; or do whatever is required to sample the company's product. Only then can an accurate and effective business strategy be developed.

4.2.2 Strategic viewpoint

Every company's top executive should have three questions constantly in mind: What is our business? What could our business be? What should our business be? How he and his top management answer these questions indicates the appropriate business strategy to move the company from its current position to its future one.[1] The BUS group's second task is to understand the business strategy, because it will identify those areas of the company that warrant careful analysis.

Of course, top management may have no strategy, in which case the BUS group, with management's permission, can help to formulate one. Having a clearly defined business strategy is so important to the company's success that I must digress to consider briefly how to formulate a strategy. The first step is for management to determine the company's business goals, such as increased market share or diversification.

The next step is to identify the company's critical success factors, those areas of the business in which high performance is required if the objectives of the company are to be met.[2] This step is not easy; no two top executives are likely to agree immediately upon what they are for a particular company. Fortunately, there are some fairly scientific ways to identify the critical success factors for your business, and even the goals that are best for your company. Among these ways is the effective use of statistics on your competitors. Until recently, short of industrial espionage, obtaining detailed data on the competition was virtually impossible. But now several organizations gather and disseminate such statistics (in a sanitized form, of course). One such group is the nonprofit Strategic Planning Institute (Cambridge, Mass.), which runs what they call the Profit

---

[1] Since a full discussion of business strategy is well beyond the scope of this book, I recommend [Porter, 1980] as an excellent text on the subject.

[2] See Rockart's ground-breaking article for a discussion of critical success factors, as well as an excellent account of the advantages and disadvantages of a total business study [Rockart, 1979].

Impact of Market Strategy Program. Suggest to your management that your company subscribe to such an organization.

After acquiring the information that is vital to your industry, be it information on quality or on rates of return, your management can determine weak areas of the company, critical success factors, and future directions for the business. The BUS group can assist greatly in this process by gathering data, interviewing top managers, and moderating management discussions in order to achieve consensus about important issues.

Unfortunately, your DP department may not have recorded the appropriate vital statistics for your company, and one of the BUS group's first priorities is to set up a project to gather them, even if that project is an isolated, ad hoc one. Later, one of the crucial sections of the plan for initiating DP projects will be the one that establishes a permanent upper management reporting system for data on critical success factors (this system, of course, will also be well integrated with other systems).

This type of system, sometimes called an executive information system or EIS, is beginning to be recognized as an essential application of information technology to modern, competitive companies. An EIS typically includes several decision support and data analysis tools, and is used by top management to measure performance in meeting critical success factors; to measure progress toward corporate goals; and to derive future goals, strategies, and critical success factors.

4.2.3 Operational viewpoint

The BUS group's third area of interest is the company's operational side, including the DP department itself. At least four techniques can be used to gather information: interviewing, performing actual jobs, conducting dataflow analysis, and performing informational analysis. The last two are also disciplined documentation techniques. Although I discuss these techniques in this section, there's no reason that you couldn't also use these techniques in areas other than the operational. Interviewing, for example, is obviously generally applicable in all areas.

One of the best ways to become acquainted with an organization is a technique called top-down/bottom-up interviewing.[3] This method dictates the order in which people in a company are interviewed. From an organizational chart of the company or department that you intend to study, interview people at successive levels from the top downward. The purpose of this sequence is to find out what questions to ask at the next, lower level. Next, interview everyone again from the bottom of the chart upward until you reach the top. The purpose of the bottom-up interviewing is to use the knowledge gained at the lower levels to be able to converse with the higher-level managers and to integrate the possibly diverse and conflicting views of people at lower levels.

Obviously, the BUS group won't be able to interview everyone in the company, at least on the first pass. Instead, the BUS group should focus on interviews with all of higher operational management and with only selected people at lower levels of the organization. As I mentioned earlier in the chapter, specialized task forces formed from the main BUS group can eventually interview more people in more detail throughout the company.

Nothing imprints itself so firmly in the mind as a hands-on experience. Therefore, fully understanding a job demands that you actually do that job. Analysts who try this learning-by-doing technique find it to be a most effective way to thoroughly understand a job and the organization surrounding that job, and it is especially valuable in uncovering those exceptional situations that are often forgotten in an interview.

---

[3]For further treatment of top-down/bottom-up interviewing, as well as suggestions on the deliverables of the interviews, see [Donaldson, 1978, pp. 52ff]. Giegold also has worthwhile ideas and references on an interviewing style called aggressive inquiry [Giegold, 1982].

Weinberg refers to this technique as "living among the natives" or the anthropologized approach to analysis [Weinberg, 1982]. However, he does caution that by living among our users for too long, we may become so like them that we lose our objective perspective. (You'll know that point has arrived when the users offer you a job!)

Studying the flow of data through a business is at the heart of the analysis technique known as structured analysis.[4] It offers several advantages for studying a company's operations: First, structured analysis provides an orderly way to study any system, be it automated or manual, simple or complex, because it advocates breaking the whole into its parts. Each part is represented by data flow diagrams, thus providing a good way to record the system and to communicate it to others.

Informational analysis is my generic term for a collection of slightly different methods for gathering information about real-world objects, their characteristics, and their interrelationships. These methods include entity-relationship modeling, information modeling, and Bachman diagramming. Informational analysis is complementary to structured analysis, since, to put it simplistically, the former models the invariant properties of data being acted upon by processes, whereas the latter models data traveling between processes. With informational analysis, you have an excellent tool for quickly gaining a firm understanding of a company's informational foundations. Informational analysis is also vital for discovering what information the company possesses, what it needs to operate and to make decisions, what the company's policies are, how to derive this information, and how to govern the company's informational resources.[5]

4.3 Devise a technologically based strategy

Once the BUS group has been established and has acquired a full understanding of the business from three major viewpoints, group members must take a third step and devise a strategy using modern technology to improve the business. In addition to members of the BUS group, participants in developing such a strategy are corporate management and senior DP management. Three components in formulating an effective strategy are these: first, projecting available resources for projects; second, identifying specific benefits from projects, either through increased revenue, reduced business costs, improved customer service, or satisfying inflexible requirements; and, third, estimating costs of projects to achieve the benefits.

As discussed in Chapters 2 and 3, the resources, benefits, and costs for each potential project are compared. If a project promises significant benefits over costs, that project's estimates should be refined with some additional analysis. Such a deeper analysis begins at the point where the BUS group's initial analysis stopped.

I now need to discuss benefits further since their identification depends upon your having a solid and comprehensive understanding of your company's business. Of the many possible methods to help you identify potential benefits, three representative methods are analyzing money flow, acquiring industry expertise, and brainstorming, as discussed in turn below.

4.3.1 Money flow analysis

A study of the flow of money in a corporation—how much goes where and for what purposes—can be illuminating, since opportunities to reduce costs are more likely to be found in those areas that consume large amounts of money. However, this type of analysis can also be

---

[4]See [DeMarco, 1978] or [Gane and Sarson, 1977] for a good introduction to structured analysis.

[5]For detailed treatment of informational analysis, see [Flavin, 1981; Synnott and Gruber, 1981; and Martin, 1982b]. The last reference is one of many by Martin on databases and information management. Its theme is planning the use of information to further a company's business, and it covers IBM's Business Systems Planning Methodology, among other topics.

frustrating. As a colleague of mine explained, ''When you start digging into people's budgets, they get aggressively defensive. A manager whose budget is under study exhibits one of four types of reaction: He either camouflages his expenditures like a chameleon and hides himself away; or like a tiger, he bites off your head; or like a porcupine, he bristles and lashes out; or like a skunk, he creates a huge political stink.''

Thus, you can occasionally lose track of the flow of cash when it disappears, like a river into a limestone valley, into an uncooperative department. To track such expenditures, you need to combine the talents of an accountant, explorer, and potholer. A simple rule of thumb to estimate these expenditures within a department is to count the employees engaged on each task and calculate the amount of money spent on each task in proportion to the number of employees.

Although large expenditures clearly deserve the most attention for reducing costs, areas with insufficient expenditures may also present opportunities. For example, if little is being spent on tracking the efficacy of advertising, advertising dollars may be wasted and opportunities to reach new markets (and thus increase revenue) may be ignored. Thus, either an automated or manual system for tracking advertising responses may be of benefit to the company by both reducing costs and increasing revenue.

4.3.2 Acquiring industry expertise

There are many sources of industry expertise, including journals and conferences, for discovering solutions to problems or for identifying new business opportunities. Especially important are conferences that address the effects of modern technology on your own industry.

Some consultants also specialize in modern trends in a particular industry, and their names and addresses are kept on file by some major computer vendors (although these consultants are not necessarily affiliated with the vendor). Check whether your computer vendor has such a file on consultants in your industry.

4.3.3 Brainstorming

There is but a fine line between creativity and insanity. What stanches creative ideas is the mind's own critical demon that prematurely dubs them to be impossible. The purpose of brainstorming is to loosen the flow of ideas—both good and bad—by deliberately silencing our carping internal critic [DeBono, 1970; Ackoff, 1978].

The BUS group may use brainstorming in order to winkle out business problems and opportunities. One guideline for a brainstorming meeting is to think laterally—that is, to make leaps of creativity, rather than follow a logical train of thought. A second guideline is to build on the ideas of others, rather than attempt to find flaws in those ideas. Following these guidelines produces a stream of unconventional proposals. Although most of these proposals will turn out to be insane, one or two may prove to be both original and workable.

To illustrate the outcome of a creative brainstorming session, let me relate how one company managed with the help of its computer system to place a hammerlock on its customers, while simultaneously making those customers very happy indeed. The Metropolis Medical Co. (not its real name) supplied medical products to hospitals. Every week, a Metropolis salesperson visited the hospitals for their orders and submitted them to a clerk at Metropolis to fill them. When a problem arose (such as a salesperson's transcription error or a shortage of stock), the clerk contacted the originator of the order at the hospital. Most problems were resolved after a few phone calls. Several days later, the requested medical supplies arrived at the hospital and were added to its inventory.

So far, this is the story of a remarkably normal distribution company with remarkably normal customers and remarkably normal problems. On occasion, however, no one was available at the hospital to give the salesperson the order, or the hospital required an item immediately and would have to phone it in. On rare occasions, a salesperson lost an order, and the hospital went to another vendor for the order.

Then, the company added a computerized order entry and inventory system and, in a master stroke born of a brainstorming session, supplied to every client a computer terminal that was directly connected to the system. In addition, Metropolis guaranteed twenty-four hour delivery time on all orders entered by the hospital itself through its on-site Metropolis computer terminal.

The advantages to the hospitals of this approach included the ability to browse through Metropolis' inventory to find the best, cheapest, or newest products, and then to order them at their convenience with quick turnaround time. If hospitals stocked only Metropolis' products, they knew their exact inventory at any time through a feature of the system. Because of this and the quick order fulfillment, hospitals could reduce the size of their inventory. Another benefit was that the hospitals didn't have to worry about lost orders or errors by salespeople and about being bothered by salespeople at inconvenient times.

The advantage to Metropolis salespeople was that instead of being walking order-takers, they could devote their time to selling. To the company as a whole, the system eliminated the army of order clerks, used the salespeople more productively, and locked in the hospitals to deal solely with Metropolis. No hospital would want to use another vendor's antiquated manual system, or to use another system and another set of terminals, or to mix their inventory from different vendors. The system, with its feature of taking the data to the people, gave Metropolis a huge competitive edge.

Before going on to the final step in implementing a data processing plan, let me recap the process up to this point: Upper management knows the company's business and what it should and could be; it has a set of goals to direct the company's activities and a business strategy for meeting the goals. Upper management has identified a set of critical success factors that are essential to the strategy. The BUS group, meanwhile, has a documented understanding of the procedural, informational, and financial structure of the company; and a technical strategy for improving the business has been formulated.

4.4 Initiate projects to accomplish the strategy

The fourth and final step in implementing a coordinated company-wide DP plan is to formulate and carry out projects based on the strategy developed in the third step. Corporate management, together with senior data processing management and the BUS group, first selects DP projects that will benefit the business and then sets a timetable for initiating those projects. For each project, top management also designates a project producer to act as a bridge between the DP project and the company at large and to champion the business objectives of the project. His technical counterpart is called the project leader or project director.

The project producer must be committed to the objectives of the project and must want the project to succeed. It's no use putting up with some warm body dragged out of semi-retirement to be propped up weekly at a meeting table. Usually, when this warm body returns to the user department, half of the users don't know who he is and the other half can't remember, and in any event, no one cares what he says. If the users cannot find anyone with the time, the authority, and the commitment required, there's no reason why the DP department should find the time to be positively committed to the project either.

The project producer must be known and respected by all the users who will be affected by the project. Ideally, he should have authority over the affected users, whether they be department managers or data entry clerks. Hence, the more important the effects of the project, the higher in the organization the explicit user commitment must be.

Thus, by integrating every DP project with the company's business and management's business strategy, and by linking the conduct of every project to the users through the project producer, you can unite data processing activities with the mainstream of company activities. The DP department, instead of being a pariah on the lunatic fringes of your corporation, can instead provide solid and indispensable support for upper management's policies.

4.5 Potential problems with establishing a BUS group

Although a BUS group may help the DP department to better serve the company at large, establishing and operating a BUS group is not without problems. I discuss three potential difficulties below.

One potential problem is a general fear that the BUS group is an elite corps intent on some secret nefarious ends. Change and rumors of change often provoke agitation among a company's employees. The prospect of computerization provokes further concern over potential loss of jobs, sometimes to the point of complete Luddism among workers who fear being replaced by some digital behemoth.[6] Corporate management's job is to dispel such understandable fears. An attitude of openness, honesty, sensitivity, and humility by the BUS group also goes a long way in this direction.

Furthermore, there is no reason why the BUS group should be an immutable cadre. Rotating several people, especially from the lower tiers of the organization, through the BUS group and setting up special local task forces to study a particular business area promote the spirit that the BUS group is representative of all interests. Remember that it's not the BUS group's job to solve the company's political problems, but neither is it the group's job to cause them.

A second potential problem is the refusal of upper corporate management to cooperate in developing a sound DP strategy integrated with the business of the company. If upper management steadfastly withholds its support for strategic DP planning, the BUS group's objectives are lost, and the data processing department will remain on the periphery of the organization, carrying out scattered and incoherent projects with divergent and irrelevant aims.

Corporate management sometimes scuttles the BUS group in more subtle ways than by an outright lack of cooperation, however. For example, management may ostensibly support the objectives of the BUS group, but set it up in a gloomy corner of the company with no real clout or authority to delve into the company's business. The reason may be that management fears what the BUS group will discover about the business. A desire to preserve secrecy may be valid, but it may also be an excuse for censorship in the furtherance of individuals' self-seeking interests. Hamstrung in this way, the BUS group soon becomes a mere United Nations-style talking shop.

Another way in which management might sabotage the BUS group is by indulging in a perversion of the divide-and-rule principle. This may entail the tacit encouragement of rival sects to tear apart the BUS group, with the BUS group disintegrating in a political bloodbath.

If a company's upper management continually refuses—either overtly or covertly—to allow data processing to serve the company as it should, the company's shareholders should ask, Do we want a modern, forward-thinking company? And, Can we get there from here with our current management?

A third difficulty in utilizing a BUS group is resistance to the data processing department's going into suspended animation for one or two years. Although I sympathize with this resistance, from my experience, many companies would be much better off if the DP departments had played cards for the past ten years, rather than turning out the termite-ridden systems that are collapsing about the users' heads.

---

[6]King Ned Ludd was the pseudonym of the elusive leader of the textile workers who rioted early in the English Industrial Revolution because of fear of losing their jobs to automated looms.

When I recommended to one data processing department manager that his staff not carry out any more projects until it formed a corporate plan for integrating DP into the overall business, I made the following suggestions: "There's a great deal of training and staff development that you need to accomplish. In addition to having some of your staff participate in the BUS group, you can have others work on prototype projects to introduce modern hardware and software technologies into your shop. In two years, you can have top-notch project teams ready to implement a new long-term company DP strategy." Unimpressed, the manager told me to take my unwholesome, disruptive views elsewhere.

Ah well, none are so deaf as those who will not hear, I suppose. This manager epitomized data processing's traditional lack of consideration for its users and the company's business. Such a manager is dangerous: He must be severed from his department before his department is severed from the company. Even if that DP manager was right in saying that a two-year data processing hiatus would be too long, without a dialogue between DP and upper management, who could even begin to say what the right length of time would be? And, of course, it takes two sides imbued with reason to form a dialogue, not two factions embittered by years of mutual distrust.

Admittedly, there is a disadvantage in spending a year or two on a total study of the business: The business itself may change greatly during the period of the study, thus invalidating some of the huge amount of information gathered by the BUS group. (Of course, this is more of a danger in new, rapidly developing companies than in mature, stable companies.) However, change alone cannot be used as an excuse for not planning. You must develop a high-level understanding of your company, together with an information model of the company, or else within a few years, the very changes that hampered the understanding of the business will leave an aftermath of computerized chaos that no one can either understand or control.

There is however a reasonable compromise between the understandable desire for an early harvest of results and a more lengthy strategic planning activity. That compromise involves the spinning off of projects in areas that appear worthwhile well before the planning activity is complete. As in any radical approach, the risks are that systems may need to be changed in the light of later knowledge. But the political benefits of being seen to be doing something tangible outweigh these risks. I concur with McMenamin and Palmer, who recommend producing something tangible within eighteen to twenty-four months of beginning the study in order to demonstrate a potential for action and not merely words [McMenamin and Palmer, 1984].

4.6 Summary

It's essential to develop a sound understanding of both the strategy and operations of your company's business before you embark on any data processing projects. In these days of pervasive technology, understanding a company's business is too important to be left solely to the users, so I propose that your company form a business understanding and strategy group, composed of both business and DP personnel.

The BUS group first develops an understanding of your company's business, and in particular its informational needs, from three points of view: external, strategic, and operational. Then, it participates with senior business and DP management to form a strategy for improving the company's business by means of modern technology. Finally, the same participants establish a schedule of DP projects to accomplish that strategy in an orderly, integrated, and lasting manner.

Unfortunately, this approach to developing and implementing a company-wide business improvement strategy has several potential problems, including a refusal by either DP or corporate management to cooperate with the BUS group, fear of the BUS group by the company's rank and file, and reluctance to delay the initiation of projects until planning is complete.

Nevertheless, the will to compromise and the desires to ward off future problems and to exploit future opportunities for the general good of the company can overcome most of these problems. Then, a BUS group can be successfully detached from the daily buffeting of politics and short-term expediencies in order to arrive at an objective strategy to advance the company's business through modern technology.

To be forewarned is to be forearmed: There must be a strategy for initiating projects that meets the goals of the company as a whole, so that no longer will a flurry of superficial, inconsistent requests fall upon the DP department from confused users. No longer will systems be periodically installed with continual major upheavals to their users, but with little lasting benefit to them. No longer will the panicked cries from users be heard week after week in the DP department, "We're not sure what we want, but do it right, do it cheap, and do it yesterday!"

Chapter 4: Exercises

1.   Who from your DP department would be valuable members of a BUS group? Whom would you choose from the company at large?

2.   What do you think is your company's business? What could it be? What should it be?

3.   What are the critical success factors of your company? Are these your own nominations, or has your corporate management published these factors?

4.   What information is needed to measure performance in the areas of critical success you identified in the third question? From which databases in your shop can you obtain this information?

5.   Form a brainstorming group to think of specific ideas for supporting your company's business strategy through information systems. (Hint: Think of the example from Section 4.3 for inspiration.)

SECTION II

The DP Project

Projects are those stepping stones across which project managers carry the users from their current situation to an improved situation. Sadly, however, some of these stepping stones are slick and dangerous. Many a project manager has at one time or another slipped off a stepping stone and deposited himself and the users in the drink.

The seven chapters of Section II are intended to guide managers safely through the project—from department organization to staffing to project reviews. First is the issue of organization: Chapter 5 explains the need for some sort of organizational structure and discusses alternative structures. It then proposes an organizational matrix structure that can simultaneously support DP projects and the development of human skills in an industry that is always changing. This structure, though imperfect, will nonetheless form the organizational archetype for the topics of the remainder of the book. Chapter 6 examines what constitutes effective project management, and highlights those management aspects that are especially important in DP shops.

Chapter 7 is iconoclastic: It seeks to break the graven image of the deadline that many project managers worship before. However, it concludes with suggestions for accommodating tough but legitimate deadlines without jeopardizing the whole project. The next chapter answers the question, Why do standards usually have the same effect on DP personnel as the brandishing of a crucifix has on Count Dracula?

In Chapter 9, ways are suggested to lighten the infamous burdens upon project members: time and project status reporting. The conduct of meetings is the topic of Chapter 10, since in many shops, meetings are ill-prepared for, poorly run, and unproductive—in short, a scandalous waste of time. Chapter 11 covers another traditional time-waster: the project review, pointing out the objectives of intermediate project reviews as well as those of the oft-neglected post-project review.

5

Organizing the DP Department

In order for a company to carry out its business, it assumes a particular organizational structure. This structure derives from how its work is partitioned into tasks and how the tasks are coordinated by managers in order to achieve useful results.

5.1 The need for organization

The term *organization* as I use it in this chapter means the structure of the components of a company or a department, as illustrated by the following example: "I think that a simple hierarchy will be the best organization for the Gruntfuttock Enterprises DP department."

Although having an organization adds to a business' overhead and consumes some of its energies, a business must have an organization for two complementary reasons: First, the work required to achieve a set of business objectives is too large or calls for too many special skills to be carried out by a single human being or machine, and so the work must be divided into tasks. This is called the *analysis* of work into tasks. Second, once the work is divided into tasks, they must be coordinated in order to achieve a set of business objectives. This is called the *synthesis* of tasks into useful work. The analysis of work plus the synthesis of tasks is what gives rise to a particular organizational structure.[1]

A human organization has both formal and informal components. The formal organization is dedicated solely to achieving the business objectives and is basically the organization as designed: the organization that appears on the company charts with positions defined by job descriptions and objectives. The informal organization is the formal organization adapted to real circumstances by the people who have to make it work. It is a structure that covers the spectrum from serving purely business needs to supporting the weave of personal friendships, loyalties, and enmities that form the social fabric of a group of human beings. Some components of the informal organization are never seen on any formal charts: for example, a phone call from a programmer to a user to clarify the length of a field; or a discussion between the VP of finance and the DP manager about data security at the "nineteenth hole" of a golf course.

In this chapter, I first explore some major disabling problems in data processing departments that are largely due to organizational maladjustments. I then discuss some different organizational structures. With that foundation, I set out a workable structure for a DP department carrying out many projects simultaneously while also developing the skills of its staff. This organizational

---

[1]This sentence is adapted from [Mintzberg, 1979], which is the most comprehensive and well researched book on organizational structures that I've come across.

model, with its advantages and disadvantages, forms the basis for subsequent discussions of DP departmental structure in the book.

5.2 Common problems arising from departmental misorganization

All organizational structures have problems. The mere partitioning and coordination of work introduce communication problems at the interface between tasks. Yet, for a given company or department, some structures cause fewer problems than others.

The flaws in a good organization are no worse than one's relatives: familiar, annoying, but possible to live with. A bad organization, however, hampers a shop's productivity and saps its staff's morale. The following sections describe eight problems of organization I've encountered most often in data processing shops.

5.2.1 The too-large job

When work is divided into tasks and then parceled into jobs, there's always the possibility of grouping too many tasks into one job so that no one person could possibly handle the whole job. Such a job can be too large in any one of its "be, know, and do" dimensions: what a person must *be,* or what his personality must be, in order to do the job; what he must *know,* or what skills he needs, in order to perform the job; and what he must actually *do,* to fulfill the job requirements [Giegold, 1982]. For example, a job holder may be required to have the forbearance of Job, the wisdom of Solomon, and the outgoing nature of Bob Hope. Or the job may require a deep knowledge of banking, together with skills in information modeling, telecommunications hardware, Box Jenkins forecasting, and graphics design. Or it may require its holder to spend twelve hours per day, every day, on its Herculean tasks.

A job may be too large either because it contains too many tasks or because each of its tasks is very large. I came across an instance of a too-large job at a corporation where the data center's manager had held that position for twelve years. During that time, no significant organizational change happened around him, although his responsibilities continued to expand with the need to have additional tasks associated with computer networks, satellite communications, and data security, and as the number of terminals, CPUs, and variety of machines increased. Obviously, his staff increased to do the hands-on work, but the job of managing all this work directly became impossible for him, even though he often put in eighty-hour work weeks. As a result of the long hours, he became exhausted, irrational, and was impossible to deal with. So, the insensitive company fired him.

The next manager lasted only six months and the one after that not much longer. At that point, the company realized it needed another management level between the data center manager and the workers. The job of data center manager was pared to a reasonable size and manageability was restored.

There are two chief causes of the too-large, non-doable job. The first is historical trend, as in the example above. The second is establishment of a special post to use the full talents of a particular managerial genius. When that genius moves on, a hole is left that no mere mortal can fill and wherein many die trying.

5.2.2 The too-small job

At the opposite extreme of the too-large job is an allotment of work that is well beneath the capabilities of a sentient being from the planet Earth. An example that I saw recently of a too-small job was the single task—assigned full-time to an experienced programmer—of maintaining the

COBOL COPYLIB on a development project. To make matters worse, a second person was assigned to maintain the project's data dictionary.

The obvious problem with a too-small job is the effect on its incumbent. The bored, demoralized worker will eventually either quit in frustration or indulge in random and probably unproductive activities in addition to his assigned job. The devil makes work for idle hands to do!

A second problem is the inefficiency of too-small tasks. Breaking work up too finely and distributing the small tasks to many different people increases the need for communication and coordination within the organization. For instance, in the above example, who ensures the conformity of the COPYLIB to the data dictionary? How does the maintainer of the data dictionary communicate changes to the maintainer of the COPYLIB? through memos or by informal meetings? Who resolves disputes between the two people? Is the coordination overhead worthwhile? Since the overhead in this example is assuredly not worthwhile, combining the tasks of maintaining the data dictionary and the COPYLIB into one job would be an improvement.

5.2.3 Too many levels of management

Too many levels of management is a special case of too-small jobs, and this problem arises when minuscule tasks are distributed vertically rather than horizontally in the organizational chart. The causes of such a phenomenon include over-staffing in middle management, awarding "harmless sinecures" as a way to move aside incompetent people, or simply poorly planning the distribution of tasks so that unnecessary coordination is needed to unify the tasks into useful work.

The result of too many levels of management is inefficiency, as a tangled web of communications develops. Endless meetings proliferate, with dozens of attendees discussing such weighty matters as the type of lock to install on the computer room door. Countless managers' approvals are required to make the simplest decisions and all managers must be consulted—even if only to avoid hurting their feelings—before any action is taken. A managerial pyramid of tiny jobs is a bureaucrat's paradise, but an achiever's Hades.

5.2.4 Too flat a management structure

Some departmental managers believe that unless they involve themselves in every decision in the department, no matter how trivial, the department will fall to pieces. This belief translates into a flat management structure: in the extreme, just the boss and everyone else. Although a nominal middle manager may appear on the formal organizational chart, if an upper manager continually circumvents him, in reality middle management doesn't exist.

A flat management structure is a classic symptom of the too-rapid growth of a small organization into a large one. Many DP departments that ten years ago were virtually one-person shows exhibit this symptom. For example, I remember a DP manager who insisted on participating in just about every decision in his department, from the location of the departmental picnic to the type of folder to be used to hold program listings. Fifteen years ago, when he was one of three people in the department, this might have made sense. But now, with a department of almost eighty people, he simply could not let go of his old way of working and gracefully delegate decision making to the right level. (This is also an example of why no organization can be perfect so long as it is staffed by human beings!) When departmental managers are so obsessed by trivia that they cannot make the tough decisions that are their primary responsibility, the whole organization suffers.

5.2.5 Separation of authority from responsibility

To be given responsibility without authority is to be assigned a job but not the wherewithal to do it. This problem has an obvious twin: authority without responsibility. The following story shows the harmful effects of both these spoliative siblings.

I was called in to investigate a company's immense DP productivity problem, which, it turned out, was due mainly to the ever-changing project assignments of its staff. Programmers and analysts were continually tossed from project to project like ingredients in a boiling vegetable stew. The reassignments were caused almost directly by the Project Approval Committee, a collection of stalwarts who viewed their job as just that: to approve every project. And why not? They had the authority to do so, but they didn't have to bear responsibility for their blanket approvals. *That* onus fell upon the DP shop members who, having achieved six impossible tasks before lunch one day, were then asked to achieve seven more before breakfast the next day.

If I had been on the Project Approval Committee, I would have behaved in exactly the same way, taking the line of least resistance. I wouldn't want to wake up to find angry users burning feasibility studies on my front lawn when I could easily pass my problems down to those infinitely absorbent sponges of suffering in DP. The fault in this case lay not with the Project Approval Committee, but with the organizational structure that separated authority from responsibility.

A great deal of high-level effort was expended to restore the proper objectives to the Project Approval Committee and to give the committee members the yin and yang of both responsibility and authority. Their new objectives were to identify the users' needs and to understand how to best address them with finite resources. The biggest change was that the committee co-opted two high-level members of the user department and the head of the DP department. For the first time in its existence, members of the Project Approval Committee had to make the challenging decisions on priorities and schedules as well as to estimate costs, benefits, and resources. Within the DP department, a manager was hired to coordinate various projects' demands for resources. These organizational changes for the first time allowed people to work uninterrupted for the duration of their assignments.

5.2.6 Inefficient distribution of expertise

If everyone in a DP department has to know something about everything to do his job, no one will know much about anything and probably no job will get done very well. This is especially true now that computer technology is advancing so rapidly and becoming so specialized.

For example, if every project in a shop has to select its own hardware, time will probably be wasted while someone carries out the necessary research. Also, the accumulated expertise will not have much value, since it will probably be outdated when the project member who did the research can use it again. If, however, a hardware-appraisal unit exists within the organization to keep track of suitable hardware and to provide advice, that knowledge could be tapped by other units whenever necessary.

Note that when I talk about an organizational unit specializing, I am not necessarily talking about people specializing. One person might hold two positions, working half-time at each, or (much more likely and useful) a person could rotate through specialized units. In that way, by working two or three years on each specialty, he would remain fresh; alternatively, he could migrate to a position he particularly enjoyed and performed well and could remain there indefinitely.

5.2.7 Organizational hypochondria

Some departments have a standard prescription for every ill: "Let's reorganize." However, reorganization is like major surgery; it is not the recommended cure for the common cold. Reorganization is difficult, extremely disruptive to production as well as to personal relationships that have taken years to develop, and—no matter how well you prepare for it—has unpredictable effects.

There are two typical problems that departments attempt—invariably futilely—to solve through reorganizing: the residual difficulties of any organization and incorrect personnel assignments. As discussed earlier, problems occur in all organizations simply because work that is subdivided must be coordinated. This results in lines of communication that can become tangled or broken and a distribution of decision points that can reduce efficiency or speed of action. Unless these problems become too severe, they must be tolerated by a department as the price of law and order. Nevertheless, some departments seem to be convinced that organizational nirvana is to be found at the next reorganization. They try a hierarchical structure and when that presents problems, they try the same structure but with the boxes shuffled around. When that, too, proves to be less than ideal, they try a matrix structure, which also falls short of perfection. And so they scrap that and try something else.

Sometimes a department tries to solve its problems through reorganization even though the problems are not caused by a poor organization. For example, I recall a shop whose remedy to the dual problems of low software productivity and the late delivery of unusable systems was to reorganize the whole department twice a year and occasionally to fire a few people. The true causes of their difficulties were their antiquated approach to analysis, their Paleolithic programming practices, and their medieval management methods. Their continual reorganizations yielded only sound and fury. The real solution to their difficulties had to await the introduction of modern software development techniques.

If you appoint the wrong person to a position, it's better by far to admit your mistake and move that person to another position. However, it's very tempting to narrow the scope of the job or to reorganize around the difficulty in order to avoid the embarrassment of acknowledging that you made a mistake. To show you what I mean, let me give you an example: I worked in a shop that had the organization shown in Figure 5.1.

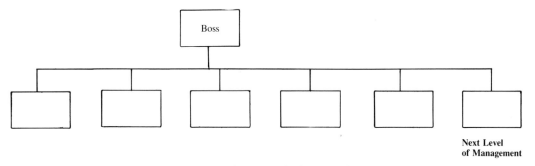

Figure 5.1. Shop organization example.

When the person promoted to be boss demonstrated clearly after a few months that he wasn't ready for the spot, upper management hired an intermediate manager, whose role was vaguely defined (see Figure 5.2). When that didn't work, the upper managers concluded (incredibly) that they hadn't gone far enough; so they promoted one of the six at the next level (see Figure 5.3), and then they came up with the configuration in Figure 5.4.

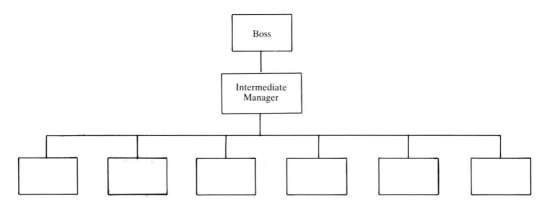

Figure 5.2. Altered shop organization.

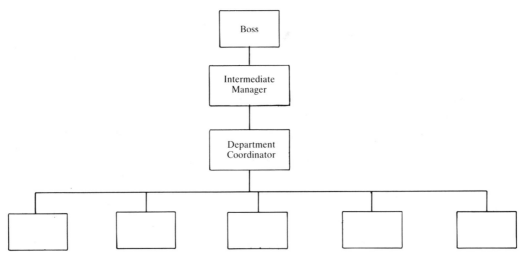

Figure 5.3. Shop organization with more intermediate levels.

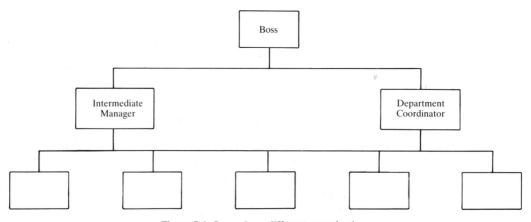

Figure 5.4. Same shop, different organization.

During the eight months that these various configurations were tried, things had not improved. When I left the company a month or so later, the managers were still engaged in these peculiar variations on the Towers of Hanoi and were getting absolutely nowhere.

5.2.8 Rampant politics

When rampant political shenanigans abound within a DP department, they are a clear sign of a weak formal organization. To be sure, there are other causes of departmental infighting: I've observed, for example, that politics are the first refuge of the incompetent. But some shops are so bedeviled by murrains of Machiavellian machinations that any lack of talents in the shop's personnel cannot be entirely to blame.

Political problems arise in a department when the formal organization is either weak or hopelessly unworkable. Then, the informal organization becomes highly distorted by social forces to the detriment of the department's business needs. Furthermore, subgroups of employees may form, each with its own social and business objectives. These objectives (which are rarely stated explicitly) are unlikely to benefit the department as a whole.

Some employees, because they don't fit into any social subgroup, may feel inadequate and alienated from the department. Denied an opportunity to contribute to departmental society, they may form small, shifting bands of renegades, which snipe at the activities of the other employees. Departments with such fractious personnel usually try to solve the problem by spending large sums of money on employee relations. This rarely works. The true way out of this civil (or rather this not so civil) unrest within the department is to re-establish a sound formal structure with strong departmental objectives. For instance, an objective for a steel company's DP department might be, "To improve the business of the Forge-Ahead Steel Company." This objective is then refined into specific subobjectives according to the jobs of the department. The subobjectives should be sufficiently detailed so that no one has any doubt about his contribution to the department's goals.

Having a sound organization does not mean your department will be transformed from a sea of storms into a sea of tranquility. There still will be politics. There will always be politics so long as there is more than one human being in your shop. However, politics in a department with a strong formal organization are constrained so they do not interfere with the smooth working of the department; they will not permit the forces of various personalities to batter the department around in random Brownian motion. (I further discuss this important issue in Chapter 15.)

5.3 Alternatives in organization

There are many possible ways of dividing labor and even more ways of coordinating the tasks. To illustrate this point, let's consider a very simplified version of a car manufacturer. The Bona Motor Co. employs fifty people and has the modest goal of producing fifty cars a week. Coincidentally, the production of a car requires fifty steps. What organizations could the Bona Motor Co. adopt? There are two obvious options: Either have each person produce one car per week, carrying out all fifty steps himself on the same vehicle, or assign each person to perform the same step of the process on all fifty cars.

I call the first option generalist style, which has these characteristics: The work offers each person creative satisfaction in producing a whole vehicle; the manufacturing process is relatively inefficient, because each worker must have his own set of tools and because of the time required for workers to switch from step to step. Every worker must be competent in all fifty manufacturing steps, and large divergences in the characteristics of the finished products can arise.

In the second type of organization, called specialist style, the manufacturing process is relatively efficient, but the work tends to be monotonous because workers don't move from step to step. Also, only one set of tools is needed, not up to fifty sets. Each worker needs to be skilled at only one manufacturing step, and the assembly line offers plenty of practice to improve that skill. Finished products are likely to be identical. At the start of the production run, the fiftieth worker remains idle through the first forty-nine steps, and the converse problem occurs at the end of the run. (Of course, this is a minor problem if the production run is long or if reassignment of workers is possible.)

The Bona Motor Co.'s management must also consider the coordination, or management, of the subdivided work. For the generalist style, little coordination is required. A manager must check that the finished products are alike and, if they're not, he must modify the procedure for the sake of future products. If the shop is short of welding tools or of paint sprayers, for example, someone must coordinate tool distribution to ensure fair shares for all. Basically, coordination is achieved by collecting all tasks for building a car into a single job carried out by one person.

The specialist style requires more and different coordination than does the generalist style. To see this, let's make the Bona Motor Co. example more elaborate. Assume that each of the fifty manufacturing steps requires a different length of time to carry out. Let's also assume that the company's goal is to turn out two hundred cars per week with a work force of two hundred. The generalist style of organization is basically unchanged, since it just becomes four times larger. But the assembly line now has six people performing some manufacturing steps and two people on other steps, rather than one person per step as before.

On such an assembly line, two types of coordination are needed. One is *synchronization:* keeping each step running at the proper speed to avoid bottlenecks in the line. The second is *integration:* ensuring that, for instance, Jules's and Sandy's gaskets are identical and that they match Cyril's engine blocks. Integration also involves figuring out what to do if they don't match. Much of the latter type of coordination can be minimized by improving *standardization,* a rigid set of schedules and product specifications to which all work must conform. When standardization is possible (as it would be on a well-understood and repeatable process), explicit coordination is reduced to handling mishaps in production.

5.4 Organizational complexity and Mintzberg's theory

One of the points of the above example is to show how complex and difficult are the decisions regarding an organizational structure. To produce two hundred cars per week for two hundred people, the Bona Motor Co. would have to choose (or compromise) between generalist and specialist styles; between lower management overhead and higher production efficiency; between a staff of creative all-rounders and one of narrow specialists; and between some latitude in product specifications and tight product and process standardization. These choices are faced by an almost trivially simple company that has to consider only two possible ways of dividing labor. A real company has to deal with far more possibilities.

When a company divides labor, it does more than split up work. It concomitantly creates needs for networks of information and channels of material flow. Coordination requires distribution of decision making and flows of authority. Mintzberg identifies five major structures that exist in any real-life enterprise [Mintzberg, 1979]. These five structures (three of which are further refined) are shown below:

1. structure of formal authority
2. structure of regulated flows
    - operating-work flows
        - operating-work materials
        - operating-work information
    - control flows
    - staff/line information flows
3. informal communication structure
    - for work
    - for social purposes
4. work/expertise constellation structure
5. structure of ad hoc decision making
    - operating decisions
    - administrative decisions
        - coordinative decisions
        - exceptional decisions
    - strategic decisions

Superimposing these five structures and their components on one diagram demonstrates vividly how complicated any realistic discussion of organizational structure can be (see Figure 5.5[2]). And even with these structures, Mintzberg is not sure his list is complete!

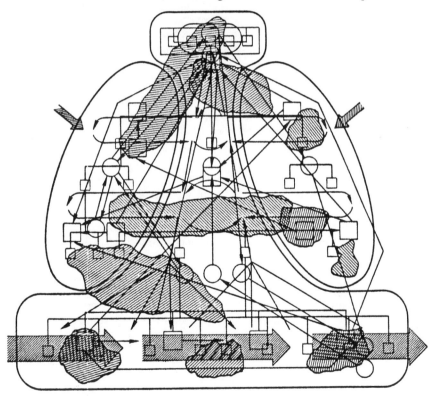

Figure 5.5. A combined overlay: the functioning of the organization.

[2]Henry Mintzberg, THE STRUCTURING OF ORGANIZATIONS, © 1979, p. 64. Reprinted by permission of Prentice-Hall, Inc., Englewood Cliffs, N.J.

5.5 A model organization for a DP department

In this section, I shall construct an organization suitable for a medium-to-large data processing department by looking at how the work of a DP department might be subdivided and then coordinated. The basic function of this department is to manufacture computer systems chiefly for the benefit of the remainder of the company. To simplify things, I assume that manufacturing and delivering a computer system, which I call a project, have three steps: deciding what to produce, producing it, and installing it and keeping it operating successfully.

The basic structure I choose for projects of this size is specialist style. Although the generalist style of operation is acceptable for a small project, for a project of any complexity, it doesn't make sense to have an unchanging team carry out every step of the work; the mix of skills required would be too great. Also, it would be uneconomical to employ a business analyst, for example, as a coder.

A specialist style project is not without its own problems. Running a computer system project as an assembly line is different from running the Bona Motor Co. assembly line. For one thing, the Bona Motor Co. assembly line produces hundreds of the same product, whereas each DP assembly line (or project) produces a unique product. Consequently, standardization at the car company is straightforward, while two DP projects, however similar they may be, are never identical. Additional coordination of DP projects is required to make up for the lack of the ability to standardize completely.

The car company has long production runs. A DP project, however, is a production run of one. If DP personnel and other resources are not shared among projects, great idleness results. (This is the start-of-run problem mentioned earlier.) Since software and hardware technologies are changing much more rapidly than car manufacturing technology, coordination is required to ensure that project members apply the most appropriate modern technology to their jobs and that their technologies match one another.

Because of these difficulties in operating a DP project as an assembly line, two types of manager are needed. The first type, called a *project manager* or *line manager,* is responsible for a single assembly line and its product. The second type is called a *staff manager,* who is responsible for providing skilled staff for each step of every project and for standardizing techniques as much as possible. He also attends to the well-being and professional growth of the people whom he manages.

With these two managers, every DP project member has a two-dimensional reporting relationship. We can show this as Figure 5.6, with line authority shown horizontally and staff authority vertically. This organization is called a matrix management structure.[3] This structure is popular throughout the business world, because it offers this advantage: Line managers retain control of their particular projects, while staff managers mediate the personnel requirements of different projects, promote high standards within a specific discipline (such as analysis or hardware acquisition), and effect standardization within that discipline. This particular type of matrix organization is termed by Sayles the *shifting matrix structure,* because its shape changes as projects are completed or canceled [Sayles, 1976]. Also, personnel shift about vertically on the matrix at regular intervals, as they are transferred from project to project. Of course, people move

---

[3]Some major companies also have three-dimensional structures that incorporate, for example, different geographical locations. Four-dimensional structures are theoretically possible, but their complexity makes them unworkable.

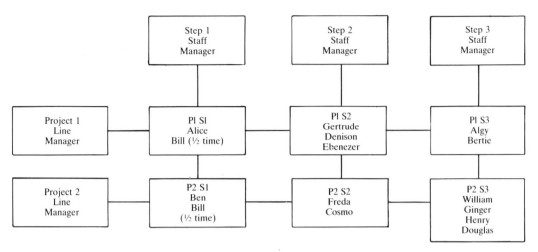

Figure 5.6. Two-dimensional reporting structure.

horizontally, too, as they change disciplines (for example, in moving from maintenance work to analysis). These shifts, however, tend to be much less frequent than the vertical shifts.

At the risk of belaboring the point that no organization is perfect, I must point out that the primary drawback of the matrix organization is that every worker has two managers: one line and one staff.[4] Additional managers are needed, increasing a project's overhead and its communication lines. Decisions formerly made by the project manager now require the staff manager's approval as well. When conflicts arise between the managers, the matrix structure requires mature managers, who are prepared, as Sayles puts it, ''to resolve their conflicts through informal negotiations among equals rather than recourse to formal authority.'' Mintzberg is blunter when he writes, ''Matrix structure is for grown-up organizations.''

The matrix organization entails a balance of power between line and staff managers. If either side gains a clear upper hand, the matrix degenerates into either a staff structure or a traditional line structure. In either case, the benefits of the matrix are lost, although its disadvantages remain.

Figure 5.7 shows a possible matrix organization for an average data processing department. Staff authority is again shown as vertical lines; line authority is shown as horizontal lines. In the example, Nelson Gabriel is the staff manager of six people, two of whom are on James Bigglesworth's project, three are on Tom Forrest's, and one is not assigned to any project. Bigglesworth is the line manager of project A, which has six and a half people assigned: two from Nelson Gabriel's staff, one half-time person from Ena Sharples' staff, three from Nigel Molesworth's staff, and one from Sidney Rumpeau's staff. (The nine people at the bottom of the chart, who are currently not working on any project, are far from idle, as we shall see in Chapter 13.)

---

[4]Advocates of the matrix structure argue that the need for extra communication is present regardless of the structure, but that the matrix approach simply makes the overhead explicit.

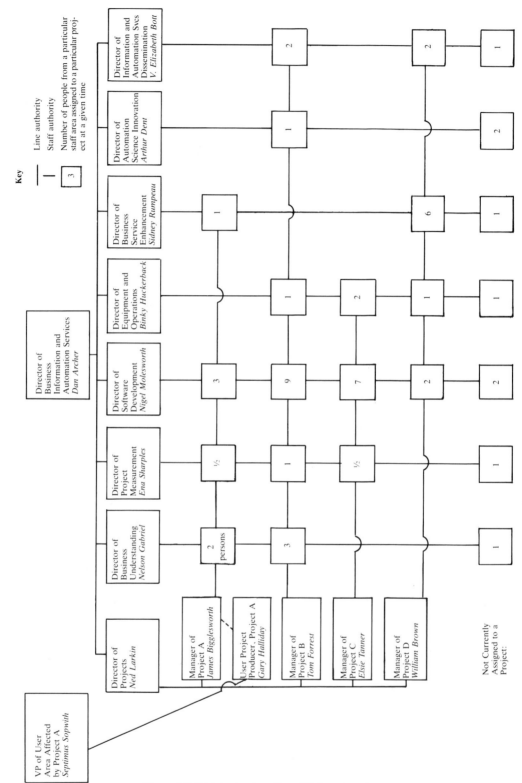

Figure 5.7. Matrix structure for a DP department.

Note in this figure the user project producer, a concept discussed in Chapter 6. This role is shown for completeness, though it is not a necessary part of a matrix structure. The producers for projects B, C, and D are omitted for clarity.

A staff manager's responsibility includes the furtherance of his particular discipline and the cultivation of his staff. Below, I show examples of the objectives of the staff managers of Figure 5.7. The responsibility of a line manager is chiefly the planning and execution of projects (the topic of the remaining chapters in Section II). His objective is to improve the company's business according to the charter of his current project.

Objectives of Staff Managers

D. Archer, Director of Business Information and Automation Services

1. To uphold the corporation's goals, beliefs, and principles.

2. To develop the professionalism of the department's personnel.

3. To improve corporate management's ability by providing timely and accurate corporate business information.

4. To enhance customer service, reduce business costs, and increase business revenue, through the integrated utilization of automated and manual systems.

5. To define and pursue excellence in the department.

6. To represent the department's interests in the corporation as a whole, in particular to obtain sufficient resources to operate the department.

N. Larkin, Director of Projects[5]

1. To balance project resource requirements with departmental resource availability.

2. To uphold management standards within the department.

3. To define and pursue excellence in staff management.

4. To define and pursue excellence in project management.

N. Gabriel, Director of Business Understanding

1. To define and pursue a thorough understanding of the corporation's business.

2. To identify opportunities to improve the corporation's business through the integrated utilization of automated and manual systems.

3. To define and pursue excellence in business analysis techniques: namely,

---

[5]This position could be regarded as either a staff or a line position.

business strategy analysis, problem investigation, procedural analysis, informational analysis, and the like.

E. Sharples, Director of Project Measurement

1.   To provide quantitative information on previous projects.

2.   To gather quantitative information on current projects.

3.   To provide quantitative feedback on current projects.

4.   To define and pursue excellence in project measurement and the quantitative and statistical analysis of projects.

N. Molesworth, Director of Software Development

1.   To define and pursue excellence in computer software development: namely, procedural design, informational design, human/computer engineering, computer/computer software engineering, programming, software quality evaluation, software quality enhancement, software tools, and the like.

B. Huckerback, Director of Equipment and Operations

1.   To acquire automation and telecommunication equipment that best serves the needs of the department and the corporation as a whole.

2.   To operate and maintain automation and telecommunication equipment to the greatest possible reliability.

3.   To define and pursue excellence in acquiring, operating, and maintaining automation and telecommunication equipment.

S. Rumpeau, Director of Business Service Enhancement[6]

1.   To analyze opportunities for providing better information to corporate management from existing products.

2.   To analyze opportunities for providing further benefits to the corporation from existing automated/manual products.

3.   To integrate projects to realize identified opportunities for improving the service to the corporation of existing products.

4.   To define and pursue excellence in identifying opportunities for improving service and in realizing those opportunities.

---

[6]More traditionally known as maintenance.

A. Dent, Director of Automation Science Innovation

1. To locate, understand, and evaluate novel or unproved techniques in the field of automation science.

2. To further the field of automation science through research and development.

3. To evaluate the department's and corporation's ability to exploit novel or unproved developments in automation science.

4. To define and pursue excellence in automation science as it might apply to the corporation's objectives.

V.E. Bott, Director of Information and Automation Services Dissemination

1. To acquire and provide education in automation science.

2. To provide education in the use of the department's services.

3. To acquire or develop and to disseminate instructional material in automation science and in the department's services.

4. To define and pursue excellence in providing pertinent education and in acquiring, developing, and disseminating instructional material.

5.6 Adapting the matrix to your needs

I certainly don't intend you to consider Figure 5.7 and the above list of objectives to be the definitive matrix structure for every data processing shop. Since no two DP departments are identical, you must tailor the structure to suit your own characteristics. For example, you could consider these possible modifications to the organization depicted:

- In a *small* shop, reduce the number of staff managers by combining some of their positions. (In the extreme case, there would be no staff managers, and Dan Archer would carry out all staff management functions. This would be a traditional small-shop structure.)

- In a *medium-sized* shop, you could break up Nigel Molesworth's software development position into several positions depending on your particular shop's requirements (perhaps analysis and design, or programming, testing, and software tools). Some reorganization might then be worthwhile, for instance, by combining some or all of the positions of business understanding, analysis, testing, and business service enhancement. (Remember that subdividing work increases communication lines and distributes decisions, but monolithic work overburdens individuals and/or prevents use of specialized expertise.)

- In a *large* shop, you may need to segment staff management positions so much that you will have more than a dozen staff managers. Having so many managers reporting to Dan Archer would be impractical. Therefore, an intermediate level of about four or five staff managers is needed between Dan Archer and the other staff managers. But if you're not careful, you can wind up with an incomprehensible labyrinth of communication and decision lines. One way to avoid such an impossibly tangled organizational skein is to have the lower staff managers responsible for staff cultivation and the upper managers deal with hiring, firing, and assignment. However, this calls for the four parties concerned—upper staff managers, lower staff managers, project managers, and workers—to behave and interact maturely and rationally. Otherwise, the whole structure is doomed to collapse in a heap of failed communication.

- A final modification is to break Ned Larkin's position into two: one to take charge of all projects, and the second to develop managerial skills. The first of these new positions could then be moved into Dan's position at the top of the shop. This would avoid any possible detachment of responsibility from authority. However, it may overload Dan's job unbearably.

5.7 Summary

In order to be feasible, the work of any enterprise must be partitioned into tasks and then amalgamated into jobs that are allocated to workers. These tasks also must be coordinated in order to achieve useful results. The basic organizational structure of the enterprise derives from the way in which the work is partitioned and the consequent tasks are coordinated.

Although the number of potential organizational dysfunctions is limitless, eight organizational problems occur frequently in data processing departments: jobs that are too large for anyone to handle; jobs that are too small to adequately occupy anyone sufficiently or that add unnecessary lines of communication; too many levels of management; too flat a management structure; the separation of authority from responsibility; a distribution of the need for expertise that requires everyone to know something about everything in order for the organization to function; organizational hypochondria, in which a department reorganizes incessantly in a vain search for perfection; and rampant politics, caused not so much by people attempting to hide their incompetence but by being left to their own devices (and mischiefs) through a weak formal organization. The formal organization is the organization as officially designated, and the informal organization is the actual organization made to work by the adaptations of its members.

Two fundamental methods of gathering tasks into jobs are generalist and specialist. The former involves dividing voluminous work into identical and independent pieces and assigning one per person. The latter involves breaking the work into distinct steps and assigning one person (or a small group) to each step. The specialist style tends to be more efficient but tends to require more coordination than does the generalist style. These two styles represent two extremes, but many intermediate mixes of specialist and generalist styles are both possible and practical.

An effective organization that I propose for a typical data processing shop is a matrix structure. The line component of the matrix consists of projects organized in a more or less specialist fashion. The staff component of the matrix is responsible for developing and coordinating the techniques on the various steps of the project, as well as for providing staff to projects and for cultivating the talents of the personnel under them.

A matrix organization, however, has disadvantages. Chief among them are the additional management and communication overhead, and the need for a way to resolve conflicts between line and staff managers before they affect the workers. Because of the additional overhead, full matrix management is inappropriate for small shops, where some staff management positions should be combined in order to reduce the number of managers needed. In very large and complex shops, an intermediate level of staff management may be necessary to reduce the span of control of the departmental head.

No style of organization is perfect. But to be without any workable organization is to invite that phantasm of a thousand faces called Perpetual Failure into your shop. To be definite, therefore, I will assume for the remainder of the book that your department has—to some extent at least— both line and staff management in its organization.

Chapter 5: Exercises

1.   Review the projects on which you've worked and try to recall instances of a specialist arrangement of work and instances of a generalist arrangement. What communication and coordination difficulties did the specialist style cause? What problems or inefficiencies did the generalist style cause?

Now consider the projects currently under way in your shop. What problems can you attribute to the project's work style? What measures are being taken to overcome these problems? What measures do you think should be taken?

2.   What is the formal organization of your department? How does the informal organization differ from it? How strongly do social requirements pull the informal organization away from the formal one?

3.   What problems in your department do you think have organizational causes? Could they be solved without the creation of worse problems?

6

Managing the Project

Although every DP project faces technical difficulties, they are not the major cause of project failures. The truly dramatic failures are due to inadequate or inept project management, which allows a project to run out of control like an unsteered car on an icy road. With no one in the driver's seat, the project crashes, its objectives unmet and its team left to shamble from the scene of the disaster in the humiliation of defeat. In this chapter, I examine what constitutes effective project management and the management activities that are vital to a project's success.

6.1 Definition of project management

What does managing a project actually entail? Although everyone has an idea of what the term *management* means, its precise definition seems curiously elusive. For example, one dictionary defines *to manage* as *to control* or *to administer*. It defines *to control* as *to govern*, among other definitions, and defines *to govern* as *to control* or *to administer*. I define *project management* to be the repeated execution of these five activities: planning, reorganizing, integrating, measuring, and revising—until the project's objectives are achieved. Since each of these five terms is also open to interpretation, let me define them as I use them in this book.

- *Planning* is establishing clear, detailed subobjectives to be achieved between the current situation and the final objective, together with a definition of the work needed to meet the subobjectives.

- *Organizing* is mapping the necessary resources for carrying out the work specified by the plan into an effective structure for executing the plan.

- *Integrating* is maintaining the unity and smooth operation of the resource structure, especially its human elements, during the actual execution of the plan.

- *Measuring* is acquiring continual feedback on the plan's execution.

- *Revising* is modifying the plan, organization, and possibly the objectives to accommodate the discrepancies revealed by measurement.

Notice that every one of these activities itself can be planned, organized, integrated, measured, and revised. However, don't take such meta-management too far, or else you'll spend so much time planning the plan that you'll never accomplish anything!

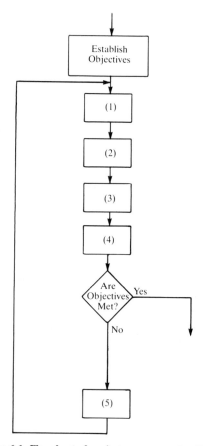

Figure 6.1. Flowchart of project management activities.

6.1.1 Project management activities

The five activities defined above are carried out in the following sequence, as expressed in the flowchart in Figure 6.1.

establish objectives
repeat
> (1) plan the tasks to achieve the objectives
> (2) organize the resources to execute the tasks
> (3) integrate the resources and begin executing the tasks
> (4) measure the progress against the plan

until the objectives are met
> (5) revise the plan, organization, and objectives as necessary

end repeat

The sections below treat each activity in detail.

6.2 Plan

A plan is to a project what a route map is to a journey. It indicates intermediate points along the way to the project's objectives and it identifies the tasks that take the project from one point

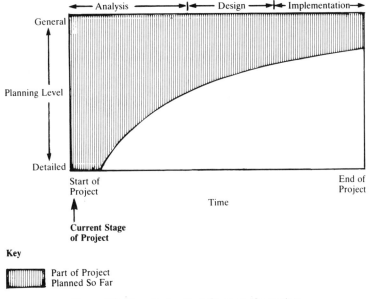

Figure 6.2. Planning levels at the start of a project.

to the next. To develop the plan, you must take into account four factors: long-term and near-term planning, the sources used to derive the plan, the tools used to depict the plan, and the appropriate project management strategy for your own project and management style.

6.2.1 Long-term and near-term planning

The first plan that you create for a data processing project consists of two parts: a part describing how to determine the users' specific requirements (including project scope definition and full analysis) and a part detailing how to implement the solution to meet those requirements (typically including design, programming, testing, installation, training, and operation).

You can plan a DP project at the general level from the start of the project to the very end, simply by listing the major activities of scope definition, analysis, and so on, as contained in your shop's methodology. However, you can derive a detailed plan only for the near term. For example, at the end of project scope definition, you can plan the analysis phase fairly rigorously, but not the design phase, because you cannot plan a solution accurately until you specify the problem in detail. Similarly, you cannot plan the programming phase in detail until you are in the design phase.

Figures 6.2 and 6.3 illustrate the principle that long-term plans are necessarily at a more general level than near-term ones. For example, assume that the objectives of a project are to improve both the efficiency and customer satisfaction in a manufacturing and wholesaling company. Before the project begins, you know generally that the project activities include project scope, problem definition, analysis, software design, programming, testing, and installation. By the time you finish the problem definition activity, you can be much more exact about the specific analysis tasks, possibly including studies of the factory floor, inventory and warehousing, order handling, stock flow and distribution, financial aspects of warehouse and inventory control, relationships between inventory and orders, inventory spoilage, and returned merchandise. The analysis activity is also likely to include interviews with warehouse managers, forklift drivers, truck

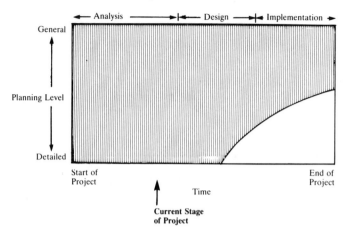

Figure 6.3. Planning levels at the end of analysis.

drivers, accountants, and even customers, and the development of data flow diagrams and data models of the relevant areas of the business.

By the end of analysis, you will have a good idea of what tasks to computerize, what procedures to change in other ways, and what areas to leave alone. You will probably also be able to outline fully what computer transactions and utility software you will need to design. For example, you may need transactions for order entry, work order scheduling, and pick list generation, among dozens of others. You may also need sets of routines to handle, for instance, the shop calendar or security requirements. At this time, however, you won't be absolutely certain (although you may have a pretty good idea) of the exact programming requirements. Therefore, you won't have a detailed plan of programming until design is complete.[1]

6.2.2 Developing a plan

There are four primary sources for creating the basic plan for your DP project: the shop's methodology, your own experience, the project team's experience, and reference books. The first place to seek out your plan is in your shop's methodology manuals. As I describe in Chapter 8, these manuals, if they're at all typical, contain every task that you could conceivably need to carry out a data processing project. From these tasks, you can winnow those that are appropriate to your project.

As I said in the previous section, you can often be quite precise in near-term planning, but over the long term, your plan becomes more general. For example, you may be able to translate your methodology's "Study user area" into "Study warehousing," "Study shipping," and so forth. On the other hand, "Design physical database" will have to remain just that until you reach

---

[1]Many project managers, however, regard a programming plan detailed to the subroutine level as being too detailed for inclusion in the overall project plan. They thus leave consideration of detailed programming plans to each programmer, with a brief review by a designer, except when a transaction is to be programmed by more than one programmer. This is a reasonable approach.

the stage when you know the components of the database, which will probably be toward the end of informational analysis.

If your shop has no methodology, you must rely on your own experience with data processing projects, supplemented by the team members' experiences and by reference books (for example [Metzger, 1973; Dickinson, 1981]). Make use of any plans or project logs prepared for previous projects to develop a complete list of tasks.

One technique that I use for planning a project for which there is a dearth of inscribed wisdom is mental rehearsal. I close my eyes and picture myself carrying out the project, step by step. For each step, I ask, What do I need in order to do this task? what inputs? what tools? what training? whose assistance? The answers to these questions lead to another set of questions: What do I need to do in order to get what I need for this task? What other tasks must I do? What meetings must I set up? What travel arrangements must I make? What hardware do I need to purchase?

The strength of mental rehearsal is that it catches the small but crucial practical details of a project that formal methodologies tend to overlook, such as arranging a meeting with remotely situated users. I find that this technique, which a friend satirically dubbed "Daydream your way to success," captures about eighty percent of the tasks and deliverables of a project. You can usually fill in the remainder of the tasks and deliverables by soliciting the aid of other project team members. Their greatest value is in planning the areas of the project in which you're not an expert.

6.2.3 Depicting your plan

I use three tools to help plan and to depict the resulting plan. These tools are the data flow diagram (DFD), the critical path method (CPM) chart, and the Gantt (or bar) chart. Below, I describe the strengths and weaknesses of each tool and then I describe how each tool fills its own particular useful role in the planning process.

The DFD is not a traditional planning tool, but it is ideally suited for that purpose because it can naturally depict general activities and their composition as detailed tasks. A second advantage in using a DFD for planning is that it shows not only tasks, but also their deliverables. Seeing how the output of one task serves as the input to another helps you to spot missed tasks and deliverables. Furthermore, you can supplement the information contained in the DFD with a data dictionary and minispecifications.

For these reasons, the DFD is the first tool to use in deriving a plan. Many modern DP project methodologies are expressed in the form of a DFD for a generic project, since it is relatively easy to tailor that DFD to a specific project. Another benefit of the DFD as the initial planning tool is that it forces you to concentrate on the intrinsic dependencies between tasks before getting caught up with the complexities of the CPM chart.

After you have a DFD that depicts the intended project activities in as much detail as is realistic, you can devise a CPM chart.[2] The CPM chart illustrates timing information that a DFD lacks, including the duration of tasks and whether the start of one task depends upon the completion of another. Indeed, from a given DFD, you can derive a large number of CPM charts, each with a different chronological arrangement of tasks. The arrangement that you choose depends first on your project strategy and second on your resources, as described below. However, the CPM chart doesn't show as clearly as the DFD how the deliverable of one task becomes the input to another.

Figure 6.4 shows a CPM chart for a DP project. Obviously, a lot is missing from this chart. For example, I've shown only some of the activities of project scope definition, problem definition and general analysis, analysis, design, programming, testing, and installation. The CPM chart is also very bland (its subject could be any project) and small (the system has only eight transactions).

---

[2]In Appendix A, I show a simple example of converting a DFD into a CPM chart.

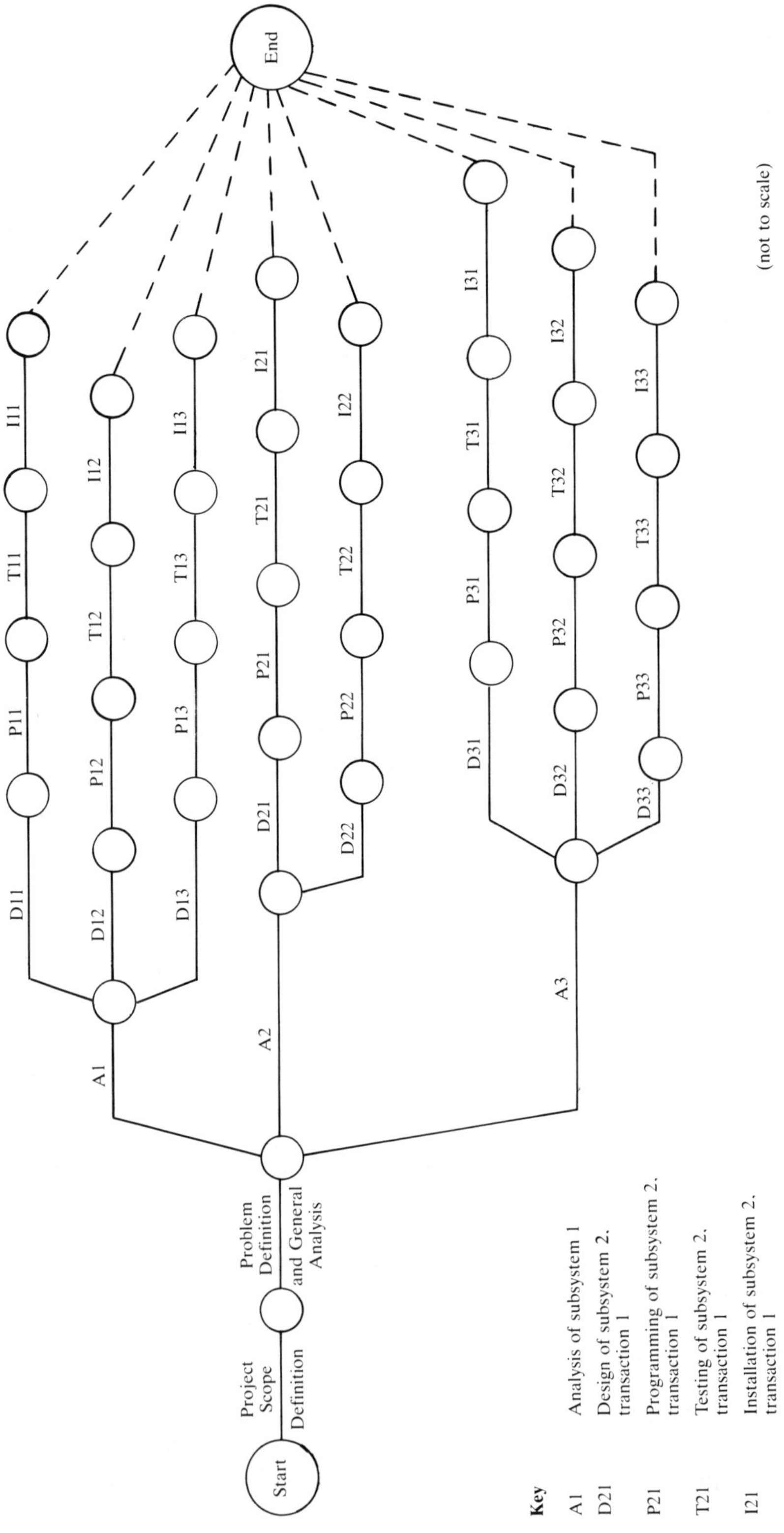
End
Start
Project Scope Definition
Problem Definition and General Analysis
A1
A2
A3
D11
P11
T11
I11
D12
P12
T12
I12
D13
P13
T13
I13
D21
P21
T21
I21
D22
P22
T22
I22
D31
P31
T31
I31
D32
P32
T32
I32
D33
P33
T33
I33
(not to scale)
Key
A1 Analysis of subsystem 1
D21 Design of subsystem 2. transaction 1
P21 Programming of subsystem 2. transaction 1
T21 Testing of subsystem 2. transaction 1
I21 Installation of subsystem 2. transaction 1

Figure 6.4. Example of a CPM chart.

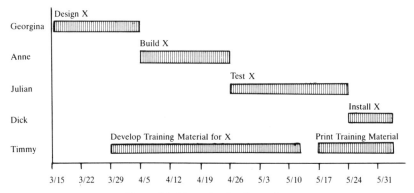

Figure 6.5. Example of a Gantt chart.

The third tool, the Gantt chart, has the merit of simplicity. It shows the duration of each task and perhaps the executor of the task, but nothing more. You cannot tell from a Gantt chart either how the deliverable of one task serves another task or how the start of a task depends upon the completion of another.

In Figure 6.5, a section of a Gantt chart shows the design, building, testing, and installation of X, which could be a piece of software or hardware, for instance. The chart also shows the development and printing of the training material for X. Because of its straightforwardness, I hardly need to describe this Gantt chart in detail. It shows, for example, that Georgina begins designing X on March 15 and completes that task on April 5.

The Gantt chart is not powerful enough for overall project planning. However, it is a useful auxiliary tool to show the relationships between resources and tasks. (I return to the Gantt chart and its important role in organizing in Section 6.3.)

6.2.4 Devising the project strategy

Project strategies lie along a spectrum, with the ultraconservative strategy and the ultraradical strategy at opposite extremes. To illustrate how the two strategies differ, I modify the CPM chart in Figure 6.4, which uses no strategy; tasks begin as soon as their inputs are available.

The ultraconservative strategy calls for each project phase to be completed before the next phase begins. For instance, the order of execution of the project tasks shown in Figure 6.6 under the ultraconservative strategy is first all the A tasks, followed by all the D tasks, all the P tasks, and so on. (In this figure as well as in Figures 6.7 and 6.8, project scope definition and problem definition and general analysis are omitted for clarity, and only part of the sequence is presented for the same reason.)

The ultraradical strategy, on the other hand, calls for completion of one section of the system before any work begins on other sections. In the project shown in Figure 6.4, the ultraradical strategy calls for the sequence of the execution of tasks as shown in Figure 6.7. The protracted length of the project is due to the unrealistic assumption that the project is staffed by only a single generalist worker. The ultraradical project strategy has a definite advantage over the ultraconservative strategy: It gets results early. You don't have to wait for a complete analysis and design to be done before you have a piece of the system up and running.

However, this strategy also has three serious drawbacks. First, because you cannot isolate subsystems from one another for the purposes of analysis, you run the risk that the analysis task

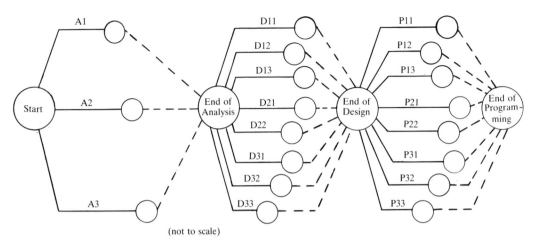

(not to scale)

Figure 6.6. Example of the ultraconservative strategy.

A2, say, will highlight some errors in A1 and possibly in tasks D11 through I13, which are already completed. In the worst case, they all might have to be completely redone, thus entailing considerable expense. Although the worst case seldom occurs in practice, the ultraradical strategy invariably causes significant extra reworking costs. This rework also tends to reduce a system's quality, since you may have to start maintaining some parts of the system even before they're installed.

A second drawback with the ultraradical strategy is that it is tough to staff. Your project continually cycles drastically from analysis through implementation and back to analysis again, with a number of design/implementation cycles interspersed. Staffing requirements may become so difficult that you're forced to adopt a generalist style of working whether you like it or not.

Third, with any normal project team, you would implement the ultraradical strategy with multiple workers, as shown in Figure 6.8. In this plan, there are five specialist workers, one each for analysis, design, programming, testing, and installation, who work in assembly line fashion. Having sufficient personnel shortens the project to a more sensible duration because more than one task can be performed at the same time. However, that means different parts of the project at any given time are in different phases. For instance, one part may be in analysis, another in design, and another in testing; this makes an ultraradical project very difficult to manage. (I once saw an ultraradical project that was in every possible phase simultaneously.) Couple this difficulty with the inevitable reworking of portions required and you have potential management nightmares. Indeed, ultraradical projects fail for just this reason, because their managers, tempted by the lure of early results, are utterly unprepared to deal with the tangled web of activities in a large ultraradical project.

Between the extremes of the safe, slow-to-produce ultraconservative strategy and the daring, fast, costly, tough-to-manage ultraradical strategy lie other, more practical strategies. The first of three such strategies is incremental implementation, which calls for the analysis and design phases to be conducted conservatively and the programming, testing, and installation phases to be conducted radically. The second compromise strategy is incremental design and implementation, which switches from conservative to radical after the analysis phase. The third strategy, which falls between the first and the second, switches from being conservative to radical after about twenty percent to thirty percent of the design phase is complete, thus avoiding much of the reprogramming needed in the ultraradical strategy. The reason for this is that by the time you've completed this

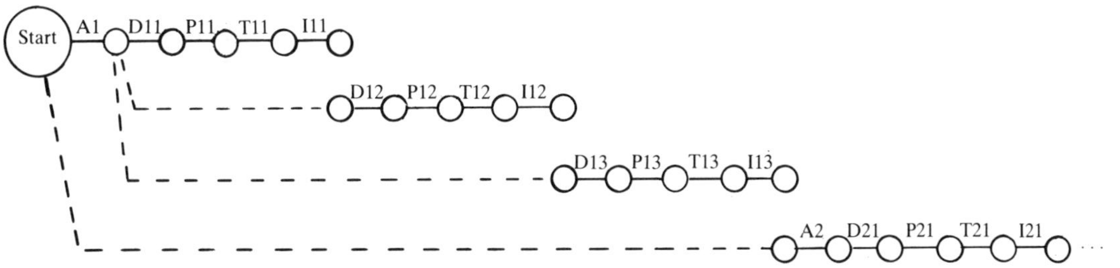

(not to scale)

Figure 6.7. Example of the ultraradical strategy with a single worker.

fraction of the design, the majority of the most widely ranging perturbations to the overall design will have already occurred. For example, your shared data locking conventions and your design for general data validation routines are nailed down by this point, since they will be required early in the design phase.

In choosing a project strategy, take into account several factors, including your particular style of project management. Naturally, if your style is cautious, the ultraconservative strategy is more appropriate; if you're comfortable with calculated risks, a more radical strategy is the choice. Another factor is your experience as a project manager; again, the less experienced, the more conservative you should be in your choice of an appropriate strategy. Do your users need quick results? If so, opt for the ultraradical strategy. Finally, consider your budget. Consider whether you have the extra cash available to carry out rework on a radical project. My own preference is for the third of the above strategies, when it is possible to employ it, because it yields the best compromise between quick results and safety.

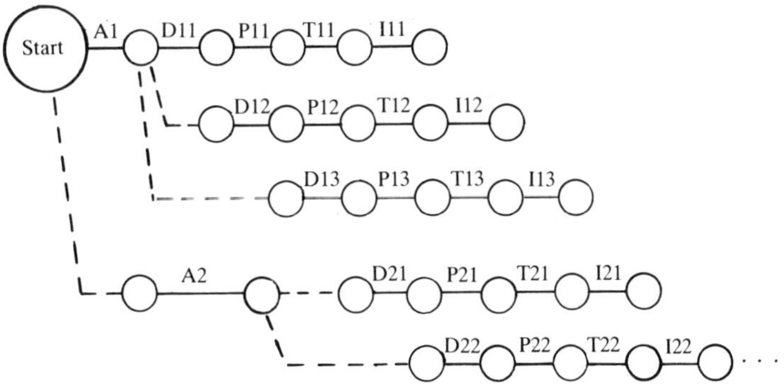

(not to scale)

Figure 6.8. Example of the ultraradical strategy with multiple workers.

6.3 Organize

If a plan is like a route map to a destination, an organization is like a vehicle to traverse the route. It is a system of cooperating parts that is called the project team. In order for a project team to be well organized, four goals need to be met: each worker's expertise is matched to the task he performs; the chosen style of working, either specialist or generalist, is achieved; the number of idle workers and the amount of idle time are minimized; and each worker performs only one task at a time.

No project organization is perfect, however, because achieving all four goals on a typical project is virtually impossible. Nevertheless, trying to reach each goal is necessary for the project to be as efficient and effective as possible. I discuss each organizational goal in depth in the sections below.

6.3.1 Match each worker's expertise to the task he performs

The first goal seems obvious and desirable enough. After all, you don't want an incompetent analyst interviewing users or a programming buffoon writing code. However, the managers who neglect to plan go so far in trying to satisfy this goal that they create tasks solely to match the expertise of the project team members.

It is comparatively easy to assess each team member's skills and assign him appropriate tasks. This approach also gives you the warm glow of knowing that you're keeping everyone busy and, better yet, busy at tasks they should enjoy doing. But assigning work to people, rather than people to work, is too good to be true, simply because it doesn't work. Before we look at the correct way to organize—that is, to plan the project tasks to be done and then assign skilled people to do them—let's look at an illustration of the ineffectiveness of assigning work solely on the basis of people's skills. In this example, a manager who hasn't planned his project takes stock of the people assigned to his project. The six team members and their job titles are these:

Bob, analyst	Ted, programmer/analyst
Alice, analyst	Bill, database designer
Carol, programmer/analyst	Rudolf, senior programmer/designer
	(joining in one month)

Another eight to ten people will join the project later. The manager ponders possible assignments: "Bob and Alice can start right away on the analysis, but I don't think Carol's actually done any analysis before. Oh well, she's got to learn sometime. I'll stick her on the analysis team, too. I'll have to come back to Ted.

"Bill is an IMS expert. I'll have him start preliminary work on the database system. I bet he'll be glad to get a head start on the job for once.

"Rudolf will be here next month. Perfect! The analysis should be well under way by then. He can join the analysis team and give 'em a bit of programming know-how. Ted's still a problem, though. I could lease him to another project, but I might lose him that way. I know: Ted can put together some software tools for us. He'll just love that and probably will work all night at it, too."

In contrast to this project manager's stream of consciousness approach to organizing, the correct way to match people and work is to begin by drafting a plan. For each task that you identify, note the skills that it requires. Some of the better project methodologies actually do this for you. Next, depending upon the resources available to you and if you're lucky, you can discuss with a staff manager a shopping list of required skills with estimates of when and for how long you'll need these skills.[3] In response, he assigns the right people with the necessary skills.

Unfortunately, life is usually not so sweet. Often, you must accept whoever is available, and make do as well as you can. Even in this case, however, refrain from creating tasks just to suit the people you get. Match your list of the skills needed with the skills received and tote up the

---

[3]Some shops deal not in single skills, but in groups of skills defined as roles. See Chapter 12 for a discussion of roles and "be-know-do" skills.

deficiencies. Your first line of attack then is to negotiate for a different set of people with a more appropriate portfolio of skills. If all negotiations with staff management fail, you'll have to fall back on project resources to get what you need. Spend some project money on training your team members in the areas that they're most deficient. Spend as little as possible, of course, since it's not a project manager's job to train people. Alternatively, you can hire temporary consultants to supplement your project team's skills.

Another complication in assessing people's skills is that although two people may appear to have the same inventory of skills, no two workers are exactly alike. Some analysts are rigorous; others not. Some programmers are fast; others slow. The differences between workers can be startling, as proved by a well-known study that showed a ratio of 25 to 1 between the fastest and slowest programmers on the same task [Sackman et al., 1968]. My own informal study of programmers in two large corporations showed a ratio of about 3 to 1 between the fastest and slowest programmers.

In my study, I also found an interesting relationship between speed and quality. As a measure of quality, I looked at the readability, understandability, and flexibility of code. Quality initially increased as a function of speed, and then declined abruptly. The overall results fell roughly along the curve shown in Figure 6.9.

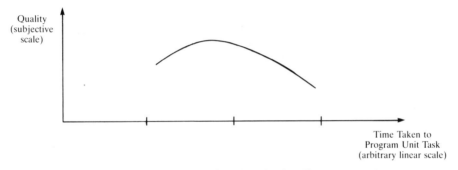

Figure 6.9. Results from an informal study of quality versus speed.

Interestingly, the points on this quality-time graph clustered into islands by programmer, as shown in Figure 6.10. The implications of Figures 6.9 and 6.10 are obvious: Programmer C can't be assigned to tasks when speed is vital; and programmers A and C shouldn't work on tasks when high quality is vital.

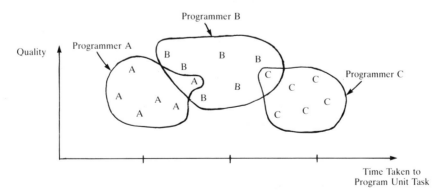

Figure 6.10. Quality versus speed by programmer.

Because of these differences in workers, you may have to re-estimate the time needed for tasks. During the planning of the project, you based the estimates on the assumption that a standard or average person would execute the tasks. Now, you must revise your estimates to compensate for the actual speeds of the workers. (I return to this topic in Section 6.6 in discussing the fifth management activity.)

6.3.2 Achieve the chosen style of working

You can organize your project either along generalist or specialist lines or somewhere between these extremes. Chapter 5 discussed these various styles of working in terms of car manufacturing, but for a DP project, let me illustrate by means of Gantt charts three ways of organizing workers.

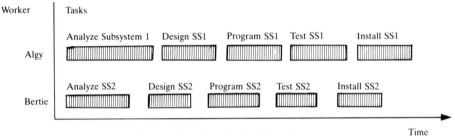

Figure 6.11. Example of a Gantt chart.

In Figure 6.11, Algy and Bertie each take a piece of the system from analysis through installation. As with the Bona Motor Co. example of Chapter 5, this generalist style has both advantages and disadvantages. One benefit is that interface problems between phases are reduced, since the same person works on design and programming, for example. Also, scheduling is easy, since each person works relatively independently of the others (although if you use an ultracon-servative strategy, you may have to have some people wait for others to finish the current phase).

Third, being able to develop a piece of the system from its inception to its installation gives people a morale-boosting sense of ownership. Finally, the project team remains fairly static for the duration of the project.

The disadvantages of the generalist approach are that it requires people with an extraordinary breadth and depth of skills to perform all the tasks adequately; and the interface and consistency problems across subsystems are increased because different people work on them. Also, a project's progress may be slow and inefficient, because each person goes through a learning curve as he moves from one phase to the next, and errors tend to be caught later, rather than sooner. For example, if Algy makes an error in analyzing subsystem 1, that error could remain undetected until after it is installed. Finally, since egos tend to become entwined in what they create, workers become overly sensitive to criticism and requests for changes to their products.

A fully generalist approach is out of the question for all but the smallest projects. In the 1950s, it was possible for a single person to know everything about computer science and data processing. But such knowledge is impossible in today's more complex, sophisticated DP world. Therefore, for modern projects, a mostly specialist approach is the only feasible one.

The Gantt charts for part of two specialist projects are shown in Figures 6.12 and 6.13. In Figure 6.12, tasks are not specialized more finely than an entire transaction, whereas in Figure 6.13, very specialized tasks indeed are pulled out for the assembly line treatment. (Note incidentally that the strategy for the project in Figure 6.12 is conservative in analysis and fairly radical afterward.)

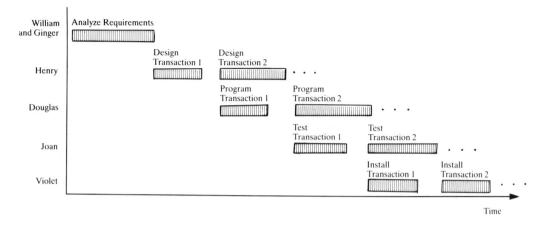

Figure 6.12. Gantt chart example of a specialized project.

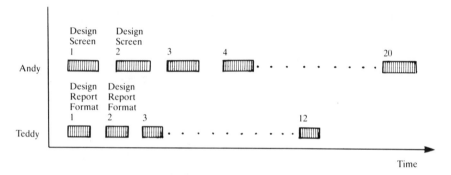

Figure 6.13. Gantt chart of a more specialized project.

The advantages of the specialist approach are these: Workers can apply a depth of acquired expertise to the project tasks and need not have a broad base of knowledge. Interface and consistency problems tend to decrease because the same person works on the same aspect of all subsystems. Each person can work with assembly line efficiency, because he doesn't have to continually switch tools or techniques and frames of mind. Errors tend to be caught in the phase immediately after they are made as the product is passed to the next person in the assembly line.

Unfortunately, the specialist approach is not without disadvantages, but since it is the only practical choice for DP projects, we need to find ways to reduce the effects of the drawbacks. The first disadvantage is if the work is too specialized, as in Figure 6.13, it soon becomes tedious and morale-breaking to the worker. This disadvantage can be easily removed: Don't break work into tiny specialties unless you desire extreme efficiency in a certain area or unless you have small tasks that require extremely arcane skills.

The second disadvantage—possible misinterpretations of documents as they pass from one worker to the next—can be tackled in two ways: First, adopt a standard methodology so that guidelines for document preparation prevent unclear or confusing contents. Second, allow workers to participate in the phase that precedes their own. For example, let designers participate in the final stage of analysis and programmers participate in design walkthroughs. If, after taking these measures, you still believe there's a problem in the transition between the two people, back off from the specialist approach and assign the two tasks to the same person. A workable scheme is to assign one person to both analysis and design or to both design and programming. That is, have persons

A and B on the analysis team and the design team, and persons B and C on the design team and the programming team.

A third disadvantage is that a worker's speed is limited by both the quality and speed of the work performed by those preceding him. To improve product quality, use walkthroughs frequently. To prevent project bottlenecks from slowing progress, build reserves at various critical points. For example, before allowing programming to start, establish a buffer of a dozen or so designed transactions.

The increased complexity of scheduling is the fourth drawback. In the generalist approach, a delay in task D1 also delays tasks P1, T1, and I1. But in the specialist approach, a delay in D1 also delays task D2, and thus tasks P2, T2, and I2. However, since each stage of the assembly line is staffed by several people, another person can be assigned to do task D2. Of course, since that might push D3 back in the queue, you must decide whether it's more important to have D2, P2, T2, and I2 completed first or D3, P3, T3, and I3 first.

The fifth disadvantage of the specialist approach is that the number of people required and their collection of skills fluctuate continually throughout the project. As the project's character varies from one phase of the project to the next (say, from analysis to database design), you need to change from analysts to database experts. This disadvantage is unavoidable if you want your project to remain efficient. In keeping with the metaphor for this chapter, as the project's terrain changes from land to water, you'd change from a car to a boat in order to keep going. (The generalist approach would call for an amphibious vehicle, which might be inefficient in both terrains.) To ensure that you have the proper mix of skills when you need it, you must plan carefully and keep in close communication with your shop's staff management.

6.3.3 Minimize the number of idle workers

The purpose of the third goal of project organization is obvious: not to waste valuable project time and money on people who are not producing. Enforced idleness usually results either because a person has to wait for another task to finish before he can begin his own, or because the project is over-staffed and occasionally no work is available for some project members.

You can avoid the first cause to some extent by building buffers of work to smooth the flow of the assembly line. This should reduce the problem from being a regular one to being only an occasional hitch caused, for instance, by the failure of a piece of hardware to arrive.

Over-staffing a project is rare, but it can occur at the start of the project when the project manager corrals all the possibly useful stray workers in the shop while he can get them. From my example in Section 6.3.1, Bill (the IMS expert) was one such potentially valuable addition, although at the beginning of analysis it was hard to see how best to use him. So, the manager shoved him into a corner to start the database design prematurely, knowing full well that the technically sound, but totally irrelevant, schemas that Bill produced would be thrown away. That's like having Bill dig holes and fill them in just to look busy.

The proper thing for the good of the shop and for Bill, too, is to return him temporarily to the staff manager. That way, he could do some useful work, like revising the database standard or assisting someone else to learn IMS. Better yet, Bill might attend a course in informational analysis so that he can return to the project and immediately assist the analysts with their studies. Having a DP professional do meaningless work is demoralizing.

One former boss of mine told me, "If you have nothing to do, don't make busy work for yourself. It's not your fault. Start reading a newspaper, and I'll soon see that my organization's not quite on track and I'll review the task assignments."

In some matrix-structured shops, the battle for people among project managers is too cutthroat for my advice to work. If you don't grab employees like Bill when you get the chance and hold on to him tightly, you lose him to another rapacious project manager. In this case, assign him to a genuine task on the project, regardless of whether he has the skills to do it. Of course, help him learn by giving him material to read or by making him apprentice to someone else. Also, most importantly, explain to him frankly why you're making this seemingly strange assignment; otherwise, he may become confused and irritated and all your good plans and intentions will be for naught.

6.3.4 Assign each worker only one task at a time

There are always those frustrating times in a DP project when you have more tasks waiting to begin than people to begin them. If you could only get those tasks under way, you'd be able to finish the project that much sooner. One way to solve the problem is to hire more people. That's risky, though, since the excess tasks might be temporary and the resultant over-staffing would be both awkward and costly.

Another way to deal with a surplus of tasks is to yield to temptation: By assigning six or seven tasks at once to each team member, you can get your project humming. The trouble is that this tactic doesn't work or even make much sense. For example, let's assume that a project manager assigns six tasks to a team member. Since each task takes about a week to do, the full assignment if done serially should take about six weeks. Done simultaneously, the assignment will take longer than six weeks for reasons explored below. Yet, an impatient manager typically hands out six one-week tasks with a deadline of only four weeks. What economies of scale such a manager expects to serve him, I can't imagine!

The problem with bulk task assignments was summed up by an analyst at a large corporation: "My boss gives me half a dozen tasks to do at the same time and he doesn't give me any priorities for carrying them out. I guess he expects me to attack them all at once. Some days, I don't know what to do next, and I think I'm going crazy." A person cannot work as efficiently on six tasks, since he wastes time switching his attention and contexts from one task to the next. He also becomes muddled by the sixfold increase in details to remember.

Establishing priorities in this situation doesn't help much either. Imagine that a boss hands a worker tasks A through F, each with a priority of 1 through 6, respectively. What happens in reality is the worker makes A the number one priority and all the rest the number two priority. He works at A fairly assiduously and he pecks at B, C, D, E, and F periodically to fend off a nagging sense of guilt. As a result, not only is he distracted from his first priority, but he also does all the other tasks poorly.

A worse problem is if a nervous or irresolute project manager continually changes the priorities of the assigned tasks. In this case, a worker spends more time switching contexts between tasks and trying to anticipate the next highest priority task than he does in actually executing the tasks.

Priorities are for managers, not for workers. Hence, for maximum efficiency and minimum distraction, give a worker a single task at a time. (An experienced worker can handle a single large task, which he can break into subtasks and rank himself with your approval.) There are only two exceptions: When a task occupies only a small portion of a worker's time, for example, if testing programs on the computer takes only three hours per day, you must assign something else to him for the remaining hours. The second exception is an emergency. However, make sure that when he returns to his normal task, you adjust his schedule to allow for the interruption.

Given my recommendation that you assign a single task at a time, what is the solution to the problem posed at the start of this section: How can you assign people tasks when you have more tasks than people? One solution is to hire temporary workers, as discussed in Chapter 12. Don't overlook the virtue of patience, however. If you keep your staff levels moderate, you may not be able to go as fast as would be theoretically possible, but your project will be more manageable and your lean, mean machine will probably result in lower project costs than would a heavily staffed juggernaut.

6.4 Integrate

Integrating is the drawing together of people to achieve a common understanding. I prefer this word and its definition by Giegold to such other terms as *coordination, communication,* or *synthesis* [Giegold, 1982]. In the context of general management, integrating is complex and multifaceted. It includes integrating one subordinate with others, yourself with your subordinates and with your boss, your department with the users, and your department with the corporation at large.

The integrating process for project management is, however, more parochial. Although you cannot entirely ignore the other aspects of integration, as a project manager you are concerned chiefly with integration within your project and especially between you and your project team. (I deal with integrating the project and the users as a separate issue in Section 6.7.)

Integrating within a project assures that everyone on the project knows what is going on, or that everyone gets into the act, as a colleague once put it. However, it doesn't necessarily mean that everyone must agree with what is going on. In our previous metaphor of a project plan as a route map and a project organization as a vehicle, integrating is like preventive maintenance to the vehicle. It ensures that the pieces are attached properly both to the vehicle and to one another and that all pieces receive the necessary oil, fuel, and electricity to operate properly.

When carried out smoothly, integrating is an almost invisible process. Hence, many novice managers tend to overlook it. But when it is neglected, its absence becomes hideously clear. For example, a project manager whom I recently advised, planned and organized superbly, but failed to communicate his ideas to anyone. The result was almost as much confusion as if he'd failed to plan or organize at all. His team members reacted emotionally to his poor integration efforts, some taking it personally (''He's trying to push me off the project''), and others reacting with contempt (''He couldn't manage his way out of a paper bag'').

To avoid this sort of management disaster, there are several helpful guidelines to integrate your project successfully. Remember, though, you as the project manager must work on two levels at once: achieving integration between you and your staff, as well as integration between the team members. My first guideline is, Share your entire plan with your project team by holding meetings and giving everyone a chance to appraise it. Then, hold another meeting in a few days to solicit project members' ideas and reactions to the plan.

Another helpful guideline is, Delegate the planning of some project tasks to senior project members. However, before assigning tasks, have the entire project team review your plan and organization to suggest improvements. Be clear and definite. To avoid misunderstandings, prepare a statement of each task in writing, including its most important goals (such as code efficiency or design flexibility), deliverables, and expected duration. Discuss the assignment with the staff member to avoid any semblance of the work assignment being handed down from on high, and have him write down his own assignment (a concept discussed in Chapter 9). This helps to integrate the worker into the project and thus enhance his motivation and commitment to the task.

After the assignments are made but before people begin work, make sure that everyone understands each other's assignments in order to know how they all fit into the project. People work together more intelligently if they understand their interfaces and if they have a chance to anticipate any interface problems before they begin work. Encourage frequent walkthroughs, so that team members become integrated with one another as well as with you.

Two additional areas for you to consider are the management activities that I haven't yet discussed: measuring and revising. Don't hide project measurements in some secret management file. Indeed, Thomsett makes the excellent suggestion that you allow team members to see the results of measurements before you see them [Thomsett, 1980]. This eliminates many of the measuring absurdities that commonly occur in projects, like corrupted time statistics, as discussed in Chapter 9.

As the project proceeds and as reality unfolds before you, it's inevitable that you will revise your plan and organization. Revisions are a constant source of frustration to the team members, who may believe that the project is floundering in indecision. Since team members also may lose confidence in your leadership, you must share the reason for the changes with the people whom they affect.

6.5 Measure

Measuring is the managerial activity of obtaining feedback on the project's progress. Just as you look at the speedometer, odometer, and road signs to track progress on a journey, so a manager needs to monitor his team's efforts at points along the way.

There are two types of legitimate project measurement: One measures the time and effort expended on tasks and the second assesses the progress achieved at any particular point in the project. (I describe how to collect both types of data in Chapter 9.) The purposes of collecting the first set of data, called time reporting, are so that time charges can be accurately allocated to the appropriate corporate accounts and so that future estimating attempts can be improved. For the latter purpose, the metrics group is responsible for these measurements, as discussed in Chapter 2.

Similarly, there are two purposes for measuring a project's progress. One is to revise the project plan, as explained in the next section, and the second is to record major deviations and problems in the project log. These measurements are collected in the form of project status reports by the project manager, as discussed in Chapter 9. The project log is a concise, written record of major highlights of the project. Since it is not intended to be a vast narrative of every trivial event of the project, the log refers to other documents, such as minutes of meetings, for details about topics.

In *Managing a Programming Project,* Metzger suggests the project log contain the following items:

> A chronological listing and very brief summary of important events during the life of the contract [project], including missed milestones, new estimates, contract changes, project reviews, equipment installation dates, important telephone agreements, meetings with the customer [user], and meetings with sub-contractors, team members, or vendors.[4]

I would add to this list any event or experience from which you and other project managers can learn. Especially important are innovations adopted for the project and how well they worked out, and problems or failures encountered and with possible reasons. The project log is used to produce the material for the post-project review, when other people will have the chance to benefit from your experiences.

With a clear understanding of what project measurement should be, let's turn to consider managerial extremes in measurement: Some managers do no measuring at all, while others make

---

[4][Metzger, 1973, p. 177].

a fetish of it. Managers of the first type must have infinite faith in these two benign laws: When ignorance is bliss, 'tis folly to measure anything. And, If anything can go wrong, with a bit of luck, it might not. Sadly, another law is, Tasks do deviate from their carefully laid out plan. Ignoring these deviations will make a plan into worthless fiction.

A project whose manager fails to measure its progress may muddle through repeated crises to completion. Tasks may overrun their allotted span and delay other tasks, jobs may be bungled and new tasks not begun, but the manager takes no notice. He sticks to his original plan, while chaos without measure rages all round him.

At the other extreme are managers who skulk about the shop, continually checking and monitoring their project team. One such person managed a project on which I worked. Just when I would be tearing my hair out over an unsubmissive design problem, he would spring up behind me with a hearty "How's it going, then?" to which there was no polite reply.

Why do some managers monitor obsessively? There are several possible reasons. One reason is ironic: They monitor excessively because they have no plan. Since the manager doesn't know what's going to happen, he has to watch closely to see what is happening so that he can appear coherent when he reports progress to his management. Their simplistic view of project management is the data processing equivalent of giving each of a thousand workers a brick and saying, "Build me a house."

Another possible reason for a manager's zeal is his belief that no one will ever work unless he regularly checks up on the team. This is nonsense, of course. Highly trained, motivated people with clearly understood assignments don't need anyone looking over their shoulder all the time to make sure they complete their tasks.

So, are there any valid occasions for close scrutiny and measurement? Yes, watch new or inexperienced workers more closely, since a novice might not even realize he's in trouble or producing a less-than-acceptable product. Even in this case, though, don't make the worker claustrophobic. Have him be an apprentice to a more experienced worker or, alternatively, allow walkthroughs to provide him with feedback. Otherwise, scrutinize a task only after its performer informs you of a problem. In this way, you make it clear that as the project manager, you are the servant both of your people and of the project and thus have little need for high-pressure monitoring.

6.6 Revise

Revising is the process of reacting to the deviations from the project plan that are discovered by measuring. It is like replanning your route when you stray off course or find a road closed.

Measuring and revising go hand in hand in the control of a project. If, when measuring progress, you observe a deviation from the plan, you have two choices: Either devise a way to return to the plan or revise the plan and organization. The first choice is preferable for obvious reasons, but there are specifically four deviations that cause a revision to a plan and organization: a slipped completion date of a task, a bungled task, a missed task, and an unforeseen change in personnel.

If a person is late in finishing a task, you have two potential problems to worry about: First, the person cannot move to his next task as scheduled; and second, a task that depends upon the delayed task may also be delayed. A delay in the completion of a task is a major problem only when it occurs on the project's critical path or when it ties up a resource on the critical path.[5]

---

[5]The critical path is a chain of tasks, each dependent in some way upon the completion of the previous one, that extends all the way to the end of the project with no gap in time between the end of one task and the start of the next. A slippage in any task on a critical path, therefore, causes an equal slippage in the whole project.

In order to prevent the slippage of the whole project, the first solution is to have personnel work extra hours, but I emphasize this remedy cannot be invoked very often. If you find that more than one or two tasks slip behind, you mustn't sacrifice your whole staff on the altar of punctuality. Accept that your estimates are wrong and that you must change your plan and/or organization accordingly. If you hang on to the unshakable belief that the project can catch up, you risk losing control of the project as it falls further and further behind.

An interesting solution to the problem of slipped completion dates is to add an expansion gap to the end of each task to allow for contingencies. This in effect removes the rigid critical path from the project and prevents the project plan from buckling under the strain of the normal task overruns. Donaldson suggests fifteen percent of a task's nominal length as an appropriate size for the gap [Donaldson, 1978]. However, never treat this gap as slack time that can be used without reason, and never include this additional fifteen percent in the target date for completion of a task.

Tasks that involve a significant component of research (for example, devising some new process control hardware) need more than a fifteen percent expansion gap. Indeed, move such tasks forward in your plan to the earliest possible time to have them completed in order to give yourself a buffer against the normal vicissitudes of research efforts.

A problem that invariably defeats even the fifteen percent expansion gap is the variation in rates for different workers discussed before. Although re-estimating task durations is necessary when you assign people to tasks and although you may possess knowledge and statistics of people's work from previous projects, you still can't be sure that workers' rates are the same. For instance, some people may have gained experience enabling them to work faster, while others may have become jaded or bored and actually work more slowly. What this means is that soon after the start of a phase, you must assess workers' rates on the particular project and revise your plan and organization accordingly.

Of course, some completion dates can't possibly be met because the deadline itself is unrealistic. (This subject is so important that I devote Chapter 7 to it.) To work toward an impossible deadline, you must have either no plan at all or a plan with impossibly scheduled tasks. When task after task misses its target date by a lot, you will be overwhelmed by changes to your plan. These changes cause even more changes, so that there are more changes than plan, and your project, like a slippery beast, wriggles free of your control and bounds away over the horizon of your budget.

The second deviation is a bungled task, which produces an unacceptable deliverable and must be redone. Completely bungled tasks are fortunately rare, since tasks are monitored and problems usually detected before it's too late. A more common and insidious problem is the partially bungled or unfinished task.

I experienced firsthand what can happen to a project when a task is partially bungled and the project manager refuses to acknowledge the fact. One project task was to document the syntax and legal values of every data element in the system so that they could be validated through central tables and thus save coding. Unfortunately, the task produced only a partial and inaccurate document, which the manager refused to have redone, claiming there was no time. The task in effect was canceled.

The result of this cancellation was chaos: Programmers coded the editing of screens however they pleased, while others ignored editing entirely. During acceptance testing, the users declared the system unusable and angrily demanded that it be fixed. Tearing out code, installing central tables, and retesting the system added almost seven months to the project, which was about seven times the amount of work that was previously thought "saved."

From this experience, I am wary of the partially bungled or unfinished task and I caution you about certain types of tasks that are notorious for exhibiting this problem, especially analysis tasks. The reason has to do with how an analysis task is determined to be finished. The determination should be based on the project plan, but in practice, it is typically based on the first analysis deadline. The effect of this determination becomes apparent in the design phase when an incomplete, inaccurate analysis document arrives on the designers' desks. The designers may appear to be slow, bumbling, and resentful as they struggle through the analysis document and come to a halt for want of valid analysis information.

Thus, further analysis is performed in the design phase, either by the designers (who may be unskilled in analysis) or by the original analysts (in which case, the designers become idle for a time). This additional analysis may erroneously be budgeted as design, which will corrupt statistics gathered for estimating purposes. Also, the design phase is prolonged, in fact more than the analysis phase would have been had it been completed, because of the inefficiencies involved in oscillating between analysis and design.

The lesson to be learned about completing a task prematurely is, Don't do it. In olden days, when analysis was a haphazard activity, I could sympathize with the project manager who didn't know whether an analysis task was complete. But today, with such techniques as structured analysis, information modeling, and prototyping available, you as the manager can determine reasonably well whether the analysis process is complete, or at least at the point of diminishing returns.[6] Therefore, you have no excuse for being panicked by a premature analysis deadline.

Two other tools to avoid the insidiously bungled task are walkthroughs and the analysis review, described in Chapter 11. Since they are well worth the time they take, I recommend that you add twenty-five percent to the duration of analysis for these tools. (This extra time is on top of the fifteen percent contingency gap.) Otherwise, you'll find yourself paying far more than twenty-five percent in both time and money when errors bog you down in the later phases of the project.

The third deviation that forces revisions in the project plan is an omitted task. This is an especially embarrassing error when such a task pops up on the critical path as the project proceeds. Regardless of how or why the omission occurred, a task must be done even if it requires you to protract the critical path for a month or two. It might take all your mettle as a manager to face the users with the truth, but your unhappy choice is to get chewed out a little now or a lot later.

Finally, a fourth deviation that causes a change of plan is a change in staff. If you unavoidably lose a project member through resignation or prolonged sickness or if you gain a new recruit to your project, reassign team members in such a way as to minimize disruption. If your resources are depleted, you will have to extend the project schedule.

Given any one of these four deviations and the necessity to revise your plan and organization, you'll be glad if your CPM charts are not on paper, since you'll have to redraw them. Magnetic boards with magnetic counters for events and string for activities are a much better medium for your charts.

For greater sophistication, computerize your CPM charts. This is invaluable on a large or complex project, when the relationships between tasks, subtasks, deliverables, resources, and time become hard to manipulate mentally. There are currently several packages that implement such charts on microcomputers. All are relatively cheap, but none so far does everything that I'd like. For example, the packages don't adequately match the skills of personnel to the skills that tasks demand, nor do they deal with the impact on schedules of reorganizing. Nevertheless, I believe any computerized aid in project management is better than none.

Whatever technique for scheduling tasks you choose, record your charts regularly—that means before you change them. If you use magnetic boards, for example, photograph them each Monday morning as well as before any changes are made. Keep this history of your plans in your project log as input to your review of the entire project.

---

[6]Prototyping is essentially the construction of various working models of the final system for the purposes of demonstration, communication, investigation, analysis, and research. For information on prototyping, see [Martin, 1982a; Squires et al., 1982; or Boar, 1984].

6.7 Technical requirements for the project manager

In order to be able to plan, organize, integrate, measure, and revise a DP project effectively, you need to be fluent not only in its management aspects, but also in its technical aspects. It's all very well to be able to spout the project's business objectives and to draw the perfect CPM chart, but without a solid technical foundation, your decisions are likely to be disastrous. How else could you know precisely what tasks to perform, whom to assign to which task, how to explain the project to your team, or what to measure? Without sound technical guidance and control, the project will lack technical coherence. It can fragment, as it is pulled in different directions by the diverse DP prejudices of the project team. Moreover, if you aren't technically current and your staff knows it, you may fall victim to snow jobs from the most convincing talkers on your team. Instead of being the project manager who is firmly in the driver's seat, you become the project donkey who is tamely led around by the nose.

I saw an example recently of how a project can run into trouble through its manager's ignorance of its technical aspects. After reading one or two articles in magazines and after hearing good reports from his staff, this manager decided that prototyping was a valuable technique and that he would use it extensively on his project. Unfortunately, he misunderstood the technique as being a way to rush into coding without the benefit of proper analysis or design.

The manager's second error was in not recruiting anyone with relevant skills, so he didn't have anyone to consult. Vast quantities of expensive code were written and then discarded in vain attempts to find the Holy Grail of the users' requirements through trial and error. I hardly need tell you the project was canceled. Although the shop's general management was partially responsible for allowing this disaster to happen, the central problem was with the project manager's arrogance and ignorance.

Of course, I don't recommend that you as the project manager be an expert on every technical issue; that is impossible for all but the simplest project. But you should understand the general features of the software development techniques currently available, including which techniques are used for what activities and the terminology used and skills required. Don't be afraid to ask for such information and advice from your inhouse experts. It's not an admission of weakness to do so, and it's far better to show humility now than to show incompetence later. (However, don't rely solely on inhouse experts; they may not always be as expert as they seem!)

Other sources of information include a good project methodology, which gives you a framework and context for the major activities in your shop. (I provide references when I discuss project methodologies in Chapter 8.) Seminars to provide a management overview are offered in almost every discipline from coding to communication protocols. Books abound, too, providing superficial or in-depth views of various techniques.

The project manager's job is already large, with planning, organizing, integrating, measuring, and revising, and meetings to attend, reports to write, and budgets to analyze. How can the manager find time to remain in control technically without having to work twenty-hour days? The solution to this problem is to adopt an organizational structure to split the manager's job and assign the parts to different people. The matrix structure, for example, removes most of the staff management burden from the project manager. Also, the metrics group helps the project manager to gather statistics and to use them to make estimates.

One immensely time-consuming activity—that of integrating the project with the corporation as a whole—can similarly be reassigned. Some shops assign this activity to someone who writes the regular status reports for users and upper managers, attends the sometimes endless *pro forma* corporate meetings, and possibly even handles the intricacies of the financial and accounting aspects of the project. This person needs strong financial skills, a flair for dealing with corporate bureaucracy, a good knowledge of the corporation's business, and a reasonable familiarity with data processing work, though he need not come from the DP department. He also needs the skills of a diplomat in order to avoid being perceived as a spy, whistle-blower, or whip-cracker.

The term for such a person is the project producer, with the conventional project manager dubbed the project director, terms coined by Brooks in *The Mythical Man–Month* [Brooks, 1975].[7] Using the director/producer team does complicate the DP organization, with the producer adding yet another line of communication. The new role also raises such nontrivial issues as how much authority he has over the conduct of the project. Can he, for instance, veto any of the director's spending or staffing decisions? Must he approve the project plan?

Shops address these issues in different ways, with some establishing mechanisms for resolving conflicts as they arise. Although the director/producer team concept has problems and although a director can never completely escape from writing reports and attending management meetings, the approach is certainly beneficial if it helps the harried, overworked project manager.

Since managing a project is a full-time job, a project manager cannot actually do the work of the project. Some managers do not believe this, however. At the slightest opportunity, they dash to the nearest terminal and pound out hundreds of lines of COBOL or rush for a vacant soldering iron. The temptation to roll up one's sleeves and pitch in is tremendous, especially at those times when the project needs all the technical help it can get. Also, coding can be a great relief from unbroken periods of paper pushing. Resist the temptation, though, for yielding to technical distractions—even for a small portion of the time—endangers the project as a whole. If you allow technical details to usurp your attention from the myriad project management problems that are your main responsibility, you run a great risk of the project's drifting out of control.

6.8 A managerial assignment

Perhaps the toughest job for a manager is taking over the management of a project that is already in progress. As the replacement manager, you're in an unenviable position, rather like a Wild West hero who must leap aboard a driverless stagecoach to save its terrified passengers. To save such a DP project, you could let the project proceed at its current pace and hope that you can learn as you go. (In the meantime, unfortunately, you're liable to make some bizarre and damaging decisions through sheer ignorance.) Or, another approach is the "new-broom" one, in which you determine to make an impact on the project from the moment you arrive. You make widespread changes, issue countless edicts, and hold monumental meetings to disseminate the New Way. Unfortunately, in this case, you may fail to understand the previous manager's plans and again are liable to make some unwise decisions.

The best approach if you find yourself suddenly to be the manager of an ongoing project is to slow the project's pace. Bring it to a halt if you must. Make everyone's first priority educating you in the project's objectives and in the plan and organization designed to meet those objectives. No doubt, you will want to change the way the project is run to match your own management style or to improve progress. But wait until you have a sound understanding of the project before making any changes. Remember what sort of manager rushes in where angels fear to tread!

6.9 Summary

Although technical problems always throw obstacles in the path of data processing projects, the major catastrophes are caused by managerial blunders. This chapter discusses the five activities

---

[7]The terms are borrowed, of course, from the motion picture industry, in which the technical aspects of lighting, camera work, and acting all are assigned to the movie's director, whereas administrative affairs such as budgeting, acquisition of capital, public relations, and generally dealing with the outside world belong to the producer. (Some shops use the terms *project advocate* or *project champion*, rather than producer.)

that are essential for successful project measurement: planning, organizing, integrating, measuring, and revising.

Planning is the establishment of intermediate tasks on the route to the project's objectives. To derive your project plan, use your shop's project methodology, your own experience, as well as that of your teams, and published references. The project plan is detailed for the near term, but is more general for the long term. The plan depends not only on the tasks you must do, but also on your project strategy, which may range from the ultraconservative approach (each phase is completed before the next is begun) to the ultraradical method (each section of the system is completed before the next is begun). The plan is depicted initially as a data flow diagram and is converted into a CPM chart with the addition of timing and task-dependency information.

Organizing is the assignment of people to the tasks identified by the project plan. The four goals of organization, none of which can be perfectly achieved in practice, are to match each person's expertise to the tasks that he will perform; to achieve an appropriate blend of specialist and generalist styles of working; to minimize the amount of workers' idle time; and to assign each worker only one task at a time. The assignment of people to tasks is best depicted by means of a Gantt chart.

The process of integrating means involving everyone on the project. It is an often neglected aspect of management, which is nevertheless essential to the smooth running of a project. Integrate your project team into the other management activities (planning, organizing, measuring, and revising), as well as into one another's activities (through walkthroughs, for example).

Measuring is the activity of assessing a project's progress, especially as it deviates from the project plan. Another facet of measuring is gathering work and time statistics, which is chiefly the responsibility of the metrics group. Neither measure over-zealously nor skimp on measuring. Rather than harass your project team members, allow them to report deviations from the plan to you. Record all the salient and instructive measurements in the project log.

Revising is the process of making changes in order to take care of deviations from the plan. It enables you to keep your managerial guns trained on the moving target of the project. There are four common reasons for revision: slipped completion dates of tasks; bungled tasks; missed tasks; and unforeseen changes in personnel. Because of this process of revising, maintain your CPM and Gantt charts on a flexible medium, such as a computer database.

In order to manage a DP project successfully, constantly educate yourself on its technical factors. Otherwise, you will have difficulty carrying out the five managerial activities. Keeping current technically does not, however, imply that you should actually do any of the technical work of the project. To find time to deal with the project technically, set up a director/producer team. The director (the conventional project manager) deals chiefly with its technical aspects, while the producer handles its external aspects.

If you are assigned to manage a project that is already in progress, you should neither hope that you can somehow catch up with what's going on nor try to impress everyone by making an instant, devastating impact on the project. Instead, make sure that you thoroughly understand the project, even slowing the project down if necessary.

Chapter 6: Exercises

1.   What activities do you consider to constitute effective project management? How do they map into the five activities of plan, organize, integrate, measure, and revise?

2.   Think of projects that have been partial or total failures. What management errors contributed to those failures?

3.   Which of the five management activities are you strongest in? weakest in?

4.   Consider the general management quality of your shop. Which of the five management activities are carried out best? worst?

5.   DP project management is itself a task that can be bungled. What effects on other tasks does bungled management create?

6.   If you find it difficult to stay on top of your project technically, what are the reasons for your difficulties? How might you overcome them? If, on the other hand, you find it easy to stay on top, what factors are working in your favor? How might other managers share in your success?

7

Setting Project Deadlines

Project deadlines have acquired mythical powers in the minds of many project managers. But I have yet to see anyone's world come to an end or any project canceled merely because of a missed deadline. Projects are canceled for patently failing to meet users' needs in a cost-effective way—not for being a month or two late in completion.

The term *deadline* is derived from a line in a prison beyond which a prisoner would be shot if he strayed. It is hardly an appropriate term to apply to the estimated completion date of a project, though this derivation may account for the terror that deadlines instill in so many managers. Worse than this dread of deadlines is the feeling by many project members that the assigned deadline is totally unrealistic. A significant number of projects fail because of a manager's fanatical devotion to a deadline that is unachievable.

In this chapter, I look first at the three lethal effects of unrealistic project deadlines, followed by a discussion of their origins. Next, I describe methods of dealing with impossible deadlines that have been imposed. Finally, I discuss strategies for accommodating those rare deadlines that are both tough and legitimate into a realizable project plan.

7.1 Effects of the unrealistic deadline

There are primarily three deadly effects of an unrealistic deadline on a data processing project: loss of managerial control of the project; production of a low-quality, ineffective system; and demotivation of both manager and workers. Because each effect is so important to the project's outcome, I discuss them in turn below.

7.1.1 Loss of managerial control

A well-run project is paced like a well-run race: The seasoned athlete begins a race by keeping back, pacing himself carefully, but moves forward slowly throughout the race until at the end he is poised for a final burst of speed over the finishing line. The tenderfoot runner, on the other hand, starts the race fast, leading the pack, and tries to win by sustaining a maniacal pace throughout the event.

Similarly, an inexperienced manager tries to meet a deadline by rushing through the project. However, having scrambled through analysis, he usually runs into serious problems during programming or acceptance testing and may either drop out or be forced out of the race entirely, without finishing the project.

Now although a project is not a race, the DP managers with the best track records are those who pace themselves early in the project in preparation for a burst of effort at the end, just like the experienced runner. Their motto is, "More haste, less speed," as they and their staff devote long, careful thought to the early phases of the project (especially to problem definition and analysis), which may yield little visible output. They then gradually pick up speed through design, until programming becomes almost a sprint. (Testing, however, always has to be executed deliberately and methodically.)

I know one manager who, in the initial stages of a project at least, tells his analysts to slow down. However, so they are under no illusions, he also tells them to be rigorous and to carefully think through every problem. He knows that a project cannot be successfully managed merely by pressing the gas pedal to the floor and careering like a madman from analysis through implementation. That approach is only guaranteed to throw the manager out of control and land him in the project hospital.

7.1.2 Production of low-quality systems

In obeying the strident dictates of an unrealistic deadline, a project manager must sacrifice the care and effort that attends the development of a high-quality system. Yet, this fact is often ignored by both data processing personnel and users alike. Indeed, an absurd tradition has arisen at all levels of DP that only sissies worry about quality, while "real" project managers are those who can develop a system by an arbitrary deadline or for an arbitrary sum of money.

I recently witnessed a disturbing example of the dominance of the deadline. In a large aeronautical engineering shop, a software system was required to operate a complex piece of hardware. Because of poor planning by the general project manager, the software manager had a seemingly impossible deadline for the delivery of his system. Yet, he not only succeeded in beating the deadline by a few days, but he actually underspent his budget. Pleased, the project manager awarded the software manager a promotion and a large pay increase.

I asked the hardware manager what he thought of the software manager's incredible feat. "That system's one of the worst pieces of garbage I've ever seen," he said. "It's badly designed, hastily coded, almost completely untested, and inaccurately documented. I'm far from convinced that it even works correctly in all circumstances."

"Ho hum, just another poor piece of software," you think. "What's so disturbing about that?" What is so disturbing is that this particular piece of software is a component in our national defense system.

Why does a deadline so often take precedence over quality? Why is the cost of system development more often considered more important than the quality of the final system, which is admittedly difficult to quantify but not hard to recognize? The answer to these questions is that low-quality systems do not exact their high tolls until they are delivered and put into production. Only then is the horrendous expense manifested of working with and maintaining such systems. Indeed, some deadline-constrained systems are so bad that it is cheaper to throw them away and start over.

Although some DP departments partition their budgetary accounting into separate cost areas, with developmental and operational costs charged back to the appropriate systems and users, few DP shops allocate their maintenance costs correctly. In the worst cases, maintenance charges are made against a giant, monolithic budget, priorities are settled by the user who yells loudest and most often, and no attempt is made to record the maintenance costs of individual systems. Even in the best cases, where good financial data are available, rarely does anyone take the trouble to relate the cost of the maintenance effort to the quality of the original development work.

In short, the wrong goals are being set implicitly for the overall good of the department. If management tells you to minimize costs and tighten schedules, the quickest way to achieve these ends is to lower the quality of the end product. Sadly, the folly in this approach is that it actually increases costs—but in someone else's budget and in another fiscal year. A poster that I sometimes see on the walls of junior programmers' offices accurately, if cynically, acknowledges the above budgetary practice. It shows an obviously frantic person surrounded by listings, ringing phones, and half-empty coffee cups, with the caption, "There's no time to do it right, but there's always time to do it over."

Some people even make a career of satisfying short-term financial expediencies by delivering products on time but of poor quality. The following story describes the quick and dirty deeds of such a deadline desperado. A contract programmer explained his views of the contract programming business to me. "I always take contracts that last three to six months," he said. "I also try to get jobs where I can code up a storm, hand over my listings right on the deadline, take the money, and run. That way, if my programs blow up, I'm well away from the scene of the crime."

I replied that I didn't think it was very professional or even ethical to do a shoddy job and then abscond, leaving bug-ridden code for some ill-fated maintenance programmer to fix up. He countered that I obviously lacked the machismo to be part of the mercenary soldier world of contract programming with its rewards for meeting deadlines.

Four years later, I met this same programmer again quite by chance, and I noticed most of his earlier bravado was gone. He confessed that he had migrated back and forth from California to New York in order to shake off his acquired reputation for poor work: It had become known that if you hired "Sloppy Joe" for three months, you'd have to hire someone else for six months to patch his code. New York City and Los Angeles, he had discovered to his chagrin, were really small towns in the world of DP.

Your duty, as Sloppy Joe eventually discovered, is to enforce standards of high quality so that everyone can benefit. Otherwise, everyone suffers sooner or later. In developing a system, of course, time is always an unwelcome pressure, but convince your management and users that they shouldn't set an unreasonable deadline, since there will be plenty of time to do it right, if it doesn't have to be done over.

7.1.3 Demotivation of employees

Unrealistic deadlines are not motivating tools, but they are commonly used by upper managers as a conscious ploy to spur the workers to frenzied production. The ploy might run something like this: "The project manager estimated completion by December, so we'll give him a deadline of June. That'll make him perspire a bit. . . . I bet we'll get the system by September at the latest." The deadline in this case is a whip used for indiscriminate flagellation.

A project manager who attended one of my seminars told me of his own painful experience with unrealistic deadlines. "My last project was a disaster," he began his tale. "My boss said at the start of analysis that we absolutely had to have the system delivered within twelve months, or else we'd be in deep trouble. I went along with his demand, because I was close to retirement and didn't want to make waves. It seemed to me more like a two-year project, but I figured the best thing to do was to staff up heavily and make overtime compulsory for everyone, with a promise of compensatory time after the project ended.

"I was amazed by the effect of my dictates on my staff. The conscientious ones sweated blood, the sane ones quit the company, and the cynics (all the rest) were totally unmoved to work a minute longer than they wanted. The staff's rate of work at least initially increased noticeably over previous projects, but its quality was significantly poorer and we produced a high proportion of junk. So, what could we do? We had no time to replace the junk and even if we had done so, what would we have replaced it with—more junk? So, we tried to patch up the mess by working around the clock. The mess, however, got worse. The deadline came and went and the project was finally and mercifully canceled, because we had nothing that worked. The original schedule and budget called for a one-year project costing $400,000. The actual project took nineteen months, cost $680,000, and delivered absolutely nothing."

How absurd to be forced to hazard the success of the whole project against the trifling rewards of an artificial deadline, and how sad that a normally kind manager should feel compelled to flog his team of willing horses to death in order to try to meet the arbitrary and pernicious demands of a deadline. What motivates a professional is not a stick on his back. It is being given the responsibility for doing a good job, being given the resources and opportunities to do a good job, and finally receiving the recognition that he has done a good job. If employees are allowed to set their own pace and to participate in their own scheduling, they rarely work unduly slowly.

7.2 Origins of unrealistic deadlines

There are four major origins of unrealistic deadlines. In order of increasing justifiability, they can derive from wishful thinking, the preliminary project estimate, the creeping commitment, and the value step. I discuss each one below.

7.2.1 Wishful thinking

A deadline caused by wishful thinking is usually based on nothing scientific whatsoever, but is merely the date by which the users would like to have their system. Some Mr. Fantasy with enough authority in the organization dreams the impossible dream and voilà! your deadline is set. Never be overcome by such a desire to please your users or your own managers that you acquiesce to this type of deadline.

I show this type of wishful thinking in the Gantt chart of Figure 7.1. If a deadline is impossible to achieve, it is also impossible to derive a workable project plan based on that deadline. Therefore, all a project manager can do is to leave the project as a giant monolith on his planning chart.

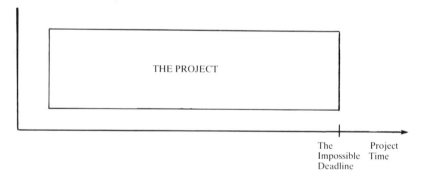

Figure 7.1. Planning chart based on wishful thinking.

In Figure 7.2, the manager allows for each task in the plan the shortest time in which that task could conceivably be executed, given ideal circumstances, and then allows no time between the tasks for review, revision, or coordination. The result is a deadline that appears to be achievable, although only under the best conditions. This type of wishful thinking is analogous to saying that first, it's possible to run a mile in four minutes; and second, if the race course is 26.219 miles, it's therefore possible to run the distance in 105 minutes.

Workers may be able to keep up a breakneck speed for one or two tasks, but they will not be able to sustain such a speed for the whole project. They will tire; time will be needed for meetings and reviews; and time will also be needed to carry out changes to intermediate products. The theoretically possible deadline of Figure 7.2 is actually totally impossible in the real world.

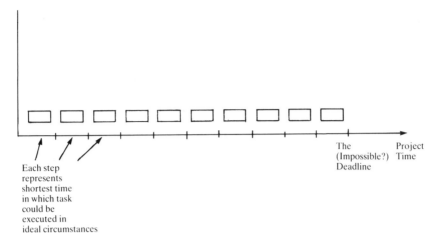

Figure 7.2. Planning chart based on ideal conditions.

I cannot blame users and DP managers for wishing that software development would proceed faster. I wish that it would, too, but there are no shortcuts to improving software development speed and productivity. The best ways to do so are to invest time and money in developing staff expertise, standardizing projects, and using tools to assist project members, as discussed in Chapters 13 and 14.

7.2.2 Preliminary project estimate

A second source of unrealistic deadlines is the preliminary project estimate. As I pointed out in Chapter 2, the earlier in the project that an estimate is made, the less accurate the estimate is likely to be. A corollary to this rule is, The earlier into the project that an estimate is made, the more likely it is that someone will enshrine that estimate as a project deadline. Be forewarned: Mentioning a date, especially at the start of a project, with no explanation or cautions, may be regarded as an immutable, realistic goal. The best procedure when deadlines are mentioned is to refer to the project plan, as described in Chapter 6. This plan, with its dozens of task completion dates, immediately demonstrates the naiveté of having a single completion date for a complex project, especially when that date is based only upon a premature estimate.

In addition, the plan eliminates a standard excuse for deadlines: that users need them in order to prepare for installation. The trouble with a project deadline is that the users believe they'll have the system by that date and make their preparations accordingly. When the deadline is missed, the users could be caught between dismantling their old system and not having the new system to replace it. If the users' needs for installation are integrated into the project plan, however, the installation details can be planned and scheduled fairly accurately as the installation date approaches.

7.2.3 Creeping commitment

Unrealistic deadlines can derive from a process of incremental extortion known as creeping commitment [Thomsett, 1980]. A user is fooled into committing to a large and expensive project by a deliberate understatement of the project's size and cost. By the time the user discovers the project's actual cost, he is past the point of no return. If he fails to come up with the extra money required to finish the project, he will lose the money that he's already spent.

Obviously, creeping commitment is a devious political trick that must be kept secret from the users in order for it to work. Often, even the project manager is uninformed about the deliberate understatement of the project's cost and receives from his management an unrealistic deadline as a nonnegotiable imperative.

I abhor the use of creeping commitment. It's an infantile ploy that creates bad feeling between the DP department and the users once the users discover they've been duped. The correct way to win users' commitment to a project is by showing them carefully detailed estimates of project costs, benefits, and resources, as described in Chapter 2. I've found that most users, faced with an objective statement of reality, will make rational, mature decisions, and it is only DP people who expect them to behave otherwise.

7.2.4 Value step

A value step is a change, usually downward, in the value of a system on a certain date. For example, the federal government may decree that on January 1, all banks shall withhold a certain portion of savers' interest for tax purposes. In this event, an automatic system for withholding interest will clearly be of more value if it's delivered on December 31, rather than January 31. The change in the system's value on January 1 is enough to make that date an irresistible candidate for a deadline.

Since a deadline based on the value step has some legitimacy, it cannot be trivially dismissed. But neither should it be given so much sway that it imperils the conduct of the project or the quality of the project's deliverables. For instance, a bank has options other than the installation of an automated system on January 1, including persuading the government to delay or revoke its decision, using a cumbersome manual system until the automated system comes up, or temporarily ignoring the rule and paying the subsequent fines. In Section 7.4.1, I explore how the value step deadline can be safely integrated into a project plan.

7.3 Ways to handle unrealistic deadlines

As a project manager, you are primarily responsible for debunking the mythical power of the deadline. If you find yourself saddled by your users or managers with an impossible deadline, your duties are to minimize their harmful effects in two ways: The first is to protect your project team from destructive pressure; the second is to reflect the pressure caused by the unrealistic deadline back to those responsible for creating it.

7.3.1 Protect the team from undue pressure

In order to shield your staff from undue budgetary or scheduling pressures that are imposed upon you by your users or by your boss, your motto should be that of Harry S Truman: "The buck stops here." Even if you feel such pressures, don't transmit those pressures to your staff.

Of course, this is a lot easier to say than to do. Being a DP project manager in many companies is like being inside a giant organizational nutcracker, where the pressures from above meet the pressures from below (and guess who's the nut!). You need a very thick shell to hold out in that spot forever without doing anything. So, many managers capitulate and force their staff members to work long hours, harangue them, blame them, and generally give them a rough time in order to meet some arbitrary and impossible deadline.

Most people like to work regular hours the majority of the time, to work hard some of the time, and to slacken off a small portion of the time. Normal people are neither able nor willing to work in crisis mode indefinitely. A manager's pleading "crisis" every time eventually becomes meaningless. One manager who realized this effect circulated a memo stating, "Since the project is now in *emergency* mode, we must escalate our work hours until we meet the delivery date." His team did not meet the delivery date, but before the manager could find a more hysterical word than "emergency," many of his team members had asked for transfers.

A talk that I once gave on abolishing deadlines was followed by a silence punctuated by nervous shuffling of feet and embarrassed coughing. After all, I'd just demolished the one abiding custom for managers in this ever-changing world. Eventually, a question was voiced: "Haven't you heard of Parkinson's Law that states work expands to fill the time available? If you take away the deadline, the project team will lose all incentive to work and the project will go on forever."

In advocating the removal of monolithic deadlines, I'm certainly not proposing to remove every deadline and thus have every project expand infinitely. Nor do I recommend that a project be allowed to continue indefinitely in the futile promise of some forthcoming gem of perfection. A project must be conducted under the firm regimen of a project plan, with the staff completing tasks on time. If schedules for tasks are slipped, you must know the reasons why. If the reasons are valid and the delays unavoidable, let the project schedule slip.

Obviously, you should try to minimize such slippage as much as you can. Since you shouldn't run a project like a leisure resort for the team members, you're certainly justified in applying extra pressure occasionally to get the job done. But to take the rigid line that no project slippage beyond the deadline is permissible under any circumstances is ridiculous. You cannot simply ignore perturbing factors that change the project plan, and such managerial inflexibility results only in casualties to your project team and to the project itself.

7.3.2 Reflect undue pressure back to its originators

So what should you do with a ludicrous deadline if you cannot tyrannize your workers and if you yourself don't want to absorb all of the associated pressure? The only sane response for your own mental and physical well-being is to reflect the pressure back to whoever created the unrealistic deadline. That means saying no to your boss or users whenever you are asked to agree to an unreasonable demand.

For example, let's say you've been granted fifteen months to deliver a computer system that fulfills a certain set of requirements. However, because of budgetary problems, your management tells you your new deadline is twelve months, but the users want the same system delivered and you'll get no additional staff members. The worst thing you can do at this point is to shrug your shoulders and put everyone on mandatory unpaid overtime. That's bad for your team's morale, bad for your own morale, and bad for your management (who must learn to respect reality, like everyone else).

When you learn of the budgetary cutback, you must look your boss squarely in the eye and say, "Only bank robbers and muggers can get something for nothing merely by demanding it. What features do you want me to cut out of the system?" Then, pull out the list of system benefits that you made at the start of the project and put your boss on the spot for a change. Make him choose what to excise from the system; make him negotiate with the users to reach a rational decision. If, after a new list of benefits is developed and a new cost estimate made, the system is not deemed such a wise idea, only then can the project be canceled for a good reason. And, you won't have to make such an important decision unilaterally.

If for whatever reason you are forced to accept an unrealistic deadline, consider asking to be reassigned to another project. One manager I know, whenever he's in this situation, says to his boss, "If you think the project can be done in half the time that I estimate, why don't you do the project yourself?" At the very least, carefully and unemotionally document your views and underlying reasons to your management and explain the situation to your staff. Otherwise, you stand to lose the respect of your staff, your peers, your management, and your users.

Saying no to bosses or to users takes a lot of moral strength and courage. But stand firm. The manager of the $680,000 disaster told me that that catastrophe taught him an important lesson: A project manager must always stand up for what's realistic, despite the inevitable managerial inquisition that ensues, and if he can't stand the heat, he should get out of the kitchen.

7.4 Legitimate deadlines based on the value step

Some deadlines are legitimate because they are based on the fact that a project completed before a certain date is worth considerably more than if it's completed some time later. The total lifetime value of any system to its users depends upon when it is delivered: The later the system is delivered, the less the total amount of benefit it will produce for the users over its working life. However, this decline in total lifetime value is relatively slow. If you deliver a system to the users in 1985, for example, it may save them $5 million over its lifetime, but the same system delivered in 1986 may save them only $4 million. (Of course, I am assuming that other factors, such as the correctness of the delivered system, remain equal.) This concept is represented as one of two lines in Figure 7.3.[1] The second line in the figure represents the cost of building a system, which tends as a crude first approximation to increase as a linear function of the time required to build the system.

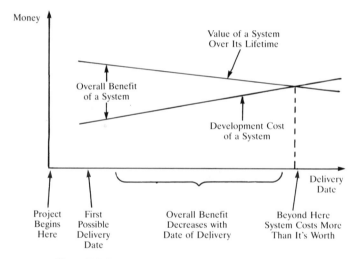

Figure 7.3. Representation of a system's overall benefit.

As these lines indicate, you can't wait forever to deliver a system. Once the two lines in the graph cross, the system costs more than it's worth. However, even when a project reaches that point, it may be foolish to cancel the project, since installing the partial system would presumably cut the users' losses. Much depends on how near the project is to completion.[2]

---

[1]Figure 7.3 is simplistic since the graph is meant to illustrate a general principle. I'm ignoring the many accounting possibilities that can also alter costs and values, such as amortization and depreciation, as well as the effects of inflation or deflation and changes in the users' business volumes.

[2]Frequently, of course, no one knows accurately how these lines are placed on the graph. I've seen systems installed with brass bands and certificates of appreciation awarded to the project team, although the systems have turned out to cost the users hundreds of thousands of dollars more than if the users had never started the project.

Incidentally, the effect of reducing the quality of a system is to decrease the value to the users of the system over its lifetime. This might be because the system doesn't provide so many functions or because it's difficult to use or because it's expensive to operate or because it's expensive to maintain or because it has any of the other deficiencies of reduced quality. So, if you opt for lower quality, you must complete the project quickly because you have less room to maneuver; the point where the lines cross approaches very soon.

7.4.1 Illustration of the value step

Although it makes little difference in the overall benefit of most systems whether they are delivered on one day or the next, there are exceptions. One such system was an automated flood warning system, dubbed Noah. It was to replace a fairly good manual system that consisted of many sensors placed in major rivers and their tributaries. These sensors measured the river height, water volume per second, local rainfall, and so on; the information from the sensors was used to predict possible flooding and to designate flood gates in the affected areas to be opened. One problem with the manual system was that bad weather made it dangerous to read many of the sensors. Another was the difficulty for humans to interpret all the rain and river data in time to do anything useful. The manual system typically provided four to six hours' warning to open certain flood gates and to evacuate designated areas. With the automated system, the information would be fed into a computer for quick analysis and then would give an expected eight to twelve hours' notice.

In the region of the country where Noah was to be installed, there were two primary flood seasons: one in November and December, and the second in March and April. So, to gain the most benefit from the system, a deadline for installation of November 1 was set. The project team installed the hardware by mid-October, had the hardware and software talking to each other during the last week of October, and delivered the system on November 1, as planned.

Unfortunately, there was no time for testing, except for the most straightforward test cases. About a month later, Mother Nature provided a boundary value test case by dumping three to five inches of rain in one day on the district covered by the sensors. The system performed magnificently, indicating to the authorities which areas should be evacuated and when, and advising them to open the gates on river A to allow water to run off via river B. The authorities carried out the system's instructions with alacrity.

The first indication that something was amiss was from an old man who'd lived his whole life on the banks of river B and who telephoned to say that the river was rising about a foot an hour; it was already spilling over its levees in several places. He added that everything had been okay until "some darn fool opened the gates up river." Fortunately, not much damage was done. The greatest expense was the evacuation of hundreds of families from areas untouched by floodwaters.

As you may have guessed, the cause of the erroneous advice was program bugs, but bugs of the worst kind because they gave reasonable data that was dead wrong. The users didn't trust the system fully for several more years, during which time a parallel manual system was also operated. How much money the automated system has cost the users is not on record.

The value of this system is not a straight line, since it falls sharply each year between the two flood seasons (see Figure 7.4). Even in a case such as this with steps on the value line, setting any one of these steps as a deadline may prove to be a false goal, because the cost of the poor quality of the system far exceeds the benefit of installing it before the apparent deadline of the flood season.

When such steps in the value line of a system occur, is there some way to take advantage of them without jeopardizing the quality and hence the benefits of the system? There is, since most systems are composed of subsystems that each have their own value and cost lines. Implementing just part of a system is often a good way to avoid the full loss of system value on a certain date. If you identify a date as a candidate for a deadline, first ascertain whether there is any significant advantage in delivering the system on or before that date. If there is, determine the minimum

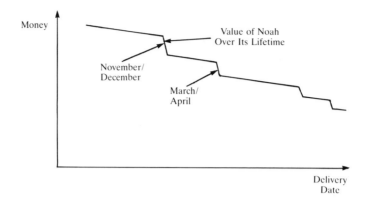

Figure 7.4. Value chart of Noah.

portion of the system that can be implemented to accrue the majority of the benefit. Finally, plan a strategy whereby you can deliver the needed piece by the crucial date with the least possible risk to the project and to the final system. In the sections below, I discuss four strategies for developing the requisite pieces in time: incremental implementation, radical development, throwaway code, and prototyping.

7.4.2 Incremental implementation as a compromise strategy

Incremental implementation, as I described in Chapter 6, simply means constructing a system gradually in pieces. First, a small working portion of the system is implemented and then other pieces are added to the working portion one by one, until the system is complete. Throughout its implementation, the system operates and its functionality increases as pieces are added. Some versions of the growing system may even be useful enough to deliver to the users.

To illustrate how you could exploit incremental implementation to deliver certain functions by a given date, let's return to the flood warning system. As the project manager, you might propose this as a feasible schedule:

October 5	install rain gauges
October 17	install river sensors
October 20	connect gauges and sensors to the computer
October 25	add software to read and to control gauges and sensors (call this sub-system 1)
November 5	do acceptance test of subsystem 1
November 8	add software to predict flooding from river flow data (call this sub-system 2)
November 30	add software to predict river flow from rainfall (call this subsystem 3)
January 8	add software to compute best flood relief tactics (call this subsystem 4)
May 15	acceptance test of subsystems 2, 3, and 4

This is not an ambitious schedule. By the beginning of the November/December flood season, only subsystem 1 is installed and tested. In practice, each piece of software is not added all at once. Small pieces of code are added incrementally to the test system under a plan derived from the software design. In this way, system testing proceeds constantly on the gradually growing system. Although this first piece of software is limited, it provides some advantages over the manual system; much more data can be captured without personal risk, and the data can be continually checked for plausibility against some sample manual data that isn't dangerous to obtain.

While adding software subsystems 2, 3, and 4 individually to the system, the project team tests them as thoroughly as possible. However, the objective of this testing is to detect as many errors as possible in the design and programming of the software. Acceptance testing doesn't take place until May 15, when a large amount of data can be compared with the actual fluctuations of the rivers over the period. In a system such as this one, the ultimate test of the acceptability of the system is whether its predictions are confirmed by reality.

This implementation of the completed system doesn't seek to deliver as much software as possible, tested or not, by a certain deadline. Instead, it aims to deliver a system worth having, with some working parts in place at the beginning of flood season, even though the whole system cannot be accepted as reliable until May at the earliest.

7.4.3 Radical development strategy

A second strategy to meet a deadline is radical development, which involves designing and implementing parts of a system without having completed the analysis of the whole system. This is a risky way to develop a system, because the analysis of the final portions of the system might require design and/or programming changes to the software that is already installed. Redoing work can be expensive.

There are three criteria for choosing when to use radical development: if there are functional pieces of the system that can be analyzed, designed, and implemented reasonably by a certain date; if implementing those pieces of the system by that date brings substantial material gain; and if enough analysis (additional to that for the pieces being implemented) can be completed to minimize the danger of having to redesign or rewrite code. If you doubt any one of these "if's," don't attempt radical development, because the method is extremely difficult to manage and tends to reduce the quality of the system that is produced.

7.4.4 Throwaway code as a strategy

One way to arrive at a solution to a problem by a certain date is to lash together some quick and dirty code as a temporary measure. This code may lack desirable qualities, such as maintainability, but it must be correct. Of course, you should write as little of this dirty code as will do the job, because it will be replaced eventually by properly constructed code, which may be part of a larger, more comprehensive system.

7.4.5 Prototyping strategy

Prototyping is similar to throwaway code as a solution to meeting difficult deadlines in that it produces a temporary system constructed from high-level languages, from database query languages, or by means of an application generator [Martin, 1982a; Squires et al., 1982]. Such a system usually cannot be operated in production indefinitely, because it may suffer from machine inefficiency, awkward dialogue, inconsistency with interfacing subsystems, or poor long-term maintainability.

The third strategy, and the fourth to a lesser extent, involve throwing something away. Unfortunately, "temporary" has a way of becoming "permanent" as in Europe, for instance, where temporary housing built shortly after World War II is still occupied. It's the same way with code. Once the code is up and running, people tend to gloss over how bad it is in order to push on with the next pressing problem. The quick and dirty code becomes older and dirtier and becomes someone's nightmare in perpetuity. The only right way to install throwaway code is to have a plan that dictates when to discard it and how to develop its replacement.

7.5 Summary

In *Controlling Software Projects,* DeMarco states that fully fifteen percent of all projects that are started are never completed. A significant factor in these project failures is a project manager's slavish subordination to an ill-conceived deadline [DeMarco, 1982].

The deadliness of deadlines takes effect in three ways: by destroying the project manager's control of his project; by ruining the quality of the project's deliverables; and by demotivating project staff. Unrealistic deadlines derive from four main sources: wishful thinking on the part of an authoritative user; the petrification of a tentative early estimate; the creeping commitment, by which users are teased or coaxed in stages toward total commitment to a project; and the value step, the date at which the value of a delivered system drops noticeably.

In dealing with unrealistic deadlines, never allow unreasonable pressures to be transmitted to your staff. Instead, firmly place responsibility for the impossible deadline back on the shoulders of the DP manager or user who originated it. The value step type of deadline, however, cannot be so quickly dismissed, but neither should it be allowed to destroy a project. The best way to accommodate value steps is to find the pieces of the system that can be safely delivered by the deadline and that also bring the major proportion of the benefits of this timely delivery. Four strategies to aid in this speedy implementation are incremental implementation, radical development, throwaway code, and prototyping. But be careful: Anticipation of increased benefits may sing as sweetly as sirens in your ear, but they may also lure you and your project onto the rocks of disaster.

Meeting a deadline is often a gamble, with quality as the stake and precious little as the payoff. One of my seminar attendees put this well when she said, "After a few months, nobody remembers whether you made the deadline or not. But if you turn out a bad system, you get a phone call three times a week forever from somebody who's mad at you." As Thomas Jefferson said, "Delay is preferable to error."

To sum up this chapter in another way, let me present the Fable of the Afghan Boots to illustrate that you always get what you bargain for. During my profligate youth, I spent some time in Afghanistan. A custom in that part of the world is never to pay the asking price for an article in a market or in a shop. Instead, you are expected to haggle over the price, much in the same way you negotiate the price of a used car in this country. This haggling is such a part of the social etiquette that for expensive articles, the process may last for several hours and involve much tea drinking and pipe smoking. After a while, I considered myself to be a skilled bargainer, often leaving a shop after an hour or two of wrangling, with the shopkeeper wringing his hands at the low price my adroitness had forced him to concede for his goods.

Afghanistan and Kabul, especially, are noted for the craftsmanship of their bootmakers. Afghan boots are made from the finest leather and are adorned with the most exquisite stitching along their sides. A bootmaker will even gladly customize your boots to match your taste and your feet. After he's measured you and listened to your style specifications, he will quote you a price for the boots.

When I decided to order a pair for myself, I visited a bootmaker, who quoted me a price. Then, remembering that I was in Kabul, I haggled with him over the amount. This particular bootmaker was a pushover, and within a few minutes, I'd knocked the price to less than half the original amount. I stopped bargaining only to prevent his further punishment. I paid the bootmaker and left the shop, chuckling at what a shrewd customer I'd become.

Two days later, I returned to collect my boots. They were atrocious. The leather was poor, the fit uncomfortable, and the needlework uninspired and shoddy. I complained bitterly. The bootmaker shrugged and pointed to the price of 400 afghans (about $7 at the time). Then, he pointed to another, superb pair of boots with a price of 900 afghans. I immediately understood: You can legitimately bargain for a product that already exists, but you cannot bargain for a service yet to be performed, since you can name almost any price and the provider of the service can simply lower his quality to meet your price.

We in data processing are like custom bootmakers to our users. If they drive down our estimates for our services too much, we merely reduce the quality of our work to match, either deliberately or otherwise. A system of low quality is unlikely to be much of a bargain either for our users or for ourselves. As the Swiss proverb says, ''The bitterness of low quality remains long after the sweetness of low price is forgotten.''

Chapter 7: Exercises

1.   Consider projects with deadlines that are currently under way in your shop. How was the deadline for each project determined? Was the deadline determined from the project plan or was the project plan determined from the deadline?

2.   Consider past projects in which adherence to a difficult or impossible deadline was the primary priority of the project team. What was the effect of this priority on the quality of the project deliverables? What have the long-term effects been?

3.   Consider projects that have missed their appointed deadlines. What were the short-term results of their lateness? the long-term results?

8

Understanding Project Methodologies and Standards

A project methodology is a plan for conducting a project, and it consists of three components: a statement of the scope of the methodology; a specification of every project activity, together with its inputs and deliverables; and a specification of how the activities interrelate. Unlike a normal project plan that is restricted to a specific project, a *methodology* is a generic plan that can be used for any project. The plan for any particular project therefore is a subset of the project methodology.

The purpose of the statement of the methodology's scope is to specify its limits. Many DP project methodologies are available, each with its own scope. Dickinson, for one, proposes a methodology intended for the projects of any DP shop, although he cautions you to restrict its scope to the needs of your own shop [Dickinson, 1981]. Dickinson's methodology is expressed in the idiom of structured analysis, using process minispecifications to specify activities, the data dictionary to specify deliverables, and the data flow diagram to show the framework of interrelationships among a project's activities.

Project methodologies and standards are often confused, and although there is no universal agreement as to their meanings, I define *standards* to be a practical implementation of a methodology. Standards have two components in addition to the three components of a methodology listed above: a specification of the tools, techniques, mechanisms, and media needed to perform and support a project's activities and deliverables; and a set of rules that govern and constrain the conduct of a project's activities and the production of its deliverables. Examples of rules are, All changes to the data dictionary must be made by the project librarian; and, All COBOL paragraph names must begin with four digits, followed by a verb-object statement of the paragraph's function.

8.1 Benefits of standards

Of the many advantages in adopting shop-wide standards for conducting data processing projects, I describe six in the following paragraphs. First, having a methodology avoids the need to replan every project from scratch and consequently saves valuable time. Although each project in your shop is unique, the similarities among projects in one shop far outweigh the differences. Therefore, you can use the shop standards to select those components that are relevant to your project's characteristics (whether batch, online, multiprocessor, database, COBOL, Pascal, and so forth). This selection, of course, consumes some time, but the time is far less than that required to construct the plan and standards anew. With the tools that I suggest in Section 8.3, you can reduce this planning time still further.

A second advantage in using standards relates to the nature of modern DP projects. Since projects are generally too large and complex for one person or even a team to carry out every phase of the project, the work must be split up and organized so that specialists can be used on each phase. A methodology that specifies activities, together with their inputs and deliverables, facilitates this specialist kind of organization, which shares the benefits of the assembly line described in Chapter 5; experts are used for each phase, for example.

However, to gain the benefits of a specialist assembly line, you must pay the price in terms of the increased coordination needed of the activities in the assembly line. The coordination is best achieved by standardizing the deliverables of each activity. With standardization, everyone knows what he's expected to produce and what he expects to get, and so communication between people at adjacent stages of the assembly line is enhanced.

Third, having a specification for a generic project framework promotes uniformity among concurrent projects, as well as between successive projects. In order for specialists to be transferred from one project to another as needs arise, as in a matrix organization, the plans for the various projects need to be uniform. Synchronization of personnel is difficult under ideal circumstances, but practically impossible if two projects are based on mutually alien project methodologies or if they use different terminologies. For example, if project A is through the new physical phase and project B is completing the external design phase, what are the implications for the matrix organization? Are the two phases the same or do they require different specialists? Or do they overlap?

If all projects in the shop work completely independently, their phases will overlap confusingly and their terminologies will differ so extensively that it will be impossible for staff managers to coordinate the requirements of multiple projects. In this event, the overhead of managing a matrix organization becomes so great that the matrix structure must be abandoned in favor of a shopful of insular projects that share very little.

Similar difficulties exist between successive projects if a generic project framework is not used. Developing good estimates, for example, means having good, reliable consistent data from previous projects to guide you. What good are the statistics, say, from these four projects: seventy person-months for structured analysis, sixty person-months for requirements definition, eighty person-months for the functional specification, and fifty person-months for general design? Not much since all these activities are similar, but not similar enough to allow you to average the efforts for use in estimating the resources needed for a future project. Furthermore, we can assume that the four projects were different sizes. If they used four different methodologies, their sizes become almost impossible to relate since their units of measurement are so diverse (number of mini-specifications or number of lines of functional specification, for instance). Trying to compare their sizes is like trying to compare two Scots miles, 800 perches, four versts, 800 poles, and half a Spanish league.

A fourth benefit from having a common set of techniques for all projects is that it ensures uniformity of hiring and training procedures. When every project uses the same standards, the roles that project participants perform will not vary in nature from project to project. Thus, only one job role analysis need be done for the same role in many projects, and presumably the best candidate for employment fits well into the "be-know-do" requirements of counterpart positions on all projects.[1] Clearly, the training requirements for personnel are minimized when all projects use the same techniques. Not only is scheduling of training simplified if every analyst needs instruction on data flow diagrams, for example, but also such training is less expensive through economies of scale.

---

[1]See Chapter 12 for an explanation of "be-know-do" requirements.

Having a shop-wide set of techniques for conducting a project conveys another benefit in training staff: informal education. Formal education is important as a base, of course, but employees gain true understanding in informal ways—through office gatherings when practical hints are shared, and through lunch table exchanges. The more people in the shop who use the same set of techniques, the greater oral transmission and enhancement of knowledge there is.

Fifth, having a standard set of tools aids in the development of these tools. By this, I mean that well-chosen tools can increase people's productivity not only in the specific task for which the tool is intended, but also in other ways related to the project. A data dictionary, for instance, can be used to track the large number of components of software under development, together with these components' knotty interrelationships.

Although using tools is good, employing a great many tools is not better. In a shop without a consistent methodology, tools tend to proliferate. Project A uses one set of tools, and project B another set, so that the shop as a whole uses perhaps twenty tools to do the job of only five or six. This is expensive in terms of purchasing or leasing the tools (even more so if the tools are developed internally), in terms of maintaining the tools, and in terms of training people to use the tools effectively. But as I show in Section 8.3, having an integrated set of tools to support shop-wide standards may yield rewards that go beyond any offered by the standards alone.

Finally, having a set of standards reduces the time spent on futile procedural debates during the course of a project. A set of rules is established at the beginning so that people on projects can work as efficiently and as harmoniously with one another as possible. Rules bring efficiency by forcing decisions from among far fewer options than without the rules. In fact, the rules may often limit the allowed choices to only one, as when a rule states, "Each part of the design must be walked through at least once before it can be programmed."

Rules also promote harmony by depersonalizing potentially heated issues (although, as we shall see in Section 8.2.6, the rules may create heated issues of their own). For instance, Wilfred may consider that one of his designs is too straightforward or error free to be walked through, but Winifred disagrees. Rather than fighting about the issue, she can invoke the disinterested, previously established rule to make her point.

8.2 Disadvantages of standards

The disadvantage of rules and standards is that their inflexibility sometimes leaves little room for common sense. In the previous example, Wilfred's design may indeed be too straightforward to yield much benefit from being walked through, but it's better to walk through five straightforward designs than to overlook one overly complex, flawed design. A rule may not always handle a situation as nicely as common sense does, but a rule that is good comes close and errs on the side of caution.

Standards may also introduce excessive conservatism into a shop (though with our industry in its current turmoil, some self-imposed restraint may be beneficial). However, the problems with standards lie not so much with the principle of having them, as with the way in which the standards are put into practice in many shops.

Many deficiencies in the form and content of a typical shop's standards jeopardize the standards' chance of success. A consultant colleague of mine was so convinced that shop standards rapidly go on the rocks that he had a stock saying, "Standards fail." To back up this unequivocal statement, he would seek out standards manuals at every opportunity. In shops where the manuals could actually be found, he would note that they often were in a dozen or so ancient binders forgotten on a lofty shelf. His most memorable demonstration that standards are born to blush unseen was when he selected a shop's standards manual from a dusty shelf and snapped it open. Much to the amusement of a small group of onlookers, an indignant spider marched angrily from the manual, swung Errol Flynn-like from a thread, and made a daring getaway behind a terminal.

Although it's far from inevitable that project standards should fall into disuse, my friend is correct that many of them do so. The reason is that standards often suffer from a number of crippling ailments. The ills that afflict shop standards can be categorized into five areas: dissemination, credibility, enforcement, execution, and modification. After I discuss each of these areas, I illustrate them by means of an actual example.

8.2.1 Problems in disseminating standards

A standards or methodology manual is a specification for a special kind of system: the system for developing improvements to the users' business, which is called a project. Unfortunately, the typical standards manual suffers from many of the faults of traditional specifications for other systems. It is often a forbiddingly long document, filling perhaps a dozen three-ring binders and detailing such things as project activities, deliverables, and techniques. In the worst manuals, the presentation is tedious, without diagrams. Some standards manuals lack even an adequate index. As one exasperated project member, confronted by a ponderous multivolume standards manual, remarked, "Once you pick up the standards manual, I'm sure it's impossible to put it down, but nobody's managed to pick it up yet."

Although most standards manuals are unbearably detailed, others are concise but too vague and general to be useful. For example, one vague manual contained the statements, "All designs must be approved" and "All program variable names should be as long as possible." I can't disagree with these statements, since it's hard to be sure just what they mean. The author of this particular manual was either fuzzy-brained or constrained by internal politics.

The worst possible problem of all in the dissemination of standards is their not being disseminated at all. For example, there may be no internal training in the shop standards, so the absorption of the volumes of standards is then left to the individual's initiative. If part or all of the standards manual is missing, or if the standards' author has left the shop, the shop will have no standards bearer and the standards are likely to fall out of use for lack of interest.

8.2.2 Problems in standards' credibility

Standards that are not credible to the people who must follow them are almost certain to be abandoned. Examples of standards that are not believable include the irrelevant ("All structure charts must be drawn by means of the SD101A template"); the nonsensical ("Every bubble on a data flow diagram must be decomposed into five lower-level bubbles"); the misguided ("All primitive processes must be specified by means of structured English"); the obsolete ("All programmers must enter their programs through the remote job entry card reader in Building 12A between 2 and 4 p.m."); and surprisingly, the too forward thinking ("Designs must be walked through before they are programmed") in a shop whose staff is not current with modern techniques.

Credibility problems in standards occur most often for one of two reasons. The first is that the standards' scope is not wide enough to cover the entire range of projects in the shop. Such a narrow scope may arise because the standards were extrapolated from the procedures used on a single type of project. For example, standards produced for batch projects do not cover the entirety of developing online systems, nor are tape processing standards entirely suitable for database projects.

The second common reason for standards' credibility problems is that the authors of the standards were not sufficiently experienced with DP projects to know what is believable and practical. All too frequently, the creators of standards glean their knowledge not by working on projects but by attending courses or by reading books. While courses and books are valuable adjuncts to experience, they are not substitutes for the practicalities of real projects. Authors who are guided only by theory are liable to misinterpret that theory and to undermine the believability of their standards in the eyes of project practitioners. For example, one set of standards that I read contained this statement: "For the sake of maintainability, each box on the structure chart should become a CALLed COBOL subprogram."

8.2.3 Problems in enforcing standards

Standards that are not enforced wither away. Or, as Donaldson puts it, "If you are not prepared to enforce standards, there is no point in wasting time on a standards manual" [Donaldson, 1978, p. 7]. But in several shops that I've visited, standards could not possibly have been enforced for the simple reason that no one ever looked at anything anyone else produced. There were no walkthroughs and little teamwork of any kind. Since standards cannot be enforced on essentially private practices, these shops in effect had no standards, despite their impressive array of standards manuals.

Consider, for example, a programmer in one such shop who rapidly turned out programs of apparently excellent quality. However, some time after he had left the shop, it turned out that he'd used bizarre program variable names in his programs, such as single characters or names of parts of the body. His programs were peppered with "MOVE K1 TO X," "MOVE FOOT TO MOUTH," and worse. This practice was in direct contravention to the published shop standard on program variable names, which called for explicit, meaningful names. This programmer's code was so unmaintainable that it had to be scrapped and rewritten by other programmers.

Even in shops whose members do conduct peer reviews of one another's deliverables, there is frequently little enforcement of standards, again for a simple reason: No penalty is levied for deviating from the shop standards. Therefore, only a minority of exceptionally dutiful and iron-willed people bother to adhere to the standards.

A small percentage of shops have a problem in heavy-handed enforcement of standards. They constitute oppressive standards nomocracies (societies governed principally by laws and lawyers). Project members in standards nomocracies spend much of their time in expensive litigation with the ominous Standards Enforcement Group, a hybrid group of standards lawyers and police with often more authority than responsibility. Because of this, project members must spend a great deal of time studying the ever-growing body of trivial legislation in the standards manual.

Although authoritarian coercion may get people to toe the standards line for a while, it often costs more in time and ill will than it's worth. Eventually, this type of enforcement collapses in anarchy, when the standards are, so to speak, overthrown by an oppressed people. I give an example of this phenomenon in Section 8.2.6.

8.2.4 Problems in using standards

A problem that stalks every implementation of standards and methodologies is one that I call the triumph of process over product. This phrase means that people lose sight of what they should be producing and instead become neurotically obsessed by the procedures for obtaining that product.

Many examples of this phenomenon occurred in shops using structured analysis. Project analysts worried excessively over drawing bubbles and arrows and over following the appointed methodology to the letter. They spent untold amounts of time producing data flow diagrams of exquisite beauty and fastidious neatness, but they forgot the intended end result: improving the users' business. They were so busy doing *structured* analysis that they failed to analyze anything adequately.

A second problem in using standards is when the standards get in the way of the job at hand. They should help, not hinder, and make a job easier to do rather than harder. But in many cases, doing things right is tedious at best and impractical at worst, even with the best will in the world.

For one thing, remembering every detail of every standard is not possible, and so a project member is forced to continually look up the correct standard in the huge document. Under the pressures of a normal project, most project workers won't.

Furthermore, people generally won't do very much for nothing; their every action is toward a perceived reward. For example, a COBOL programmer obeys the syntax of the language when he codes, because he knows the program won't compile if he doesn't. There is no similar benefit for a programmer who obeys the syntax laid down by a standards manual. Neither does a maintenance programmer gain much short-term benefit by recording his changes to programs. In fact, since it causes him double work, he loses. Of course, recording changes helps him in the long run, but some maintenance programmers are myopic in perceiving future benefits. Using most shop standards requires great discipline, and thus, apart from some of the most obviously beneficial and easily applicable ones, the majority of standards will lapse because of their obscurity, their difficulty to follow, and their lack of immediate returns.

8.2.5 Problems in updating standards

Every rule should have an underlying reason and the reason should be known so that when circumstances change, rules that are no longer reasonable can also be changed. For example, consider the programming rule, "Constant portions of expressions within iterative statements should be moved out of the iterative statement and expressed as a partial result just prior to the iterative statement." In plain English, this means that if a piece of an expression within a loop has the same value on each iteration of the loop, in order to avoid continually recomputing that value, make the computation once, before the loop begins. My reaction to this rule is, Why do we want to move such a piece of code from its natural, logical, understandable place to a less natural one? The reasons are that the object code will be more efficient if we do so, and that some compilers aren't smart enough to move the computation automatically to increase the efficiency of the object code.

If you weren't told these reasons, you would be obliged to follow the standard blindly, even if efficiency were less important to you than legibility in the particular piece of code you were writing. What if your shop bought a new sophisticated compiler that optimized its object code as much as possible? In that event, the main reason for the rule would be nullified.

Yet, despite this consideration, many standards manuals contain no reasons for their standards, no sunset clauses on standards' applicability, no list of rejected alternative standards, and no mechanism for correcting and updating standards. Without these, and especially without the feedback mechanism to change standards, they soon suffer from most of the credibility problems mentioned before and fall into disuse. As British Chief Justice Coke said, "When an Act of Parliament is against common right or reason or repugnant or impossible to be performed, the common law will control it and adjudge such an Act to be void."[2] Coke's words echo through the years into many modern DP shops. Unreasonable, repugnant, and impossible standards are voided by the laws of common sense. But such standards shouldn't merely be abandoned or ridiculed. They should be put right through the closure of the loop between practitioners and legislators. Only in that way can standards be kept in line with practice and reason.

8.2.6 A mortifying example

In a large corporation that was plagued by systems of poor quality and diverse development styles, management established a Quality Assurance (QA) group. Its charter was not to assure

---

[2]Sir Edward Coke, "Bonham's Case," *Rex v. Dr. Thomas Bonham, 1610.*

quality as you might imagine, but to develop and enforce standards. The group followed that dictate to the letter, cranking out new standards on almost everything, including the correct diameter for a bubble on a data flow diagram, the percentage of total effort on each phase of the project, and the number of spaces to indent after a COBOL ELSE.

The QA group enforced their standards with pedantic zeal and became the major force at code walkthroughs. At each session, a QA representative pointed out such felonies as a PIC clause beginning in column 31, rather than the standard 32. Code was continually sent back for re-editing in order to ensure its conformity to the ever-mounting volumes of increasingly petty standards. The re-editing actually introduced bugs, but the QA people didn't care about bugs.

Diplomatic relations between the development people and the QA people were hardly cordial, and open hostilities occasionally broke out, with raised voices and fists slamming on tables. One morning, this message appeared on every terminal: "Those who can't program write programming standards." The war between the two departments didn't remain secret for long. Higher management and users stepped in to impel an armistice, whose terms were, "Strict standards will not be enforced by the Quality Assurance group on projects with time-critical deadlines, but will be applied to those projects at the discretion of the project manager." In other words, standards were abandoned. (The QA group, however, lingered on for years with a single person until it disappeared in one of the periodic corporate reorganizations.)

8.3 A solution to some standards problems

Two of the problems from Section 8.2.4—that standards often become the master rather than the servant of a project and that they are often so complex and detailed that people can't remember them—give us clues to a cure for the endemic failures of standards. What we need is a tool that has a superhuman ability to record and recall a vast amount of detailed information and that is a selfless, impersonal, nonpolitical, ever-ready assistant to any project member at any time. What we need, therefore, is a computer to take care of standards.

I'm surprised that no one has yet admonished the DP industry with "Physician, heal thyself," because ironically, in our breathless rush to automate every other business, we seem to have forgotten to automate our own. We have a few tools such as compilers, text editors, and data dictionaries; but we don't have anything nearly as sophisticated as, for instance, computer-aided design or computer-aided manufacturing (CAD/CAM) systems that are used for hardware design, car manufacturing, and numerous other industries. In fact, we hardly have a system at all; most of our tools do not work in an integrated fashion.

Systems are just beginning to be introduced to help us in our DP systems development business. These systems go by various names, such as computer supported methodology (CSM) and computer-aided software engineering (CASE).[3] Although in their infancy, they are already starting to offer significant advantages not only in the implementation of methodologies, but also in DP project management. Below I briefly cover these advantages in the five areas of standards dissemination, their credibility, enforcement, use, and modification, and the area of general project management.

8.3.1 Standards dissemination

A CASE system helps most in disseminating standards by making them easier to learn and to understand and more palatable to use. Of course, the prospective user still needs preliminary

---

[3]For a concise overview of CASE systems, see [Pressman, 1984]. For further details on commercially available CSM and CASE systems, contact a major vendor of DP project methodologies.

training in the methodology and must read the accompanying manuals, but a CASE system offers such computer facilities as indexing and menu schemes to tame the mob of details in the typical DP project methodology.

With these features plus an online help facility, for example, a CASE system eliminates the frustration of a missing or too long manual. All the information that's necessary is stored in the computer. In this way, a CASE system can become the custodian of the documentation of the standards, as well as the primary information resource, thus improving the standards' chances of survival.

8.3.2 Standards credibility

There is no fundamental reason that CASE-implemented standards should be more credible than any others, but in practice, they are for two reasons. First, since a CASE system itself is presumably developed by its own methodology and bootstrapped into existence by its own tools, the system's creators therefore are practicing DP project members, who temper theory with practical experience.

Second, you can easily constrain the scope of an automated data processing project methodology to fit the characteristics of your particular project and thus make your own methodology credible. At the start of the project, as project manager you might configure a CASE system for your own needs, with a list of options on a menu, such as, Are you a conversion project? Are you a maintenance project? Are you a new development project? A CASE system would then establish the correct parameters and tools for use on the type of project that you choose.

8.3.3 Standards enforcement

If you conduct your data processing projects through a computer system, the enforcement of standards is almost automatic, since the computer examines closely every deliverable of the project and gives rapid feedback to project members on any errors or omissions. The computer can also ensure that incomplete or incorrect work is rectified before it is used in other activities.

Many of the political problems of enforcing standards evaporate when the computer becomes the guardian of the standards. People seem more prepared to accept an enforced discipline from a computer than from within themselves or from another person. (For example, imagine the problems in your shop if COBOL syntax were enforced not by the COBOL compiler but by a group of human preprocessors.) With a computer system, very often the only possible way to carry out work is the way dictated by the standards. Thus, enforcement becomes a moot issue.

Enforcement is an unpleasant word, redolent with notions of threat and punishment; as noted earlier, this is in fact one reason that standards fail. A CASE system, on the other hand, can sugar the pill of enforcement with a coating of helpfulness: The system provides valuable assistance and in return the person follows the standard methodology.

8.3.4 Standards use

Although many manual implementations of standards actually interfere with the work that they purport to enhance, a CASE system implementation helps project members with their work. Among the many ways possible, I mention only three examples here.

First, the CASE system can form a framework for integrating the various software tools that a project uses. For example, it can use information in a data dictionary for the test case generator. Second, by bearing part of the burden of the process of conducting a project, a CASE system relieves project members to concentrate more on the product of the project and to be more creative. For example, a CASE system could assist greatly with document preparation and the endless revision to documents that a project requires. It also could automatically take care of the hundreds of standards trivia, such as PIC clauses always starting in column 32. That way, the coder could place the PIC clause almost anywhere and the program formatter of the CASE system would shepherd the errant clause into its prescribed standard position.

Third, a CASE system can provide a central point of communication for project members. By making project information available to them in a clear, unambiguous way at all times, it would reduce much of the chaos concomitant with the haphazard communication carried on in many DP projects today. Other ways in which a CASE system can be of great use to project participants range from the maintenance of an inventory of off-the-shelf software modules to reducing people's reporting loads, as discussed below and in Chapter 9. In most of these ways, a CASE system serves as assistant to project members, a position that counterbalances its dominant position as enforcer of a project's standards.

8.3.5 Standards modification

Modifying a CASE system to reflect changes in the conduct of DP projects is tougher than modifying standards on paper. However, because of this difficulty, CASE modifications are more likely to be disseminated and enforced, just as the CASE system itself is. Also, the concept of version releases is well understood and accepted in the data processing industry.

One significant difficulty in making major changes to a CASE system stems from its having not only a set of procedures for carrying out projects, but also a data store of project information and statistics. If a change to the CASE methodology is serious enough, it may require a conversion of the data in the CASE database as well. Such a major change cannot be undertaken lightly.

8.3.6 General project management

Having a CASE system is an immense boon to you as a project manager. Not only does it provide you with guidance through a project, as any project methodology does, but it also eases your reporting and estimating duties. A CASE system can automatically handle much of the routine status reporting by keeping track of key data and printing a report regularly, thus eliminating much of the time spent on the activity. This frees project members to concentrate on reporting any potential problems that you need to be aware of. A CASE system can also help greatly in producing your project status reports for higher management.

As I will discuss in Chapter 9, a number of difficulties accompany the reporting of time spent on project activities, including the correct apportionment of time to various categories, such as analysis activities, meetings, and so forth. A CASE system with its built-in framework of activities in the project methodology is a natural way for capturing and processing this project time data. It also can serve as a tool of the metrics group for developing project statistics to be used in future estimates.

Overall, a CASE system contains an integrated database, which holds information on as many aspects of a data processing project as possible. The system is to a project what a data dictionary is to a computer system. However, since it encompasses so much more than a typical data dictionary, a better name for this core of a CASE system is a project management encyclopedia. This database provides a further great benefit derived from having a computer-aided software engineering system.

8.4 Summary

A project methodology is the designation of a system for conducting a project. Standards are the implementation of a methodology by the addition of tools, techniques, rules, and so on, for conducting a project. Having shop-wide project standards yields several advantages to the shop and its projects, including avoiding the need to replan every project from scratch; facilitating a specialist type of organization; promoting uniformity among concurrent projects and between successive projects; making hiring and training procedures uniform; aiding the development of tools; and reducing the time spent on futile procedural debates.

However, although standards should confer many benefits to a shop, they often fail in practice. The areas in which methodologies are vulnerable include dissemination (the length, tedious style, or even misplacement of the standards manual, as well as the unavailability of training in standards); credibility (irrelevance, absurdity, outdatedness, or unacceptable progressiveness of standards due to an inappropriate scope of the standards or an unfamiliarity with DP projects of the standards' authors); enforcement (lack of enforcement, perhaps through lack of vigilance or, alternatively, oppressive over-enforcement); use (the triumph of process over product or simply the unwieldiness of application); and updating (lack of reasons for having the standards or absence of a mechanism for modifying the standards).

Of the above list of problems with standards, the complexity of standards and their hindrance of the process indicate that the solution lies in the computer implementation of standards. A computer system (such as a computer-aided software engineering or CASE system) would overcome problems in many areas of the practical deployment of standards: in dissemination, credibility, enforcement, use, and modification. A CASE system would also ease the status reporting and statistical recording problems that plague the management of most DP projects. In fact, such a system could go much further, providing statistics for a metrics group and even a project management encyclopedia to aid the entire project management process.

A CASE type of system is probably the best hope for the successful adoption of shop-wide DP project standards. It can provide the advantages of having standards, while at the same time avoid many of the problems inherent in the traditional establishment of standards. The scope for the continual refinement of such a system is also immense. Eventually, a CASE type system could evolve into an expert or knowledge-based system that could supplement a project manager's skill with years of distilled knowledge in the effective conduct of data processing projects.

Chapter 8: Exercises

1. Consider the standards of your shop or of other shops in which you've worked. How successfully were they implemented? What problems occurred in their implementation? What could you have done to avoid those problems?

2. What tools does your shop use to support the conduct of projects? Which are automated? How well do the tools fit together? What would you suggest to integrate them fully?

9

Reporting Project Status and Time

As a project manager, you obviously need to know what's happening on your project: which tasks have been completed, which tasks are in trouble, how much time was spent on each task, and so on. However, some project managers make their teams' procedures for reporting project status and time spent on tasks into oppressive bureaucracies. Such burdensome reporting systems often consume an unconscionable amount of the project team's available time but deliver very little useful, accurate information to the manager.

In this chapter, I explore typical problems with reporting of both project status and time spent for project tasks. I also suggest ways to streamline both reporting activities and to improve a report's conformity with reality.

9.1 Project status reporting

The clearest, simplest guideline I can give for efficient project status reporting is, Emphasize the extraordinary and downplay the ordinary. But before I consider this and other guidelines, we need to look at what project status reporting is not. Some project managers believe that their team's status reports must be adorned with all the trappings of officialdom, regardless of the time wasted. For example, some managers demand excessively lengthy reports, presumably on the ground that verbosity of itself conveys authority. Others demand remarkable polish of presentation (reports being typewritten, for instance, with centered titles all in capital letters), although the reports are of only ephemeral interest and have but a tiny circulation. Most project managers require a monthly or weekly status report regardless of whether there is anything significant to report at that particular time. In contrast, but equally bad, is the manager who provides no formal means to report anything before the end of a month.

In composing his own status report for upper management, many a manager wants to create a work of joy, containing nothing but good news. This is a difficult task if his subordinates' reports are full of doom. Thus, the managers in some shops censor their project teams' status reports for the sake of impressing, or at least not alarming, upper management and the users.

Many project status reports are basically superfluous in that they tell the manager what he already knows, including such statements as, "Task ABC is going according to plan." This kind of pap reaches an extreme in reports that have been bowdlerized for the sake of upper management's delicate sensibilities.

9.1.1 Project status reporting gone amok

One project manager incorporated most of the above failings into his project status reporting system, including an uncontrollable passion for typewritten reports. Every Friday morning, each of fifteen project members submitted a detailed, typewritten report on what he was supposed to do, why he was doing it, what percentage of it he'd done, and how well it was going. Then, after lunch, the manager would discuss (*argue over* is a better description) the details of each report with its author. A sample of the discussion follows:

Boss: From your report, Sue, I see you're still programming module T2714P3. How come? You were supposed to be done two days ago.

Sue: Remember last week I said that I had some problems unit-testing T2714P1? I got delayed there for about four days, what with that maintenance job you asked me to do on the RATS system as well.

Boss: Okay, so you say you're twenty-five percent done on T2714P3. Only twenty-five percent?

Sue: I wrote that yesterday morning. I guess I'm forty to fifty percent done by now.

Boss: Let's try to be more precise. How long have you been at it?

Sue: Three days, give or take.

Boss: So, given our five-day estimate for the job, that's more like sixty percent, isn't it?

Sue: All right, sixty percent.

Boss: [He crosses out twenty-five percent and writes sixty percent.] You say here that you're having some difficulties with the T2714 specs. What sort of difficulties? Are they slowing you down at all?

Sue: Well, I guess not too much. I'm just having some problems with the interface to T2712. Dave wasn't always too clear.

Boss: You know it looks bad to say "difficulties" in a report. You and I know what it means, but my managers tend to panic when they see stuff like that. Let's reword this and say, "Work is proceeding reasonably well." [perusing through the report] I'm looking at the "Tasks to Be Initiated in the Coming Week." Why have you got unit-testing T2714P3 in there? That was on last week's list.

Sue: But I just told you: I fell behind on T2714P3 and I can't possibly start testing it before next Tuesday or Wednesday.

Boss: Okay, but let's just cross it out and say nothing. If it shows up on the "Initiate" list twice in a row, they'll smell a slip in the schedule. Best to keep quiet and make up the slip later. Less grief for all concerned. I see T2716 is on your "Initiate" list for next week. What happened to T2715?

Sue: Remember we had that meeting two weeks ago when we changed the plan to do T2716 before T2715?

Boss: Oh yes. Well, that's about it. Just get Carol to type up the changes and slip the report back in my mailbox. We'll talk about it again next week. Thanks, and good work!

That was a mild sample. In worse cases, the manager would complain about a report that wasn't submitted on time or that wasn't long enough or that omitted a crucial item. Several people told me they spent eight hours a week in writing, correcting, discussing, and changing their weekly report; that seemed to me to be an underestimation.

9.1.2 Guidelines for efficient project status reporting

First and most important, as I indicated earlier, good project status reporting highlights the exceptional and downplays the ordinary. Think of the analogy to a manufacturing plant, in which there is little point in regularly reporting voluminous data to prove that production is within expected tolerances. The only data worth reporting are the exceptions when production falls outside its set limits, along with perhaps a graph showing production trends. Similarly, in the manufacture of a DP system, the project manager knows the targets for production from his project plan. The project plan represents what the military call the "nominal," that is, what a manager can assume to be true unless he hears otherwise.

A manager doesn't need a regurgitation of his own project plan. So long as the actual development of the system proceeds within a narrow margin of the nominal, a manager needs no detailed information. But he does need plenty of details on the tasks that fall behind (or even go too fast) and the problems that need to be addressed. If you look at the dialogue in the preceding section, note that the boss tried to do that in his own way. He waded through the information he already knew in order to find the new details that he should attend to.

In addition to emphasizing the exceptions, a project status report should report details as explicitly and objectively as possible. The report should not contain answers to such broad and meaningless questions as, How is the task going? and, What percentage complete is the task? Reporting on progress in terms of "reasonably well" and "excellent" is a waste of everyone's time.

Also, a less obvious but equally significant waste of time is writing specific percentages such as forty percent and eighty-two percent, because the remaining five percent of a task could require fifty percent of the time needed. Although it's a beautiful dream to imagine that such precise numbers have any significance, the only truly significant information is in answer to, Is the task done? and, Is the product of sufficient quality to fulfill its objectives? If you find that you cannot report without resorting to fictions like "percentage complete," you clearly haven't broken down tasks into units fine enough to properly track progress.

Traditional status reporting tells what has gone wrong when it's too late to fix the problem, if it reports deviation at all. Thus, the third guideline for status reporting is, Announce deviations from the project plan as early as possible. Ideal status reporting reports something going wrong as soon as it starts to go wrong, regardless of whether it's time to report the status.

What information should your staff members report to you? My fourth guideline is, Report as little as possible, as simply as possible. A simple scheme for tracking project tasks uses a two-part card, like the one in Figure 9.1. As the project manager, you fill out the top half of the card, since you have all the necessary information, and the assigned worker fills out the bottom half and returns it to you.

Advise your staff to report on as many problems as possible, especially those that require your help to solve, and more important, to report expected changes to the task completion date as soon as possible. In Figure 9.1, for example, the designer estimates that the task will take one elapsed day more of work than intended. By encouraging your staff to use the card to report a problem immediately, you can keep informed with a minimum of misunderstanding and the maximum of forewarning.

A final guideline in reporting project status to higher managers is, Be honest. If you insist on fabricating your reports in job security language, go ahead, but be warned that it is tough to corrupt the crisp details of a proper project status report into a trite "everything's groovy" kind of project narrative. If you work in a company where honesty is punished and covert activities are rewarded, reporting project status as described above may not be for you. Then again, the company may not be for you either (more on this in Chapter 15).

Document No.: _D124/T5/2_   Today's Date: _10/28/84_

Manager: _B. EPSTEIN_

Task No.: _D124_   Task Description: _To design M124_

Scheduled End Date: _11/10/84_

Task Deliverables: _M124 Structure Chart   Updated DD_

Functional descriptions as necessary

Task Goal(s): _Generality with respect to customer type; overall maintainability_

Task Status: _IP_

Estimated Work Till Completion: _10 E-DAYS_

(after today) _(+1 E-DAY)_

Problems: _SPEC 1.2.7 is unworkable_

How can I help? _Get Pat to fix 1.2.7 - meet with users?_

Key

I.P.	in progress	*An elapsed day is the passage of 24 hours. It represents about
E-Day	elapsed day*	five to seven working hours (or however much time for work an
+1 E-Day	one elapsed day beyond schedule	average person in your shop has for work in an average day).

Figure 9.1. Scheme for tracking project tasks.

9.2 Time reporting

Reporting the amount of time that an employee spends on each task serves several useful purposes. This information can be used for totaling the hours worked for an hourly employee, or for improving estimating ability and future estimates, or for chargebacks against various corporate budgets.

Unfortunately, the different uses of a time report tend to distort its figures in different ways. For example, an employee might use the time report to exaggerate his working hours; or a project manager might distort the report's figures to make his previous estimates appear better; or another manager might decide to change the description of a task so that it can be charged against a corporate overhead category, rather than his own rapidly dwindling budget. When all the falsifying forces act at once, a time report may become so distorted that it serves none of its intended purposes properly. Worse yet, it may fall to the harried project team member himself to cook the figures to suit everyone's whims.

9.2.1 A time reporting example

One DP shop I'm familiar with has taken this art of statistical lies to a new extreme. Every Thursday noon, all employees are required to list the hours worked on tasks and assign to each task a confusing array of codes. Among the codes are one for the corporation as a whole, one for the department, and one for the current project. The weekly festival of figures typically begins at 11:50 a.m. each Thursday, with the frantic scribbling of mostly erroneous hours worked alongside largely arbitrary codes. Employees take little care to choose the correct code for reasons that will soon become clear.

Within a day or two of the submission of the timesheets, a group of shadowy characters from the corporate accounting department tracks down employees to correct their timesheets. This group looks for such faults as failing to sign the form, using a nonexistent code, using the code for an almost empty budget, and recording hours that total more than thirty-five for the week. The last two violations deserve further explanation, for they epitomize timesheet corruption. Within that department, there was little point in pondering for long what code to assign, because the codes often overlapped. When an analyst attended a meeting, for example, was he to use the code for analysis or the one for meetings? The answer was that he had to choose the code for the budget containing the larger balance of funds.

The thirty-five hour work week rule is a shabby trick that shops use to avoid paying overtime or awarding compensatory leave. For example, a worker may toil seventy hours one week and twenty or thirty the next, but he is expected to chop or pad (again, skewed by the obesity of the budget involved) as necessary. This alone makes a mockery of keeping track of the time spent on the different tasks of a project and hence undermines all chances of making good project estimates in the future.

In this same department, the tedium and futility of this time reporting method resulted in employees trying to avoid the enforcers of the timesheets, known as the Time Police. When a programmer spotted a time cop, he instantly vanished through a far door and went to lunch. The effect was hilarious, with time policemen chasing tempus fugitives in and out of the doors of the programming shop like a Marx Brothers routine.

9.2.2 Guidelines for efficient time reporting

Time reporting should not be the star act in a political circus, but its aim should be the recording of the most accurate data possible on the amount of time spent by every person on each task. To make this reporting system effective, keep it as simple as possible. In principle, all a reporter needs to report is what he did, for how long, and on which project. From this information, someone with more time to spend than a busy project team member can consolidate the figures as needed to charge the appropriate budget.

That someone may well be a computer. There are several advantages to an automated or semiautomated time reporting system. One benefit is immediate recording of the data in the computer by the project participants, as they carry out the tasks, rather than waiting for an end-of-the-week timesheet collection. They also can receive help directly from the computer from online menus, for example, and have errors indicated immediately to them. Since the computer is obviously a much better number-cruncher than a human/pocket calculator combination, it can quickly calculate how many person-hours were spent on a particular design task, for example, or on the design as a whole.

Another benefit in using a computerized system is having the database as an excellent medium for storing data. Timesheet data is valuable years later for analysis in different ways by the metrics group, whose job is virtually impossible if all it has to work with is fading figures on yellowing paper.

However, a computer system cannot entirely replace manual recording. A project worker cannot dash off to the nearest terminal every sixty minutes to report his last hour's activities. Instead, he should keep an informal desk diary and, at the end of each day at the very least, note to the nearest quarter hour how the time was spent on each of the day's tasks. Then, when time permits, he can update the computer timesheet from his informal log.

A simple computer system may still require the use of codes for tasks. If so, make sure that the codes will allow you to indicate, for instance, that you attended a meeting and it was for the purpose of analysis. Finally, you need some identifier in the code to identify the analysis task you were pursuing during the meeting. An example of a simple task code that fulfills these requirements is AM1234, with A indicating analysis, M meeting, and 1234 the particular portion of analysis. Again, a computer system with a help and/or a menu facility would aid a team member in generating the appropriate code.

Even with the discipline in time reporting and recording that a computer system offers, you may still be able to manipulate the budget that is charged. That's up to you and perhaps the project producer, who must carefully watch the project's financial data. No valid time reporting system, however, ever allows you or anyone else to corrupt task time data at its source, since any information that's altered before it's recorded is lost forever. Task time data is not the property of a single project, for it belongs to the department as a whole. Because of its great value for years to come, no one should be allowed to destroy it for the sake of some petty, short-term financial maneuvers. And certainly, no project manager should force his project team to carry out this vandalism for him.

9.3 Summary

Traditionally, project status reports have been simultaneously verbose but vague, polished but inaccurate, and regular but partially outdated. They have also consumed a great deal of project members' and managers' time. Worst of all, however, they have typically dwelt obsessively on the ordinary, at the expense of what managers really need to concentrate upon: the exceptional.

Efficient project status reporting highlights the extraordinary and downplays the ordinary, stressing departures from the project plan as soon as they occur or even before they occur if possible. It emphasizes problems that need management resolution and never tries to hide difficulties in order to protect the image of a project team member or the project manager.

Time reporting has often been driven more by parochial, political, or financial goals than by a desire to capture actual data about time spent on tasks. This has led to so much distortion of the figures at their source (the project team member) that the figures have become all but useless. Thus, not only is valuable departmental information lost, but also project members' time is wasted in the composition of suitably spurious data.

The chief aim of effective time reporting is recording the most accurate data available on the amount of time spent by each person on each task. Time reporting also is relatively simple for the reporter himself to carry out. A good system is to have each project member jot down his task times on a desk diary and transfer that information to a small computer system whenever his schedule permits. The computer can then store the data indefinitely and also consolidate it for both statistical and budgetary purposes. Another role of the computer system is the protection of this departmental asset from the moment that it is entered.

Chapter 9: Exercises

1. In your shop, which reporting systems are the most cumbersome and time-consuming? How could they be streamlined?

2. What political forces in your shop work to distort the accuracy of reported project status and task times? (Do such distortions matter, or is reporting merely a *pro forma* ceremony in your department?) What suggestions can you make for improving the accuracy of status and time reports in your particular environment?

10

Holding Successful Meetings

Meetings, if poorly conducted, can be spectacular time and money wasters. However, if well conducted, they can be equally spectacular successes in exercising the collective intellect of your shop. In order to conduct productive meetings, you must ensure that certain common mistakes do not occur in your shop.

This chapter suggests guidelines for removing the most conspicuous faults from data processing meetings, beginning with an example of a poorly run meeting to illustrate many of those faults. However, since the conduct and sociology of meetings are surprisingly deep subjects, I recommend that you follow up the advice of this chapter with that of a book such as [Doyle and Straus, 1977].

10.1 Wally's meeting

Boss: [The time is 2:50 p.m.] Shirley, tell everybody on the JERKS project that we're having a meeting in ten minutes in the conference room.

Shirley: Wally, you know that Mary and Rob are at a users' meeting and won't be back until around 4. What shall I tell everybody the meeting's about?

Boss: The meeting's about the project status. Oh, and just leave a note for Mary and Rob to join us as soon as they can.

Boss: [It is 3:20 p.m., and the meeting still hasn't begun]. Harry, will you try to find Jeff and Carol. I want to get this show on the road.
          [Harry leaves the room. Two minutes later, Jeff and Carol appear. Jeff settles into Harry's seat.]

Reg: Er, I think Harry's sitting there, Jeff. [While Jeff gets a chair, Harry reappears to stifled giggles. The meeting now comprises twelve of the total fourteen members on the JERKS project.]

Boss: I think it's about time we had a project status meeting to touch base with everybody. Sally, let's start with you. How's it going?

Sally: Okay, I guess.

Boss: Jeff?

Jeff: Pretty good.

Boss: Judy, how's the database schema coming along? What percentage complete would you say you are?

Judy: Hard to say exactly; about fifty percent.

Boss: What about the customer order data? Have you talked to Mary or Rob yet?
          [A lengthy, meandering discussion ensues until Betty, leader of the SMARTS project, enters the room.]

Betty: Excuse me, Wally. We've got this room booked from 3:30 on.

Boss: Just give us a few minutes. We're nearly through.

Betty: Sorry, Wally. It's already 3:40.

Boss: Okay. Let's see if anyone's in Room 3.
          [Like the tribes of Israel, the project members wander through a wilderness of hallways, until they arrive at the Promised Land of Room 3 and sit down.]

Boss: Darn. I just remembered Mary and Rob will be joining us. Harry, could you put a note on the door of Room 1 telling them where we are? [The long-suffering Harry sets off.] All right, as you know, analysis is coming to an end. We've got to get our act together for design and programming. I was just talking to Joe about screen standards, right, Joe? [Joe nods.] So, do you think we should keep the number of screens to a minimum and put as many fields as we can on each screen?

Joe: No. An article I read said every screen should capture a single definite idea. [The conversation continues among the five screen dialogue enthusiasts, but goes in no particular direction. Mary and Rob, lead analysts, arrive.]

Boss: Ah, you found us. We're discussing the project status. [He gives a recap of the meeting so far.] What happened with the users?

Mary: We sorted out some of the criteria for classifying products, but we're meeting with them again.

Boss: Great! Sounds like it's going well. Are you about ready for the analysis review?

Mary: We're in pretty good shape, but we need more work in the customer area.

Judy: I need to talk to you about the customer data.

Rob: It will take a while to prepare and send out the documentation.

Boss: How long before we're ready?

Mary: A month, maybe six weeks.

Boss: I'd better get together with both of you on that.

Marvin: [Stands and grabs his pen and pad of paper, containing doodles of the U.S.S. *Enterprise* and E.T.] Gotta go, Wally. Car pool and I'm driving this week.

Boss: Just a minute, Marv. I want to talk about programming standards a bit. [Marvin reluctantly sits.] Those old standards of ours need to be overhauled. For one thing, all that old DOS stuff can go for a start. [Boss produces a copy of the standards and leafs through it.] And there's nothing much about structured programming that

I can find, only some stuff about the ALTER statement.

[Before he gets any further, there's a knock at the door, and a face peeks in.]

Face: Uh, excuse me, is Marv—? Oh hi, Marv. You gonna be ready soon?

Boss: I'd better let you go, but I want you programmers to set up a standards review group. Is there anything else to cover today? [Silence] All right. Good meeting, folks. See you tomorrow. [As everyone leaves, Wally puts his hand on Joe's shoulder.] Joe, do you have a few minutes to talk about screens?

Wally's "Good meeting, folks" was in fact a fiasco, for which Wally himself was entirely responsible. In the remainder of this chapter, I offer guidelines to be followed before, during, and after the meeting in order for it to be productive, and I counterpoint the requirements with illustrations from Wally's ill-fated gathering.

10.2 Before the meeting

10.2.1 Arrange for a convenient meeting place

Before even calling a meeting, attend to such practical details as where to meet. Make sure there is a meeting room available at the time of the meeting. Surprisingly often, this elementary point is overlooked. Wally succeeded in generating considerable confusion merely by not checking that the first conference room was available for the full duration of the meeting.

10.2.2 Find out if all participants can attend

Make sure that each of the meeting's participants will be available at the scheduled time and place of the meeting. There's not much point in arranging a meeting for a time when two of the meeting's key attendees are elsewhere. Also, try to sort out participants' availability before circulating invitations to the meeting. Otherwise, needless mayhem results if you continually change the time and place of a meeting as you discover various attendees' inability to attend at the scheduled venue.

10.2.3 Give plenty of notice

Circulate notice of a meeting, preferably in writing, well in advance of the meeting. How much advance notice depends on your shop's protocol and your own common sense. Wally's ten-minute warning was so short that it didn't even allow time for Mary, Rob, Jeff, and Carol to be informed of the meeting. And, it certainly didn't allow anyone time to ponder the topics of the meeting, or even to find out what they were.

10.2.4 State the meeting's agenda explicitly

Unlike Wally, who failed even to state an agenda for his meeting, the manager calling the meeting should prepare a written agenda of the items to be discussed and circulate it to the meeting's participants. Wally did mutter something about project status, but that hardly constituted an explicit description. Each item on the agenda should have a clearly stated purpose. For example, "to decide how many and which models of terminals to install at the various types of user workstations" is a valid agenda item. "Terminals" is not; does it mean, Shall we buy terminals for the programmers? Or, does it mean, Why hasn't the vendor fixed the two terminals that broke last week? If each agenda item is not specified clearly, every attendee will be ready to discuss a somewhat different topic. This will create confusion.

10.2.5 Limit the number of agenda items

Keep the number of items on the agenda to a minimum. One item is ideal; even four may be too many, depending upon their complexity. A too long agenda presents two problems: First, the more items there are, the longer the meeting will be. After an hour or two, most people's attentiveness deteriorates into daydreams about lunch or the weekend. As a result, the last items of the agenda tend to get short shrift.

Wally's meeting dealt with at least six major items: the progress of each team member; the database schema; the plan for design and programming; the screen standards; the analysis review, including Rob and Mary's latest analysis discoveries; and the programming standards. There was no time for more than laughably superficial discussion of any of these items, especially the last item, curtailed by the interrupter from the car pool.

The second problem with numerous agenda items is that unless the items are closely related, every attendee is not needed for every item. Thus, a meeting with many items demands many attendees, who thus waste a good deal of their time sitting bored in a meeting when they could be working more productively. In addition to the huge waste of resources, a meeting that covers too many disparate topics is unfocused and muddled.

If you find that the list of attendees for your meeting looks like the Great Gatsby's guest list, it's probably because you have too many items on your agenda. Break up your meeting into several meetings and save everyone's time. A single agenda item rarely demands the presence of more than seven people. One exception to this guideline is for a press conference type of meeting, discussed in Section 10.3.4, when many people need to be given some information.

10.2.6 Be specific in selecting attendees

After you limit the number of agenda items, carefully consider who can seriously contribute to the discussion of each item and invite only those people. If you fail to specify the attendees carefully, you will waste people's valuable time, as I said before. Marvin, who spent most of Wally's meeting doodling, is a good example of the superfluous attendee. (Occasionally, however, you may have to include a superfluous person or two for the sake of politeness or politics.)

I once had a manager named Alf who, like Wally, invited everybody to his meetings. Every meeting was like a Woodstock experience: It had throngs of attendees; it seemed to last days; people slept through portions of it; and it featured dozens of acts on the bill. Alf defended this practice with the light bulb argument: It's cheaper to have a light burn continuously, rather than risk damaging the bulb by switching it on and off many times. He believed it was more efficient to get everyone together at once for one gigantic meeting, rather than have them meet in several smaller groups for shorter periods. Regardless of the argument's validity regarding light bulbs, I certainly know that long meetings with dozens of attendees are not productive and that Alf's meetings were no exception.

10.3 During the meeting

10.3.1 Adhere to the agenda

The most important rule of an effective meeting is, Do not digress from the items on the agenda. Although it's tempting to stray when an interesting or contentious side topic comes up, don't. With too much digression, the meeting will become an uncontrolled free-for-all. In attempting to go everywhere, it will go nowhere. Wally's meeting exemplifies this (though I can hardly accuse him of digressing from an agenda that he never had to begin with). If a topic does arise that warrants substantial digression, record and table it for a subsequent meeting. That way, you not only avoid disrupting the present meeting, but you also give participants time to think about and research the new topic.

10.3.2 Nominate a moderator

When a meeting diverges from its appointed agenda, often no one notices because everyone is so engrossed in the digression. Therefore, the person calling the meeting should name a moderator or facilitator, who signals whenever the discussion drifts off the topic and who redirects everyone's attention to the agenda item.[1]

10.3.3 Assign a recorder

Although a meeting can generate many good ideas or successful resolutions, no one may be able to remember them an hour or so later. That's the chief reason for having a recorder to write them down and keep track of the meeting's progress. It's useful for the recorder to note the main points on a large board to serve as the focus, or graphic memory, of the meeting. This helps to promote a common understanding among the attendees of what actually is being said and resolved in the meeting. (The recorder and moderator may be the same person, although this may not be a good idea when the meeting is large and the discussion controversial.)

10.3.4 Follow procedural rules according to the item type

Each item on an agenda can be categorized into one of four types, depending upon its objective. An item can be established for either planning, communication, problem solving, or deciding. Each type has its own set of procedural rules, which I discuss below.

Planning

The outcome of the planning type of agenda item is a strategy for reaching a previously agreed-upon goal. The tangible product of a planning item is, for example, a CPM chart. A meeting to discuss a planning item generally has few attendees (perhaps two to five) and tends to be long, especially for major plans. Such long meetings are typically broken into several sessions, with the first to develop an overall plan. Subsequent meetings work out the more detailed levels of the plan, and a final session integrates the parts into one plan.

A danger with any planning meeting is the temptation to do the work, rather than just to plan it. Wally succumbed to this temptation in his meeting by trying to establish the screen standards to use, rather than simply planning for the development of screen standards. Clearly, the planning of work should precede its execution; otherwise, what's the point in having a plan?

Communication

The objective of the communication type of agenda item is to disseminate information to a group and to receive feedback on the results of some course of action, rather like a press conference. The components of effective communication are preparation and listening: The person

---

[1]For a detailed discussion of the moderator's role in a meeting, see [Doyle and Straus, 1977].

transmitting the information organizes his thoughts coherently and omits irrelevant information. The person receiving the information works actively to understand it, echoing phrases in his mind and preparing questions about anything he doesn't understand.

Wally's mistakes in communication were that he failed to allow his staff any time to prepare their oral reports on the project status and that he listened only superficially to the information they did impart. For example, he allowed such comments as "Pretty good, I guess" to pass unchallenged and unclarified. Wally also further complicated the communication by holding a catchall type of meeting in which everyone was dragged into the meeting, regardless of whether they were needed. He thus created a spaghetti bowl of communication lines at the meeting.

Problem solving

In the movie *Butch Cassidy and the Sundance Kid,* Butch's assailant says, "There ain't no rules in a knife fight." Butch thus reasons he need not fight with a knife and he quickly defeats his opponent with a well-placed kick. Similarly, some people assert, "There ain't no rules in a problem-solving meeting," and anything goes so long as the problem is solved. This is only partially true. While solving problems demands creativity and creativity demands flexibility, there still must be some ground rules.

The most important of these rules is, First identify the problem to be solved. How else can you look for a solution if you aren't sure you know what you're solving? A problem-solving meeting that does not abide by this rule soon goes awry by dwelling upon the inconsequential. To help distinguish between a problem, its symptoms, and its causes, I use a cause-effect diagram, described in Appendix B.

Once you identify the true problem, begin to seek a feasible solution. An overall guideline for this stage of a problem-solving meeting is for every participant to nurture the weak and feeble seeds of ideas that others plant in the meeting. Resist the all-too-human tendency to scoff at or to snuff out others' partially thought-out ideas. Several techniques that formalize this guideline include lateral thinking and brainstorming. In lateral thinking, a person tries to make creative leaps of thought rather than to pursue a logical sequence of thoughts [DeBono, 1970]. Brainstorming is described in Section 4.3.3.

Nevertheless, despite the rules and techniques to formalize problem-solving meetings, the act of solving a problem is a creative endeavor that can never be completely orchestrated. Therefore, with the caveats of the last three paragraphs in mind, I agree that so long as you address the true problem, there "ain't no rules" in a problem-solving meeting.

Deciding

The purpose of an agenda item of the deciding type is to select a course of action from a list of options. A meeting of this type can be divided into four distinct stages:

- First, identify potential courses of action and achieve a common understanding of what each option is.

- Second, identify each option's ramifications, including both its advantages and disadvantages.

- Third, discuss and evaluate each ramification.

- Fourth, select the most advantageous course of action.[2]

---

[2]Some people consider only the third and fourth stages as constituting the decision making proper, and categorize the first two stages as problem-solving and/or communication meetings.

Of the several ways to organize these four stages, a typical arrangement is the following: Accomplish stage one in a preliminary meeting; conduct the necessary investigation in stage two outside the meeting; and carry out stages three and four in a final meeting. For a simple decision, however, with all the relevant facts at hand, you could combine all stages into a single meeting.

In the final, actual decision-making stage, the meeting's chairman begins by soliciting the previously researched pros and cons of each potential course of action from the meeting's participants. The chairman is the person responsible for the decisions being made and is usually the convener of the meeting. For ease of reference, these pros and cons should be written on a large board in full view of the meeting's participants. Then, the meeting's attendees compare the various courses of action by weighing their respective advantages and disadvantages against an agreed-upon set of criteria.

In order for a high-quality decision to be made, the chairman aggressively inquires into the views of every participant.[3] Unfortunately, many managers refuse to spend the time and effort to probe below the superficial in seeking counsel and, as a result, they decide in haste and repent at leisure. An hour spent in hammering out facts before making a decision is worth ten hours in not having to repair the effects of a poor decision.

How a meeting's chairman makes his decision depends upon the weight of the decision and his own management style. At one extreme, an autocratic chairman makes a unilateral announcement of his selected course of action. At the other extreme, a democratic chairman abides by a vote of the meeting's attendees. Of course, a chairman may instead determine that more or better information is needed before a decision can be reached. However, the chairman's style of management is less of a factor than it may appear—if the decision emerges from the four-stage process outlined above. Then, in the majority of cases, the superior course of action becomes so apparent after the discussion and consideration that no reasonable person can ignore it. If such a revelation does not take place, probably the season is not yet nigh for bringing forth a decision and more work is probably necessary to find the best option.

The participants in a decision-making meeting are those whose advice is valuable in making the decision and those who are affected by the outcome of the decision. If the second group of people is very large—it may even be the whole company—invite one or more representatives from every interested area. Not only can the representatives offer valuable advice in the decision, but they also can be very effective in selling the outcome to those affected by the decision.

The above description is the ideal way to make good corporate decisions. Unfortunately, in reality, human frailties conspire to reduce the quality of the decision-making process. For example, in the "yes, boss" phenomenon, no one in a decision-making meeting is prepared to contradict the viewpoint of the most senior person present. This is dangerous, in that it breeds sullen resentment in those who feel obliged to stifle their opinions. Worse, it reduces the quality of the decisions made while at the same time falsely reassures the boss that his decision is based on the consensus of the whole group.

As a manager making decisions, your duty is to encourage diversity of views before you reach your conclusion. Find some way to remove the fear, diffidence, or devotion to the boss that harmfully homogenizes all the opinions at a meeting. In doing this, you not only improve the final decision, but also promote fellowship and understanding between you and your staff. In one shop where I worked, we each wrote down our evaluations of a course of action anonymously and then passed them to the recorder, who summarized them on a large white board. This method broke the ice; over the subsequent weeks, an atmosphere of openness and trust gradually developed among us all.

---

[3]For a discussion of aggressive inquiry, see [Giegold, 1982].

However, it's important to distinguish between dissidence expressed before a decision is made and dissidence expressed afterward. Encourage dissidence beforehand, but make no mistake: After a course of action is selected, you're entitled to full cooperation from everyone in carrying out the action, regardless of their original views.

10.4 After the meeting

Many meetings end raggedly, leaving their attendees greatly bewildered about the resolution of the meeting. Wally's meeting, which was brought to a close so hastily, is a splendid example of a poorly concluded meeting. Many meetings also seem to exist on a plane of reality apart from everyday working life. Whatever resolutions they make are quietly forgotten when the participants return to their shop. Again, I suspect that Wally's meeting also suffered from such a ghostly disembodiment, in that nothing discussed in the meeting had any effect at all upon subsequent work in the shop.

There are three details that you must attend to if you want to avoid the confusion and disembodiment that I described above. These are to note action items, assign responsibilities, and distribute the minutes.

10.4.1 Note action items

A simple, but often neglected, rule is to write down all future actions agreed upon in a meeting. These are called *action items*. For example, an action item in a problem-solving meeting may call for additional research into the causes of a problem and for a subsequent meeting to consider the outcome of this research.

The purpose of this rule is for there to be a record of the actions called for and their purposes. Wally's meeting yielded several action items, including the planning of the analysis review, the establishment of screen standards, and the modernization of the programming standards. Since none of these were recorded, I bet the programming standards task in particular would quickly slip into oblivion.

10.4.2 Assign responsibilities for action items

Like any other task, an action item must be specifically assigned to someone for execution. However, many managers who, though they would never think of leaving a normal task unassigned, continually fail to attach names to the action items of a meeting. Presumably, this is in the hope that action items will somehow execute themselves.

Wally failed to assign the programming standards tasks to anyone in particular. To be sure, he addressed the action item in the general direction of the programmers ("I want you programmers to set up a standards review group"). But any one of the programmers could dodge responsibility for that action item with a clear conscience. Wally should have assigned the action item to, say, Marvin, with the directive to form a small review group and to report back to him by a specific time. Better yet, Wally should have treated the action item as a normal task, using a task assignment card like the one shown in Figure 9.1.

10.4.3 Distribute the minutes

Minutes are a written record of the proceedings of a meeting, and distributing them can serve several purposes. First, they serve as a continuing group memory for those who attended the meeting. Second, they serve as objective documentation of the meeting's discussion for those who weren't present. Third, they serve as a means of continuity between one meeting and a subsequent related meeting, and, finally, they serve as archives and audit trails by which future generations can review the evolution of a decision and be informed of the reasons for rejecting alternative causes of action.

The necessity for minutes is greater for some types of agenda items than for others. Decision-making and problem-solving items, in particular, warrant good records to keep track of the sometimes bewildering array of actions that are candidates for evaluation. Communication items, on the other hand, may not need much minute taking, since they are often based on existing documentation. However, the question and answer sessions of such meetings are well worth recording. Planning items also usually require few minutes, since they tend to generate their own documentation as part of their primary output.

At one of the companies where I've consulted, however, we've found minutes of meetings to be so valuable as long-term group memories that we generate written minutes for almost all formal meetings. Sometimes, these minutes have been created in unconventional ways, for example, as transcriptions from audio or video tapes of a meeting. Tape recordings often lead to more accurate minutes and allow people to replay a meeting in its entire human subtlety.

10.5 Summary

Meetings are extremely powerful managerial tools, but they can cause great damage if they are mishandled. Simply by closeting a dozen or so people in a room with the salary meters ticking, a manager may waste vast sums of money unless he ensures that the meeting is highly productive. In this chapter, I offer several important guidelines for meeting with success.

First, before the meeting, secure a meeting place, and set a time that is convenient for all attendees; advertise the meeting with as much notice as possible; circulate an agenda with few and specific items; and invite only those people who can seriously contribute to the meeting.

During the meeting, adhere to the agenda and appoint a moderator to enforce it. The conduct of the meeting depends upon the type of agenda item, be it planning, communication, problem solving, or deciding. A recorder is useful to create and preserve the meeting's group memory in the form of minutes.

Finally, at the end of the meeting, write down the items identified for action during the meeting and assign responsibility for attending to each item. Soon after the meeting, and certainly before any follow-up meeting, have the meeting's minutes circulated for review both by the participants and by other interested observers.

Chapter 10: Exercise

1. What problems recur most often in meetings in your shop? What are the effects of these problems? Set up a series of meetings to find solutions to your problems.

11

Reviewing the Project

A project review is a major and formal checkpoint in a project at which you take stock of the work done to date, evaluate its quality and relevance to the project objectives, and set an appropriate strategy for the next stage of the project. The media, mechanisms, and participants of project reviews depend upon the stage of the project being reviewed.

Although some people confuse a project review with a walkthrough, they have distinct differences. A project review is more formal and more major in scope than a walkthrough. Whereas a walkthrough is intended to improve the quality of a deliverable or piece of a deliverable, a project review examines the status and quality of multiple major deliverables.

Most project reviews are attended by senior people from outside the main project team, while most walkthroughs are attended only by the project team, with perhaps a user or two. A walkthrough may of itself result only in recommendations for improvements to a particular deliverable; a project review, on the other hand, may recommend more drastic actions, including the cancellation of the project.

11.1 Structure of a project review

A project review resembles a meeting, both in its structure and in its criteria for success. A project review has three parts and, as with a meeting, its prelude and postlude must be attended to as diligently as the review itself. The basic structure of a review and its major activities are as follows:[1]

Components	Activities
Prelude:	Notify participants of the venue and the objectives; select and circulate the review materials.
Review proper:	Read the review materials; present the materials and hold a question and answer session; make the necessary decisions and plan the strategy.
Postlude:	Circulate the action items and minutes; execute the action items recommended by the review.

In the prelude, notify all the attendees of a review well in advance of its date and location, as well as of the objectives of the review. Bear in mind that since a review might be a grueling

---

[1]For additional details on the structure of reviews, see [Freedman and Weinberg, 1982].

session lasting several days, choose if possible a location that's free of distractions. That rules out your normal workplace, but it also rules out resort hotels.

The materials selected for circulation to the review participants naturally depend upon the work being reviewed. For example, the analysis phase generates its own documentation that serves as the review material. However, you are not limited in the review to written documents. Don't overlook the possibility of demonstrating any prototype models created during the analysis, for instance. If you are reviewing the acceptability of the final system, the review participants should study the system itself before the review.

By circulating the materials well before the review, you give everyone the opportunity to study them thoroughly before the review. Unfortunately, this is an opportunity that few people take, as most participants skim through the first twenty or so pages of the documentation just before the review, make a few notes, and feel that they've discharged their duty adequately.

One solution to this problem is the forced read: Gather all the review participants, except the documentation's authors, in a room and assign them to read, say, ten pages of the materials for perhaps fifteen to twenty minutes. Then, assign them the next ten pages. Being frog-marched over documentation in this way is tedious, of course, but it works.

Today, however, the ordeal of a review is not so intimidating as it once was, simply because modern techniques of software development emphasize the benefits of regular communication throughout the project and not just at major checkpoints. Techniques to improve communication on a project include use of graphic documentation, walkthroughs, incremental implementation, and prototyping. As a result, review participants are already familiar with most aspects of the project and are not confronted with mountains of unfamiliar documentation. The benefit of the review derives from the participants' being able to see all the pieces of documentation in full ensemble.

Begin the review with all participants, so that everyone can see the big picture. Later, break the group into smaller specialized working groups to tackle particular issues. For example, in an analysis review of a manufacturing system, there might be subreviews of the order entry, warehouse management, and financial control subsystems.

If the review material is rather long, split it into sections and conduct the review of one section at a time. To help you decide how to divide the material, a good rule of thumb is for each section to be able to be presented in about an hour. In the question and answer session that follows, participants ask questions based on reading the review materials, as well as on hearing the presentation. The questions that are asked by participants probably indicate omissions or ambiguities in the documentation, and the pertinent sections should be clarified. After all, what else but the documentation will answer these questions when the documents' authors are no longer around?

The review generates action items of varying magnitude, from simple documentation corrections to major decisions on reworking previous phases. The course of the project after the review depends upon the magnitude and number of action items that the review raises. Typical choices are to let the project proceed and simultaneously work on the action items; to let the project proceed once the action items are completed; to repeat the review once the action items are completed; or to cancel the project immediately.

The review therefore raises issues that require decisions to be made. Who makes these decisions depends upon your organization and your project methodology. In any case, it's important that as little review time as possible be spent on making decisions. Resolve minor issues in the working groups if possible, but defer more major decision making, especially when the issues are unclear or require more research, to meetings following the review. Also, use the review primarily to identify problems, rather than to correct them.

Unless there are many major action items to be worked on, you will want to decide the basic strategy for the next project phase before the review adjourns. (This does not mean, however, producing a detailed plan during the review.) Using your experience from the previous phases, decide whether you want to adopt a more radical or more conservative strategy for forthcoming phases. Then, determine the order for working on the major portions of the project in those future phases.

In the postlude to the review, circulate a list of action items and minutes of the review to all review participants, all other project members, any affected users, and anyone else affected by the action items. Probably the best way to acquire the minutes is to tape record the review and transcribe the minutes afterward. As project manager, you have the principal responsibility for managing the action items and ensuring their successful completion. Managing most of them will be trivial, while others will require a significant amount of effort.

11.2 Types of project reviews

The eight reviews to be conducted during a typical data processing project are, in chronological order, project scope review, analysis review, design review, programming review, system review, acceptance review, periodic production review, and post-project review. This set is fairly typical, but your shop's project methodology may call for a different set of reviews.

Furthermore, you may tailor the precise sequence of these reviews to suit your project strategy. For example, if you adopt an ultraradical strategy in which you design subsystem 1 before you analyze subsystem 2, your sequence of reviews might be thus:

> project scope review
> general analysis review
> subsystem 1 analysis review
> subsystem 1 design review
> subsystem 2 analysis review, . . .

In the following sections, I describe each of the eight reviews, their purposes, and their participants. I devote special attention to the periodic production review and the post-project review, for many shops handle them badly or omit them entirely.

11.2.1 Project scope review

Purpose

The basic purpose of a project scope review is to determine whether the project is addressing an appropriate set of problems and opportunities to improve the users' business. If the scope is approved and the project is ordained to continue, a secondary purpose of this review is to affirm a set of preliminary objectives to improve the business, as well as a feasible project strategy. If the project's scope is not approved, this review might recommend enlarging, diminishing, or shifting the scope of the project to address a different area of the users' business; adjourning the review for further study; abandoning the project; or shelving the project for a period of time.

Participants

The participants in this review include at least one person from each of the following groups: BUS group, metrics group, senior DP management, senior user management of the area to be affected by the project, the project manager, and the members of the project survey team.

Description

The project scope review analyzes information gathered during the project survey,[2] as well as other findings of previous or concurrent project surveys to evaluate the worthiness of a project. Using this information, the reviewers determine which set of problems and opportunities in and around the project area offer the most promising benefits, given the resources available, and which of the feasible approaches outlined in the survey seems the most propitious. The decisions made during the project scope review are not final, but represent the working assumptions under which the project's analysis phase is begun if, of course, the project gets a green light from this review.

11.2.2 Analysis review

Purpose

Like the project scope review, the primary goal of the analysis review is to check whether the basic problems the project is intended to solve are adequately addressed. The difference between the two reviews is that the preliminary information available for the first review is likely to be well defined for the second. Additional purposes of the analysis review are to determine whether the deliverable of the analysis phase, the requirements specification, is of good quality and does justice to the project's business objectives; and to list the most important qualities of the system to be developed.

Participants

The reviewers are the same as those in the project scope review, with these additions: several operational users from the business areas affected by the project; business auditors; hardware and software designers; representatives from the user training and computer operations areas; and the entire analysis team.

Description

With better, more detailed information available, the analysis reviewers re-examine the issues considered in the previous review in order to validate the decisions made, including the project's objectives. In many respects, this review is a point of no return, because after this point, it is difficult to alter the project's objectives. This review is also the last point at which the users should cancel the project for business reasons, unless there are dramatic changes in the users' business problems or opportunities during the later phases of the project. After the analysis review, the project should be canceled only for technical, political, or financial reasons (such as hideous cost overruns or unforeseen bankruptcy). Also, the analysis review is the last review until the acceptance review when user representatives are present in force.

Because many DP project managers perceive this review to be their last chance to sign up the users for the remainder of the project, the analysis review may become no better than a sideshow. Although an all-too-typical review is a wretchedly jolly, back-slapping affair, I've noticed a sobering phenomenon: The more euphoric the review, the more likely the project is to end in tears.

---

[2]A project survey, which some shops call a feasibility study, results when the BUS group identifies a problem or opportunity to be addressed by a project. This survey looks at the estimated costs, benefits, and available resources for the project, and broadly outlines feasible ways to exploit the opportunities or attack the problems. The project survey does not yield definite and binding conclusions, but rather only indicates whether it's worthwhile to carry on the project.

The following story illustrates the worst kind of analysis review, which was no more than a brainless sales pitch. Several years ago, the manager of a project to develop a large customer billing system invited me to attend the analysis review as an unbiased observer. It was to be held in a month in (and this should have raised my suspicions) a Las Vegas hotel. I agreed to attend and was promised that the review documentation would be sent immediately. It never arrived, even after I called four times to ask for it. Despite my misgivings about being fobbed off with such excuses as "the copier broke down" or "it's in the mail," I missed the second warning signal.

The review was scheduled to last for three days from 10 a.m. to 4 p.m. each day. The attendees were the project manager, the project analysts, project librarian/scribe, four members of the user department, and me. These four users seemed remarkably senior to be attending such a review, and I wondered how such high-level people could realistically comment on the detailed analysis document without the aid of some more operational managers. (Later, I learned that two of the users weren't even in the departments directly affected by the project.)

The review began at about 11 a.m. on the first day, with the coincident late arrival of both the documentation and two of the users (who wandered in, muttering, "Is this where they're holding the mutt 'n' donkey show?"). By the time the project manager had reported on how well the project had gone so far and how pleased he'd been with the cooperation of the users, it was lunchtime.

During the subsequent technical part of the review, some of the users fell asleep and I concluded that any questions from me were definitely not welcome. Apparently, I was there only to add credence to the analysis document and not to detract from it by pinpointing flaws. On the second day, three of the users rolled in bleary-eyed at lunchtime, and they all dashed in and out throughout the afternoon to make "important phone calls." After the afternoon coffee break, one user disappeared completely.

The review ended in a scramble of hearty handshaking earlier than planned on the third day, probably because two of the users had landed in a hospital: Having discovered a sudden interest in agriculture, they had driven their rented car off the road on the way back from a ranch on the outskirts of town. That was the only acknowledged blemish on an otherwise "perfect" review.

I submitted a report on the review to the project manager, saying that I needed a further week of study before I could submit a report on the analysis phase. I never heard from him again, but I later heard through the grapevine that the project had failed, with only twenty-five percent of the system having been delivered, and even that part failing to meet the users' business needs correctly.

If you skimp on the analysis review, or make it into a comic revue, your project runs the risk of straying drastically from the users' business needs. If that happens, I guarantee that the fond memories and photos of people drinking champagne in Las Vegas won't help you much. But hang on to the photos, because your users might try to deny ever having met you.

11.2.3 Design review

Purpose

The design review's goal is to determine if the design fulfills the requirements specification, is of acceptable quality, and can be implemented easily.

Participants

Those who attend the design review include the project manager, at least one analyst, a member of the metrics group, a technical auditor,[3] a representative from the user training and computer operations area, one or more senior programmers, a representative from the production support department, and the entire design team.

Description

The design review is the last checkpoint to ensure that everything is in good technical shape before you open up the programming guns and move the implementation forward along a broad front. Metzger describes the situation at this review: "You're about to commit major resources (programming manpower, testing manpower, and computer time) and you'd better have a warm feeling that you're really ready. Once you begin implementing that baseline design, it's exhausting, expensive, and morale-busting to have to stop to do a major overhaul." [Metzger, 1973].

As stated above, the reviewers first ensure that the design meets the specification, the whole specification, and nothing but the specification. Second, they check that the design meets the standard for the qualities established for the system (for example, flexibility, user friendliness, or efficiency). Third, they assure that the design is programmable and not obscure or littered with weird algorithms. (In practice, this is rarely a problem, since the programmers participate in the design phase in order to familiarize themselves with the design and to keep the designers honest.)

Finally, at this review, the project manager devises a basic strategy for implementation, that is, the order in which portions of the system will be constructed and installed. As manager, you are guided by technical considerations, as noted in Chapter 6. But what is most helpful in deriving an implementation strategy are the estimates provided by the metrics group for the implementation times of each part of the system. Using these estimates, you can better orchestrate your resources during the implementation period.

11.2.4 Programming review

Purpose

The programming review's goal is to determine whether programming is complete, to review integration test results, and to decide whether the system is ready for system testing.

Participants

Reviewers include the project manager; at least one analyst; at least one member of (though, more likely, all of) the design team; the entire programming team or the senior representative, with the rest being on call; and the technical auditor.

Description

During the programming phase of a modern DP project, coding is not the only activity carried out. As each piece is coded, it is also tested and added to the system for testing again. This so-called incremental approach reveals errors in an orderly, controlled way rather than in a devastating mass

---

[3]A technical auditor checks the technical quality of the system (for example, its database or design), whereas a business auditor checks that functions of a system are in line with company requirements or federal laws, for instance.

at the end of programming. Thus, the programming/testing phase prepares the way for a system test that is not beset by swarms of logic, data structure, and interface bugs.

Therefore, the programming review ensures that not only is the coding complete, but that testing was rigorous. In order to do this, review the test data used for unit testing and for testing during incremental implementation, together with the test log for the programming phase.

The test log should depict a system that is settling into an equilibrium. It will no doubt record the discovery of several problems at the start of the programming phase, including design errors or even analysis errors, as well as problems in the new software being added to the incrementally growing system. But each such problem should appear only once or at most twice in the log.

As review participants, watch for alarm signals that indicate the system is not yet settled enough for system testing. Such signals include the failure of the number of known bugs to fall asymptotically toward zero (this may indicate a premature end to testing); areas of code in which bugs continually appear; severe analysis or design errors that were revealed during programming; and areas of code that are riddled with errors.

Do not allow a system to proceed to formal system testing if you're not comfortable with what you see. Instead, send it back for further testing in specific areas, or for recoding, or for redesign, or even for reanalysis of certain portions. Such courses of action are always unpopular, troublesome, and expensive, but to rush ahead with a system exhibiting numerous major faults is to enter into a season of mistakes and muddled fruitlessness that is premature system testing.

11.2.5 System review

Purpose

The goal of the system review is to decide whether the system is ready for acceptance testing.

Participants

The reviewers include the project manager; at least one analyst; at least one member of (and probably all of) the design team; senior programmers (with the others on call); the technical auditor; a representative from each of the user training, documentation, and computer operations areas; a representative from the production support department; and a senior DP manager. (If the system review is combined with part of the acceptance review, as described in Section 11.2.6, other attendees include a senior user, several users in operational areas, a business auditor, and a member of the BUS group.)

Description

This review examines the results of the system test phase of the project.[4] Since testing is performed throughout the incremental construction of the system in the programming phase, you might conclude that the system test phase is superfluous. Not so! This phase concentrates on detecting system-level flaws, including volume problems, such as transaction throughput, response times, and effectiveness of the physical database; multiuser problems, such as conflicting updates; and production software that may not have been well tested earlier, such as reconciliation subsystems and conversion subsystems.

---

[4]For good accounts of system testing, see [Donaldson, 1978] and [Perry, 1983].

Other components of the system to test include the technical, operations, and user documentation; the procedures for security, operations, cutover, restart and recovery, and manual backup; and the production JCL. Even the user training courses can be tested.

Separating the system review from the system test itself is difficult, because much reviewing goes on during the actual testing. However, once you as project manager decide to call system testing to a close, hold a formal review of the test results with all the review participants. The reviewers will then decide either to move on to the acceptance test or to redo some testing, programming, design, or analysis in order to bring the system to an acceptable state. If any work is redone, a system review must be held again before you move on.

11.2.6 Acceptance review

Purpose

The acceptance review's goal is to determine whether the system is ready to be put into production.

Participants

Reviewers include the project manager; at least one analyst; the technical and business auditors; a member of the BUS group; a senior DP manager; a senior user; several users from the affected operations areas; and a representative from the production support department.

Description

The acceptance review looks at the results of the acceptance test phase of the project. This phase is the users' chance to ensure that the system works within their environment and that it satisfies their business requirements (see [Metzger, 1973]). In practice, however, acceptance tests are ineffective, because they lack both the thoroughness of system testing and the authenticity of everyday operation. In an acceptance test, the users may be given a chance to run only a few transactions against some test data, and they can thus discover only what is glaringly amiss with the system. However, since the test is usually far from comprehensive and since the users probably have only a cursory familiarity with the system, they can glean only a superficial idea of the system's qualities. They are hardly qualified to predict how the system will perform in its real business environment.

The formal acceptance procedure therefore becomes a fatuous, meaningless ceremony and, unless the system goes crazy or crashes completely during the test, the project team typically browbeats the users into signing an acceptance document. Everyone may euphorically wave this document as promising peace of mind for all time, but, like the 1938 Munich agreement, hardly is the ink dry on the document than the system may run amok in production and terrorize the users for years to come.

So, what does it mean for the users to accept the system? Does it mean that they abrogate their rights to complain about its weaknesses once it's in production? Of course not. No user will grit his teeth and silently tolerate production failures just because he signed an acceptance document. Does users' acceptance thenceforth free the DP department of all responsibility for the system? No again, even though a signed document is often used by DP personnel as an excuse for obduracy or tardiness in correcting system errors. For this reason, the users who sign a document for what proves to be a less-than-acceptable system are likely to be blamed by their own management. This will contribute to deep and long-lasting acrimony between the users and the DP department.

The solution that I offer to the two problems of the traditional acceptance test—that it lacks thoroughness and it lacks the authenticity of true production—is to split the acceptance test into two parts. The first part merges with the system test and the second part becomes a periodic production review, which I describe in Section 11.2.7. To merge the acceptance test with the system test solves the thoroughness problem, but it means that the users aren't involved and the test isn't conducted in the users' business environment. Therefore, the system test and its review should be carried out at the users' site and by the users or, more likely, their technical and business auditors. Of course, you will want to hold your own test and review at your own facility before going to the users' site.

A valuable way to involve the users early in the implementation is to adopt incremental implementation or prototyping strategies. That way, the system will not be a last-minute surprise to the users. By involving the users in the testing, the acceptance test reviewers can obtain a clear picture of whether the system lives up to the qualities originally agreed to as the production criteria.

However, even though the system may be ready for production, it might not fulfill the users' long-term business needs in every way. This is the purpose of the system's final review, the periodic production review.

11.2.7 Periodic production review

Purpose

The periodic production review is intended to identify enhancements to the system following installation and to evaluate the system's potential to further improve the users' business.

Participants

Reviewers include at least one BUS group representative; a member of the metrics group; the production support team responsible for the system being reviewed; the technical and business auditors; and at least for the first one or two reviews, members of the original development team.

Description

As mentioned before, the users' signature on an acceptance document is not a true measure of the system's worth. All the document signifies is that the system appears to the users to be in good enough shape to be put to use. Another commonly but equally ineffective yardstick for judging a system's success is how well the system meets the functional specification produced during the project's analysis phase. This criterion merely ties the system's quality to the quality of its specification.

What is therefore needed in order to effectively judge the installed system is a means to close the loop from the delivered system to the original business objectives. This procedure takes place in the periodic production review, which consists of reviewing three aspects: the operation of the system, its technical quality, and the fulfillment of the users' business requirements. A periodic production review should be conducted regularly throughout the lifetime of the system, with the first review occurring about a month or two after the system is installed. This review concentrates on the system's operation, and particularly any operational difficulties. Three to six months later, the next periodic production review deals chiefly with technical aspects of the system. Subsequent reviews are held every six months to one year, when attention focuses on how the system is improving, and can further improve the users' business.

In the sections below, I discuss each of the three parts of the periodic production review, followed by a discussion of the relationship between this review and system maintenance.

Review of the system's operation

After the system has been operating for a short period, review its installation. Check, for instance, that every piece of the system was installed properly, and that the correct version of each piece of software was installed. Check also that the hardware is operating correctly.

In addition, review how well people are using and operating the system. Are all the training, user documentation, and operating procedures suitable for and comprehensible to all users and operators at their respective levels? Check the users' ability to make the best use of the system. Do they understand it or have they developed bizarre notions of the system's behavior? For example, some users suggested this cure for a rather temperamental system: "If the screen suddenly goes blank, turn the terminal on its side for twenty seconds and the screen will come back." Do the users know about the help facility or do they need the agility of a video game fanatic to get what they want from the system? How is the system's response time? long? inconsistent?

Don't forget to check the most obvious point of all: Are the users actually using the whole system? Surprisingly often, users overlook many potentially valuable portions of the system for whatever reason. In one startling example, two months after its installation at their remote site, the users were using *none* of the system! No one had officially told the users the system was ready for use and no training had been provided. The unusual problem was detected by an astute production support manager, who noticed that nobody had complained about the system or requested that it be changed in any way.

Also, review the efficiency of the running system. When you see the system operating on real data in a production-style database and on a real machine with a real number of users, you may spot some inefficiencies that didn't appear during testing and that can be traced to procedural or database design shortcomings. At this point, watch for physical data disorganization, which may come, for instance, from many deletions and additions, and which will cause system performance to deteriorate.[5]

Review of the system's technical aspects

In the inescapable rush to get the system into production, you may have neglected or deliberately compromised some of its technical qualities. Although you can never again fix the system as cheaply as you could before installation, you still have a chance to rectify some of its problems even when it is in production. Therefore, this part of the periodic production review has two technical purposes: identifying technical flaws in the system and targeting areas for preventive maintenance.

First, review the bugs that users report as a matter of course, and check both the system's output and database for evidence of undetected errors. If a portion of the system harbors many errors, a good idea is to recode that portion, whether you've corrected them or not. The chances are good that additional errors are lurking in that portion. Also, review how well your procedures for recovering from system failures work in practice.

Second, review the system's maintainability. The reason is that if you tune the maintainability of the system soon after its deployment, you reap benefits for the entire productive lifetime of the system. For example, with just minor redesign, some modules could become universally useful library modules. Don't forget to review the maintainability of data structures as well as the structure of procedural code. Even if the project used a technique such as structured design, the system won't be perfectly maintainable. For instance, the designers won't always have factored out functions with the right balance between restrictivity and generality.

---

[5]See [Donaldson, 1978, pp. 253–55] for additional operational features that you should review.

Later in the system's career, review those parts of the system that undergo extensive changes, since modifications will result in degraded structure and maintainability. Consider recoding or even redesigning or reanalyzing parts in order to restore their maintainability. While it may seem cheaper to go on patching and plugging veterans of alterations, in the end lavishing vast sums on intensive care and repair is not worthwhile. Instead, assess the merits of replacing the expensive old maintenance-guzzler with a sleek new subsystem.

Review of the system's business aspects

The periodic production review closes a feedback loop by comparing the problems and opportunities earmarked at the beginning of the project to the solution actually achieved. It gives a chance to measure the successfulness of the system in practice, as well as an opportunity to search out imperfections, business problems that remain unresolved, and new business problems created by the introduction of the system or by other causes.

During this review, try to quantify as accurately as possible each business benefit. In this way, you can then evaluate to what degree you have accomplished the original itemized benefits of the system. To make additional measurements, ask such questions as, What unanticipated benefits does the system produce? What new problems arise from the new system? What functions fall short of expectations? Can deficient benefits be restored by revamping these functions?

In this review, don't forget to measure the costs of the system in production and to compare these with the originally estimated costs. Ask the metrics group representative to provide the original figures and to conduct the current measurements.

Periodic production review and maintenance

To make the periodic production review far more than a passive series of measurements and comparisons, follow each review that you perform with remedial treatment of the faults that you find. A periodic production review is like an annual medical checkup, which is followed up by your doctor's prescribing courses of treatment for any ailments that he identifies. The ailments that periodic reviews uncover are anything from bugs to unsatisfied business needs.

If you think that a periodic production review seems to be akin to the functions of maintenance, you're right, except that the former is a proactive activity, whereas the latter is a reactive one. Traditional maintenance means waiting for a user request for a fix or an enhancement to a system. Such requests are often irksome, because they may be hasty, ill-thought-out, badly expressed, and so limited in scope that they must be followed by further requests. A maintenance department usually has a jumbled backlog of hundreds of such requests and yet no coherent picture of the users' essential needs for system improvements.

With a periodic production review, by contrast, you in the DP department take maintenance to the users. This yields three beneficial results: First, your political relationship with your users improves, since you appear to be on the users' side (you're actually on the side of business as a whole), and you're less likely to receive those angry early morning phone calls. Second, by planning the maintenance function, you can organize and schedule a coordinated set of system enhancements and thereby reduce the expense of maintenance. The disorganized way in which many shops currently make maintenance changes to systems is like the way uncoordinated utility companies make changes to the sidewalk: One week, the water company digs it up to lay a pipe; the next, the gas company breaks it up again to fix a leak; and a week later, the phone company redigs it to lay a cable. By planning maintenance, you need dig up a system only once, make many changes to it, test all those changes, and put it back into production as a well-defined new release of the system. Thus, you reduce maintenance overhead significantly, although you do pay a small price by having to delay the implementation of some enhancements until the next system release is ready.

Third, the maintenance job becomes more interesting. No longer does maintenance have to be the job that no one wants. With active reviews, maintenance work can actually become a training ground for new project members to learn the company and business. In fact, since this new activity is so unlike traditional maintenance, I prefer *production support* or *business-service enhancement* as more modern and more accurate terms for the activity.

A production support department that employs periodic production reviews has similar activities to the BUS group. Both study the business interests of the corporation, for example. The greatest difference is that the production support department seeks opportunities for improvement in automated systems, whereas the BUS group pursues such opportunities in manual systems. But this is an artificial distinction that will undoubtedly blur into insignificance as automation makes greater inroads into businesses everywhere.

Until that time, both groups need to work together, ensuring that the information garnered in periodic production reviews is available for the BUS group's continuing review of the overall business. Also, the production support department should have a firm presence in the BUS group, a presence that will grow with the increase in computerization.

11.2.8 Post-project review

Purpose

The purpose of the post-project review is to take stock of the lessons learned from the project and to communicate this knowledge.

Participants

Among the reviewers are the entire project team, senior staff from other projects, staff managers, and anyone else who can gainfully learn from your project experiences.

Description

The post-project review is a vehicle for conveying practical information and eliciting intelligent debate on reliable ways to conduct successful projects. A primary objective of the post-project review is to dispel some of our industry's extraordinary fanaticism, which feasts on the ignorance and misunderstanding of our own business. Open almost any popular trade journal and you'll find at least one rabid article on, for example, prototyping versus deep up-front analysis, COBOL versus Ada versus Pascal, and the lovable, ever popular GOTO statement.

A colleague of mine once lambasted a shop that boasted among all its employees a total of fifteen person-centuries of DP project experience. He mused, "How much further ahead is your shop now than 1,500 person years ago? About ten to twenty person-years, I'd say, because you learn—if at all—only from your own triumphs and mistakes, not from other people's. So, year after year, your shop repeats the same hackneyed triumphs and the same time-honored mistakes, with each person believing that he is striding through frontier territory by his actions."

Though a trifle harsh, my colleague's point is well made. Most shops—as well as our industry in general, for that matter—know very little about what factors make some projects whir like delicately tuned clockwork and other projects grind gruesomely to a standstill. Why do we know so little of the causes either of successful projects, or of unsuccessful projects, or of the many projects whose outcome is somewhere between the two extremes?

It's hardly surprising that we know so little about unsuccessful projects. The manager of such a project normally does his best to hush it up and to save face politically or else he'll be exiled to a low-priority salt mines project or demoted or simply fired. The manager of a failed project won't willingly cooperate in an explicit review of the project unless he's assured of amnesty. That's too bad, since the only benefit of the mistakes of the project—education—is lost.

But why, conversely, do we know so little about fairly successful projects? One reason is that DP managers are often nervous of what close scrutiny of the successful projects will reveal. So, if the review of a successful project occurs at all, it usually is a superficial celebration that runs along these lines: "Mr. Manager, to what do you ascribe your success?"

"On this project, I decided to use the latest Angus Prune project estimating methodology coupled with the James Riddle structured debugging techniques, and, of course, I couldn't have done the project without my hard-working, dedicated crew." The arbitrariness of such a reply reminds me of a television interview between a rather condescending young reporter and a hundred-year old man. The reporter asked the inevitable question, "To what do you attribute your extraordinary longevity?" With a twinkle in his eye, the man replied, "Every night for the last eighty years, I've drunk a fifth of bourbon and sucked on a raw onion."

A post-project review is intended to share knowledge rather than to continue to dwell in ignorance. If you regard this objective as being too altruistic for your taste, consider the personal benefits of holding a post-project review. If your project was successful, you have a chance to apprise everyone of that fact. If your project was a catastrophe, you also have a chance to direct people's attention away from you as a scapegoat and toward the true reasons for failure. But don't lie or try to whitewash the problems or make yourself look better. If you made mistakes, say so; if you don't admit them, someone else will eventually say so for you. Even if you've done such a bad job that you must leave your managerial post, you'll perhaps be able to leave with head held high, and you'll have made a valuable contribution to others: You may have saved them from pitfalls that lie in the path of their projects.

The main sources of the project review material are the project log and the material and views contributed by project members (for example, specifications from analysts or testing problems from testers). The chief topics to cover in the review are these:

- brief overview of the project
- a comparison of the estimates made at various project stages with the actual results, with assistance from the metrics group
- the tools used and their respective strengths and weaknesses (but don't blame the tools for project difficulties, unless you can prove a genuine case)
- what you would do differently given the same project again
- other lessons from the project

Hold the review about six weeks or so after the system is installed, while it is still fresh in everyone's mind. Unfortunately, after only six weeks, the production system is still in its infancy and so you won't know a great deal about the project's success in terms of its business objectives. Anyone who can possibly learn anything from the review should be allowed to attend. Since the post-project review is an automatic event independent of the successfulness of the project, no one can construe the review as a kind of judgment on the success or failure of a particular project.

Don't be tempted to turn a post-project review into a carnival, as did one project manager who delivered a system that was a poor answer to the users' business needs. Nevertheless, this manager threw a post-project review that turned out to be an extravagant party. He invited senior user and DP managers to the party and won great acclaim and eventually a promotion. Although lower-level users soon learned of the system's deficiencies, they were loathe to point out that the project emperor wore no clothes. After all, senior management who had attended the success party could hardly admit the project to be a failure.

Avoid the temptation to make the post-project review a travesty of objectivity, for it helps no one in the long run. Even this crafty project manager was eventually politically assassinated by a conspiracy of frustrated users.

11.3 Summary

A project review is a major checkpoint at which to examine the work done to date and to set a strategy for the next stage of the project. The project review consists of three parts: a prelude, when the material is circulated for the review; the review itself, when the material is presented and discussed and the project's disposition is determined; and the postlude, when the action items from the review are performed and another review is set up, if necessary.

There are eight standard project reviews, although your own project methodology may call for a somewhat different set of reviews. The primary purpose and benefit of project reviews is as serious project tools, and not as opportunities for seedy public relations stunts. The analysis review is particularly prone to being abused in this way, as it gives the project manager the chance to sell the project to the users, before they become less centrally involved in the following two phases of the project.

The traditional acceptance review does not truly ascertain the acceptability of the system, which can be determined only after the system has run in a live environment for a while. Also, traditional acceptance reviews have been based on scanty acceptance testing results. The acceptance review should be at least as thorough as the system review, which can serve as an in-shop dress rehearsal for the acceptance review conducted at the users' site.

The periodic production review evaluates the successfulness of the system in its operation, technical construction, and most important in continuing to meet its chartered business objectives. This review has some beneficial side effects, including improving the DP department's relationship with its users, improving the quality of and interest in maintenance work, and allowing maintenance tasks to be planned and coordinated more effectively. For greater effectiveness, the production support group should be guided by the advice of the BUS group.

The post-project review is intended as a forum for the project team to share with other project team members what it learns from carrying out the project. By holding objective post-project reviews, you and the other managers in your shop increase your understanding of the factors that influence a project's success. Such understanding increases everyone's chances of triumph on future projects.

Chapter 11: Exercises

1. What reviews does your shop routinely conduct as part of a project? What is the objective of each review?

2. Think back to the last half dozen or so reviews that you've attended. Given these reviews and the discussion in this chapter, how could the reviews be conducted more effectively? What changes, if any, in the course of the project (or other projects) resulted from these reviews? Was any of these a post-project review and were any of the lessons learned communicated during this review?

SECTION III

People: A DP Department's Greatest Resource

A classic description of a manager is someone who achieves results *through his people*. Therefore, how you perform as a manager depends chiefly upon how you use (or abuse!) those who work for you. Your management performance also depends greatly upon how you react to those alongside you as well as above you in the organizational hierarchy and upon how you react to the personal pressures of your managerial position.

Chapters 12 and 13 consider an employee's path through a DP department, emphasizing the tremendous risks that exist for squandering valuable human resources in the poorly planned hiring, training, promotion, and dismissal of people. Chapter 14 addresses another cause of such wastage—the shackling of potentially productive people in counterproductive working conditions.

Chapter 15 introduces the concept of a *mediocracy,* a term that I use for a major organizational dysfunction that can drastically erode the potential of every person in a department. Mediocracies, which are unfortunately common, not only create products of low quality at very high prices, but also are difficult to rectify even with concerted efforts.

Chapter 16 deals with the inability of some project managers to accept an unpleasant reality. In some cases, this inability may reach the point of psychosis and throw an entire project out of control.

The tremendous toll that being a DP manager can take on yourself, your family, and your co-workers is the topic of Chapter 17. Although silently taking punishment appears to be a noble stance, it is laudable in intention only. Instead, it often turns out to be an action of self-destruction. This final chapter discusses strategies by which you can avoid becoming yet another kamikaze DP project manager going down in a blaze of glory.

12

Hiring and Firing

A shop's employees are its most valuable assets. They represent a huge financial investment in the time and effort to hire and to train them. They also represent an investment in terms of worker continuity: In as little as six months, an employee absorbs much of the shop's unwritten culture and develops invaluable working relationships with co-workers. Therefore, hiring and firing employees are not actions to be taken lightly.

In order for managers to determine when and which employees to hire and fire, they first must know what specific skills are needed for the positions in their organization. Only by placing people with the right skills in each position can they hope to make the organization live up to its potential effectiveness. This chapter addresses the issues of how to define the people that you need for your department and how to secure those people through effective hiring practices. It also discusses the reasons, both good and bad, for firing an employee.

12.1 Hiring

Hiring a person to fill a new or a vacant post involves six steps: defining the job to be filled, advertising the job, selecting the interviewees, conducting the interviews, selecting the recruit, and integrating the recruit into the department. In the next sections, I discuss each of these steps in their natural sequence and then describe some other aspects of hiring employees.

12.1.1 Defining the job to be filled

Before hiring anyone, regardless of the position being considered, you must first define exactly what the job entails. If this first critical step is not done thoroughly, you will be unable to draft an accurate advertisement and to select the best candidate from among the applicants.

Many shops are lax in specifying jobs, some shops undertaking the hunt for a new employee with only a job title and an administrative grade. A job title alone is no substitute for a clear definition of a job, since it often reveals only a person's nominal role in the department, rather than his actual contribution to the department's business.[1] Titles such as ''programmer/analyst'' or ''systems specialist'' are often meaningless, with the owner of such a title expected to do miscellaneous, hastily assigned tasks. A job title without an accompanying job definition cannot

---

[1] I consulted at a small software company that realized its job titles were irrelevant and so allowed its employees to choose their own titles. One programmer had his card printed with the title ''grand wazir.'' Not to be outdone, his colleague printed his card with ''senior grand wazir.'' A title that appealed to me particularly was chosen by someone from the word processing department; it was ''text engineer.''

possibly specify the real objectives and activities of a job. Administrative grades reveal little more: typically only an approximate salary range, length of service with the company, and position in the departmental pecking order.

An excellent way to specify a job definition is by means of a *role grid*. This grid allows for the fact that very few jobs are monolithic but instead consist of several distinct roles. For example, the job of a senior systems analyst may comprise these roles: participation in the BUS group, quantification of business opportunities, presentation of data processing plans for approval by management, and explanation of new systems to all who are affected by them.

A portion of a role grid for this position might therefore look something like Figure 12.1. The size of the role grid depends upon the diversity of the department. A grid that I saw recently in a large shop had about 50 columns for jobs and about 250 rows for roles. It was held in a computer file and maintained by a small but useful set of programs.

Figure 12.1. Role grid for the senior systems analyst position.

The next step in job definition is establishing the *be-know-do grid*, based on Geigold's terminology [Giegold, 1982]. This grid specifies for each role in the shop the personality of that role's holder; his skills, qualifications, and experience; and the activities involved in the role. An example of part of a "be-know-do" grid for the senior systems analyst position and others is presented in Figure 12.2.

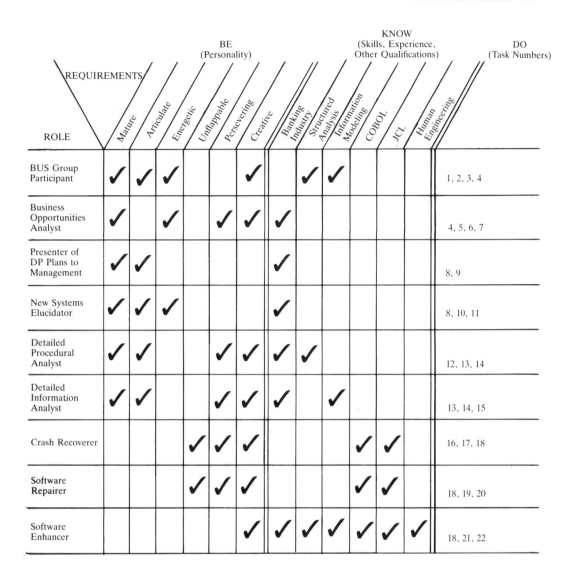

Figure 12.2. "Be-know-do" grid for the senior systems analyst position.

ROLE	BE (Personality)						KNOW (Skills, Experience, Other Qualifications)						DO (Task Numbers)
	Mature	Articulate	Energetic	Unflappable	Persevering	Creative	Banking Industry	Structured Analysis	Information Modeling	COBOL	JCL	Human Engineering	
BUS Group Participant	✓	✓	✓			✓		✓	✓				1, 2, 3, 4
Business Opportunities Analyst	✓		✓	✓	✓	✓							4, 5, 6, 7
Presenter of DP Plans to Management	✓	✓				✓							8, 9
New Systems Elucidator	✓	✓	✓			✓							8, 10, 11
Detailed Procedural Analyst	✓	✓		✓	✓	✓	✓						12, 13, 14
Detailed Information Analyst	✓	✓		✓	✓	✓			✓				13, 14, 15
Crash Recoverer				✓	✓	✓				✓	✓		16, 17, 18
Software Repairer				✓	✓	✓				✓	✓		18, 19, 20
Software Enhancer						✓	✓	✓	✓	✓	✓	✓	18, 21, 22

Note that in the "do" section, each role is described by several numbers, which are defined in the form of a task description. An example of a description for a task in the role of BUS group participant is as follows:

TASK NO.:   3
TASK NAME: Participate in banking conferences.
TASK DESCRIPTION: Form short list of relevant conferences.
                    Determine most important topics.

Some shops depict the "be-know-do" dimensions of a role somewhat differently. One good way is to show only the "be" dimension as a grid and the "do" dimension as a data flow diagram.

The tasks then are described in the form of minispecifications of the DFD, with the "know" requirements contained in the minispecification for the individual task.

Another variation on the role grid is to treat requirements more precisely than the simple binary checkmark or no checkmark of Figure 12.1. Some shops have a scale of necessity from, say, 0 (not required) to 5 (essential) for the "be" dimension, and a similar scale from 0 (total ignorance is acceptable) to 5 (solid expertise is required) for "know." Such precision as this, of course, calls for much more thought about roles than does the simple "yes or no" approach. But this precision pays off especially well when you are selecting new people to fill a role.

Although developing and maintaining job descriptions is the staff manager's responsibility, each person in the shop should ensure that his own job description is correct. In fact, the best job description emerges if the actual job holders write their own descriptions. You, as staff manager, simply act as the final editor. In this way, people develop a greater pride of ownership in their jobs than if their roles and tasks are defined by inflexible, and possibly inaccurate, edicts from on high.

12.1.2 Advertising the job

Once you have the description of the job to be filled, you will know both the job's roles and the "be-know-do" dimensions of each role. This knowledge enables you to compose an advertisement that accurately portrays the vacant post.

However, I must add a warning at this point: Don't be too rigid in the "know" requirements. Remember that a recruit can contribute not only experience but also potential to his new company. Shops that employ people solely for their previous experience and that spurn candidates with valuable potential miss tremendous opportunities to hire talented people who can be trained in specific skills. As a general rule, I prefer to hire someone with little experience but who can think, rather than someone with ten years' experience but who cannot think.

Although flexibility to future demands is especially important in the DP industry, I have seen some strange advertisements for positions in DP trade journals, requiring applicants to possess extraordinarily specialized backgrounds. For example, one ad demanded experience in SNIBBOL 3.7.1/B running on a 3033N under MVS/TSO. I think that someone knowing SNIBBOL 3.7.1/A could easily pick up SNIBBOL 3.7.1/B from the SNIBBOL vendor's manual, and I suspect the true reason for such a specific requirement is that the ad was written with a particular applicant's experience in mind.

Another advertisement, which appeared when the HP 3000 minicomputer had been on the market for just about a year, stridently called for someone with "two years of COBOL on the HP 3000 under MPE," a call that can have moved few to reply! Some shops are pleased to ask for someone with, perhaps, "five years' experience utilizing COBOL under DOS/VSE" without any further clarification. This type of advertisement tends to attract people with six months of relevant experience that was repeated nine times.

However, I'll be the first to concede that solid experience is absolutely necessary for some positions. For example, I wouldn't recommend that you hire someone with lots of potential but no actual database experience as the lead database designer on a project. Neither would I recommend hiring people with potential if you lack a serious plan for tapping that potential. Otherwise, you will stifle their drive and probably frustrate them into resigning before very long. Thus, an important objective of your department's hiring policy should be to maintain a healthy balance of past achievement (experience) and future achievement (potential).

12.1.3 Selecting the interviewee

Soon after you've advertised the position to be filled, applications and resumés presumably will come flooding in. (So, too, will the calls from warm-body traders with lavish tales of somebody or other in their throngs of itinerant miracle workers who happens to be just perfect for the job.) The next step is to divide the resumés into the likely candidates for interview and the also-rans, using the "be-know-do's" in the job description to do so. Since resumés often tend to exaggerate their author's achievements, read through them with healthy skepticism. Some resumés are indeed worthy of the Pulitzer Prize for fiction. I recall one applicant whose resumé claimed in so many words that he singlehandedly wrote all the software for the NASA Apollo Program. When I quizzed him about this astounding *tour de force,* he looked abject and confessed, "My head-hunter rewrote my resumé. I haven't actually seen it yet."

With that caution, use the resumés to separate the sheep from the goats. If there are too many likely candidates, select the resumés for the best six or so. If there are none, you'd better weigh carefully how urgently you need to fill the vacant post and look closely at your requirements in case they're too unrealistic.

Following this step, don't throw away the resumés; they provide valuable material for use in conducting the actual job interviews, such as in suggesting questions about the techniques that the candidate has used on previous projects.

12.1.4 Conducting the interview

The most important step in conducting an interview is to plan what you want to ask and what specific information you want from the candidate. In order to accomplish these two goals, you should have a planned structure for the interview. You don't have to follow this structure mechanically, but always be aware of it during the interview and try not to omit any parts. Too many job interviews that I've experienced myself have been so much meandering through largely irrelevant terrain that by the end of the interview, all the interviewer could possibly know about me was that I was a fairly reasonable sort of bloke.

The following is my own suggestion for a five-step interview structure. First, put the interviewee at ease. Begin by describing the shop and the company. Tell him about the shop's goals and plans, and how they fit in with the company's business. Describe the technical facilities and general working conditions of the shop. (You may even want to take him on a short tour in order to let him experience the general ambience.) Explain his career possibilities within the company, and his likely job assignment and co-workers. If there is a range of possibilities, tell him of all of them. Finally, tell him the shop's overall policies and organization; for example, the criteria for promotion, for training, specialist areas of the shop, and other such opportunities. Stress that these openings are available if he proves himself to be suitable.

Second, ask questions about the candidate's background and his personality. I like to mark interesting items on his resumé with a highlighting pen and jot questions in the margin. I use these questions to delve deeper into his background. Be politely aggressive in your inquiries. Remember, don't merely ask the questions, but also listen carefully to the candidate's responses to the questions. Make a questionnaire using the "be" and "know" categories of your "be-know-do" grid and have the candidate rate himself from 0 to 5 in each of the categories.[2] This tells you at least how he himself views his strengths and weaknesses.

Third, ask him to answer additional questions related to the specific job. For example, if the interviewee is currently an analyst and he is applying for an analyst's position, your list might contain such questions as these:

(a) What does an analyst do?

(b) What specific talents does an analyst need?

---

[2]See [Singer, 1982] for more information on this recommendation.

(c) What kind of personality do you think is best suited to the job of analyst?

(d) Describe the personal characteristics of the best analyst whom you've ever met.

(e) If you took this job, what tasks would you need the most help with?

(f) If I replaced you on your present job and you had only a short time to brief me, what aspects of the job would you emphasize?

(g) What are your career development goals over the next two to five years?

(h) What abilities do you need to have to meet these goals?

(i) What aspects of this shop and corporation do you think you would like most?

(j) What would you dislike?

(k) Why are you leaving your current job? (Ask him also why he left a previous position.)

Questions (a) through (d) help to determine whether you and the candidate are on the same wavelength in understanding the ''be-know-do'' dimensions of an analyst. The answer to question (e) reveals what the candidate feels his weaknesses to be, while the following question explores how well the candidate understands his present job and how clearly he can sum it up. Questions (g) and (h) ask the candidate about his envisioned career path; question (h) asks specifically what he considers his strengths to be. Questions (i) and (j) elicit the candidate's perception of your shop and corporation. (If his perception is wrong, feel free to correct him.) The last question gives you an idea of what in a job is important to the candidate and what would cause him to leave your shop.

I think that it's only fair to leave the applicant fifteen or twenty minutes to think about his answers or to jot some notes next to each question before you ask for his ideas. However, it's also fair to spring other questions on him to test his ability to think quickly.[3]

Fourth, ask to see a sample of his work, an obvious but important point, since there is no better evidence of the candidate's abilities. If the job candidate claims in his resumé to have recent experience with structured analysis, for example, ask him to bring along to the interview a small piece of a structured specification that he's worked on. If you're interviewing a potential manager, have him show you perhaps a sample of a plan that he's developed. Even if the candidate has no DP experience, ask him to supply some work from a previous job or from his university. Have him explain the piece of work to you and ask him probing questions to make sure that it really *is* his work. For instance, when I asked ''Mr. Apollo'' mentioned in Section 12.1.3 about the Apollo 13 lunar landing and he wasn't quick to remind me that it failed to land on the moon, I began to suspect that he wasn't the central pivot of NASA that his agent had professed him to be.

Finally, take care of administrative matters, such as the interview expenses and the procedure for notifying him of the results of the interview. If a second interview is needed before making the decision, ask him when he'll be available.

Conducting the interview with more than one interviewer is a good idea, and it offers at least three benefits: First, you have someone else with whom to compare notes following each interview.

---

[3]For more discussion of the above questions and what you can learn from the answers, see [Giegold, 1982, pp. 122-24] and also [Steger et al., 1975].

Second, if the position demands a wide range of skills, your colleagues can explore different aspects of the candidate's character and technical abilities. Third, your own idiosyncrasies and biases will be averaged out with several interviewers.

12.1.5 Selecting the recruit

With the "be-know-do" grid that you developed in the first step, you know the ideal personality of the incumbent, the ideal talents and experience, and the activities the job encompasses. These can serve as the criteria by which to measure each candidate that you interview. Immediately after the interview, you and your colleagues should note (on the 0 to 5 scale) how strong you consider the interviewee to be in each of the "be" and "know" categories. You will probably find that all your judgments are very similar, except they may be skewed by your different personalities. (Plot the scores on a graph for easier comparison.) If there are great differences among your evaluations in any crucial category, call the candidate back for further interviewing.

After you've interviewed all the candidates, decide which one best matches the profile of the post you want to fill. Since you will rarely, if ever, get a perfect match, you will have to accept deficiencies in certain categories, particularly those in the "know" category, since these can be overcome by training. However, deficiencies in personality are difficult to correct, so serious weaknesses in crucial "be" categories should eliminate a candidate from further consideration. To decide whether to eliminate a candidate, first consider his potential by looking at his record of achievements, his intelligence, and his overall enthusiasm. As I advised earlier, a regulated infusion of these qualities into your shop may be worth years of experience in some narrow field of endeavor.

If the Fates are frowning upon you, it may happen that no candidate seems suitable for the job. In that case, you will have to widen your catchment area in order to attract additional applicants. Possibly you advertised insufficiently or in the wrong media or in the wrong geographic location. Perhaps you offered too little money for the job (though your hands may be tied by corporate pay scales), or you focused on older, more experienced people (who tend to command higher salaries), rather than on talented newcomers. Possibly, the job itself is not doable and requires a superman to fill it. Find the reason for the dearth of suitable candidates first, and then try again.

Occasionally, a candidate may turn up who is perfect—but for another job. For example, a prospective analyst may appear with the personality and skills of a software toolsmith. If this occurs, you may want to offer the candidate the toolsmith job (qualified people are hard enough to get without letting one slip through your fingers) while continuing, of course, to search for a new analyst.

Finally, when you and your co-selectors have decided on whom to hire and how much to offer him, that's not quite the end of the story. Check his references if you've asked for them. (If you don't intend to check them, don't ask for them.) Keep in mind, though, that companies today are wary of giving qualitative opinions on ex-employees, and previous employers often will only provide the dates of an employee's employment, his job titles upon joining and leaving the company, and the salary ranges for his job grades. Even this information is worth the phone call.

12.1.6 Integrating the recruit into the department

Having accepted your offer and arriving for his first day, the new employee needs to be integrated into the shop and usually given some sort of training. The training need not be formal, but it should be planned and not glossed over in the haste to make the recruit productive. At the least, printed information explaining normal working hours, corporate facilities, and company benefits and rules must be provided. Additional training may simply be time allotted for reading and for talking to co-workers. Of course, training shouldn't stop once the employee has settled in, but should remain part of the job itself.

Monitor the recruit's performance and assess your hiring decision after six months or so. Compare the "know" qualities of the employee with what you expected when you hired him. Try to account for any discrepancies and use these conclusions to polish your hiring techniques.

12.1.7 Further recommendations

There are three further do's and don'ts of conducting an interview and hiring personnel: First, don't bait the interviewee with spurious expectations or promises. Early in my career, I was interviewed for a job by a company that specialized in developing scientific and engineering software. The interviewer was an outrageously merry old soul who seemed to regard the world as the greatest place he'd ever set eyes on. Most of the interview consisted of a lunch that transgressed the normal bounds of noontime festivities. During the lunch, others from the company joined us and cigars and drinks were passed around liberally. People I'd never met came up to me and told me what a splendid fellow I was and how well I'd fit in with the gang. By that time, I was ready to be carried around in a sedan chair and to sink my incisors into a slice or two of fatted calf.

I accepted the job, not only for its apparently convivial working conditions, but also because I'd be joining the fledgling Engineering Automation Department as the second programmer/engineer. I was particularly attracted to that position, because I was promised during the interview that within a year the department would be split in two, with me heading one of the offspring departments. Looking back, I can't believe that I was so credulous. I didn't even ask what reasons they had for planning this odd amoeboid split.

Upon arriving, I found the day-to-day atmosphere to be worse than I expected, but the work was reasonably stimulating. (I discovered that because staff turnover was fairly high, they turned interviews into jamborees to trap the unwary.) After about eight months, another programmer/engineer was hired into our department. Two months later, someone else was hired as manager of the department. After six more months elapsed, during which nothing much had happened, I was feeling rather puzzled. Why hadn't they divided the department and installed me as one of the managers? Why had they hired a manager over me? I approached my interviewer, who by now had moved to another part of the company. When I reminded my interviewer of his promise, he feigned memory loss, and my new boss comforted me with "We all have to take the rough with the smooth, don't we?" I felt angry, naive, and betrayed. Within a month, I resigned, vowing never to believe interview promises again.

Sadly, the practice of making detailed promises in interviews continues. I recently met a programmer, who was told when she was hired that at the end of project A, she would be promoted to project analyst and then to project leader on project B. Neither promotion came to pass. Instead, after she finally complained, she was grudgingly made programmer/analyst on project C. She experienced the same emotion that I had felt—betrayal—and was actively seeking a job at a different company.

It is unacceptable for you as a manager to tempt prospective recruits with the lure of personal advancements that you cannot honestly predict, control, or remember. If you do make extravagant personal offers that the candidate can't refuse and you can't deliver, you will soon have a bitter employee who views you as an unreliable manager.

My second rule is, Beware of the recommendations of a current employee. Treat a candidate who is a friend or an ex-colleague of someone in your shop in the same way that you would treat any other candidate. (This, of course, may be rather difficult if the candidate is the nephew of the department head!) But don't be swayed too much by a personal recommendation, since a friendship can cloud a person's judgment of another's professional ability. However, if the candidate has worked closely with someone in your shop, you can obtain some valuable direct information on the candidate's strengths and weaknesses.

During the interview itself, avoid all reference to your shared acquaintance. Otherwise, you bias the interview and falsely raise the candidate's hopes. When you come to selecting the new employee, be ready to turn down your colleague's protégé. If you're not prepared to do this (because you want to keep the peace with your colleague), don't accept the personal recommendation at the start.

Finally, consider hiring temporary rather than permanent help. There are three basic cases for hiring someone as a consultant or a contractor. The first case is when you need special skills that you cannot justify as a full-time or long-term position in your department. For example, you may need an expert in the internals of your operating system to measure and optimize the flow of production through your hardware. This work would take just a few weeks and might be needed only once a year. Clearly, if this was the only reason that you needed an internals expert in the shop, you could hardly justify paying him as a full-time employee. It would be better to hire him as a part-time consultant when you needed him.

A second case for hiring temporary help is when you need an objective view of internal issues. For example, an external consultant can be impartial about analyzing the efficacy of your shop's organization. Not only is he probably better qualified to do the work, but an internal employee is likely to be too embedded in the shop's organization and politics to be able to see its structure objectively. There is, however, a danger in hiring an outside consultant: His objectivity might be more like complete unfamiliarity. Unfortunately, I've seen consultants with an insalubrious blend of arrogance and ignorance enter a shop and try to impose solutions to problems that they evidently hadn't truly understood.

The third case for hiring temporary employees or guest workers is to deal with the increased work load about two-thirds of the way through a project. Widely used in Europe until very recently, the practice of hiring guest workers means that country A, going through a period of high activity, has many jobs that its citizens cannot or will not do. Therefore, country A invites workers from country B (which presumably has high unemployment) to work at these surplus jobs for the duration of the boom. Following the boom, the workers from country B return to their homeland.

"Guest worker" translates in the DP vocabulary to "contract programmer." You can hire extra programmers as guests and then let them go toward the end of the project. Thus, you can effectively level off the need for your own programmers, which in turn makes your staffing somewhat easier. Furthermore, you can assign interesting and challenging work to your own employees, and relegate the grunt work, such as tabulating data validation criteria, to the outside workers. I also like to use contractors for routine testing, which few of my programmers seem euphoric about having to do. This enables your shop's staff to pursue more fulfilling career paths.

But every solution creates different problems. In this case, the amount of supervision must increase for contract workers, for example, to ensure that their work meets the quality and standards of your shop. For this reason, some shops rarely hire individual contract workers, but instead obtain their "guests" from contract programming companies that foster standards of excellence in their own employees and wish to develop a long-term relationship with the shop.

Many DP managers worry that by inviting contract programmers into their shops, their own programmers will be lured away to the contractor world. This happens far more rarely than managers fear, and the programmers who do leave would probably have left anyway. Don't try to discourage your people from becoming contract workers, but merely point out that by doing so, they will be sacrificing continuity of assignment and probably stunting their careers, as well as perhaps losing a guaranteed paycheck.

A more realistic danger of using contract personnel, however, is that you may be overrun by hordes of consultants and thus lose some control, especially if the consultants come from different companies. Another damaging effect is that you may lose the impetus to develop your own staff if you rely on consultants as your chief source of talent. As a consequence, your best employees may go elsewhere to be challenged by interesting tasks and to be rewarded for their efforts.

12.2 Firing

Since a shop's employees represent a huge financial investment in the time and effort to hire and to train them, casting out such large investments is not an action to be taken lightly. Yet, there are managers who will agonize over a $20 expense item, but who won't think twice about dismissing an employee of ten years' standing. Such managers disregard not only the huge capital loss to the company caused by their actions, but also the great stress and emotional damage to the fired employee, as well as possibly to his colleagues. One manager I met even held the incredible attitude that it was beneficial occasionally to "execute" a worker in order to inspire others to "fight harder." This manager never even considered alternative means to motivate his people or otherwise increase their productivity.

Why do managers fire an employee? They typically choose dismissal as a solution to one or more of these problems: a worker's poor performance, his unmanageability, or his negative attitude. However, summarily firing an employee with such problems is often the worst solution.

Since firing an employee can be simultaneously cruel, wasteful, and unproductive, understanding the true reason that the employee failed is imperative. The best way for you to do this is to ask the employee himself for his thoughts on the causes of his poor performance or poor attitude. However, he may only have vague feelings that he's not being managed very well or he may be reluctant to voice his true feelings to you as his supervisor. He may also be reticent about telling you about any personal problems that detract from his ability to work effectively.

If open communication with the employee fails to yield results, try to elicit the cause of the problem yourself. Ask such questions as, Is his poor performance isolated to a particular type of task? When did his poor performance begin and were there any significant events that coincided with the deterioration in his performance? How poor actually is his performance? How did I measure it? What data did I use? What are the detailed symptoms of the problem? Have I seen such symptoms elsewhere? What hypotheses can I form for the cause of the problem? What would I expect the symptoms of each hypothetical cause to be? To help you answer these questions, below I suggest nine probable causes of an employee's poor performance, causes that derive as much from how an employee is managed as from the employee himself.

To illustrate my point, let me present an instance of an employee's poor performance that was due almost entirely to my bad management. I once assigned the task of designing the dialogue and screen formats for a large online interactive system to a programmer/analyst named Charlie. After he'd been on the task for about six weeks, I went to find out how he was doing. He was doing terribly. The dialogue he'd come up with was counter-intuitive and awkward, the fields on the screen were arranged in an unnatural order, and each screen was so crowded that it was all but impossible to comprehend. I had no alternative other than to scrap Charlie's work and assign someone else to do the task.

Unhappily, because of its having been delayed, this task found its way on to the project's critical path, and I found myself called into the boss's office. Annoyed, he asked what had happened to the dialogue and screen task and I told him. Then, he got angry and suggested that it might be better if Charlie no longer graced the department's upholstery. I ruefully agreed and prepared to dismiss Charlie.

That evening, however, it occurred to me that of everyone concerned in this ignominy, Charlie was the least to blame. Almost all of the causes for his failure had been established by me. I knew that Charlie was inexperienced in human engineering, but no one else was available for the task. Yet, I hadn't provided him with any training or reading material. Although I could hardly devote much time for ad hoc training, that didn't excuse my lack of planning. I knew months earlier of my need for human-machine interface skills, and I should have arranged before the project began for Charlie or someone else to get the necessary training.

Worse still, when I assigned Charlie the screen task, I failed to set any objectives, nor did I check his progress until far into the project. When I told him that his task had failed, Charlie was astounded. He'd been telling everyone how much he enjoyed doing it and how he was actually proceeding ahead of schedule. Rather than firing him, I reassigned Charlie to do programming tasks. He was visibly hurt and his self-confidence was shaken. My boss thought me an idiot for keeping Charlie. "Covering up for him won't do you any good in the long run," he told me darkly. Nevertheless, I'm glad I realized my mistakes in time to avoid destroying Charlie's self-confidence completely. Even so, Charlie never trusted or respected me as a manager again.

12.2.1 Possible causes of an employee's failure

An employee may perform poorly because, like Charlie, he lacks objectives for tasks. There's an old expression "Let the dog see the rabbit," which means if a person sees his objective clearly, he is better motivated to work toward that objective. Because I didn't show Charlie the objectives of the screen-formatting task and because he lacked the experience to set worthwhile objectives himself, he drifted off in the wrong direction. Instead of creating screens that captured well-defined sets of information in a comprehensible way, he attempted to break the world's record for cramming the greatest number of fields onto a single screen.

A second possible cause of failure is if the employee lacks adequate training to do a task well. Even if I'd assigned Charlie a clear objective for the screen-formatting task, he would probably still have done the task poorly, for he had no experience or training in it. How, for example, would he know what a well-defined set of information was? As project manager, it was my responsibility to make sure he had the training before he began the task, since the success of my project depended on it.

A worker may be judged a failure if his performance is not measured accurately against the objectives set for him. So, if you intend to fire an employee for poor performance, make sure you measure that performance correctly. What first appears to be a lack of productivity may be due instead to a faulty or incomplete measuring technique.

For example, a programmer named Jim acquired a reputation for extreme slowness in a shop where coding speed was of the essence. He had once been the leading light of the programming staff, but now he often took two or three times longer to code a program than other programmers in the shop. However, when Jim's new manager closely examined his supposedly poor performance, he found that Jim was spending well under twenty percent of his time on the job. The rest of his time was taken with unofficial training of new programmers, who were told to "see Jim if there's anything that you don't understand," with meetings on programming standards, and with advising the maintenance group on enhancements to an ancient system in which he'd been marginally involved. Given the amount of time he was allowed to do his primary job, Jim's performance was in fact excellent, in both quality and quantity.

If you intend to evaluate an employee's performance against an objective, ensure that the objective is the same one that you set the employee. I know firsthand of being set one objective implicitly and being measured against another one explicitly from working in a shop like Jim's, where speed of completion was always the unstated primary goal of any task. On one occasion, management gave my fellow programmers and me an especially tough assignment. We did what we thought was a superb job; we turned out some fairly decent code and didn't miss the deadline by much at all.

But our self-congratulation soon turned to horror. Our manager had attended an inhouse management course, from which he learned (correctly) that after a task is accomplished, its results should be measured against the task's original objectives. Unfortunately, he interpreted these objectives in an unexpected way: He called in a team of hot-iron boys to measure the machine efficiency of the code we had written. Of course, this team of microsecond hunters found a bounty of redundant defensive code, slow COBOL verbs, and other spectacularly irrelevant indictments of our work.

Needless to say, we were bitter. Thenceforth, we insisted on having written statements of the objectives of every future assignment. If our performance was to be measured, we also insisted that it be measured against our stated goals, rather than some retroactively trumped-up ones.

Another possible cause for the poor performance of an employee is being set objectives that are either too large or too small for his skills. Performing a task with major objectives can be a challenging and rewarding experience, so long as the employee knows that the task requires careful planning and organizing. However, if the employee fails to realize this, he'll battle on, with dour professional pride until he gets into deep trouble. The moral: Never let an employee loose on a major task without first seeing his plan for the task. That way, you can determine whether he understands the job's scope and whether he can handle it.

Continually receiving trivial tasks, on the other hand, is frustrating for an experienced worker. He may feel slighted, lose interest in his work, and do nothing, or he may decide to greatly enlarge the scope of his tasks or do something completely different from his assignment. His attitude may become negative, as he belittles the work of others who have more interesting tasks. To remove this problem, replace the scraps of work with a challenging job by which the worker can be fulfilled. Neither the too-large nor the too-small job is an effective use of a worker's talents and skills.

Occasionally, an employee is fired because he is judged on his behavior, rather than his performance. An old and probably apocryphal story about Henry Ford goes this way. In an attempt to improve the efficiency of his company, Ford called in an ergonomics expert to study its organization and the employees' productivity. After several weeks of intensive research, the consultant submitted a preliminary oral report to Ford: "I'm happy to say, Mr. Ford, that you have very few problems in your firm and most of those problems are minor. There is, however, one exception. Down the hall, there's a man who does nothing but lounge in his chair with his feet on his desk and stare fixedly at the ceiling. Why, that man is wasting thousands of your dollars every year."

Henry Ford replied softly, "The man you speak of once had an idea that saved us millions of dollars. When he had that idea, his feet were planted right where they are now."

Ford demonstrated in this story that he possessed a talent essential in a good manager: the ability to distinguish between an employee's performance and his behavior. What's important is the worker's contribution to the department's overall assignment. Behavior within limits of acceptability is at best secondary and in some situations irrelevant, as Mr. Ford realized.

Data processing people, and programmers in particular, are notorious for their aberrant and sometimes bizarre behavior. As a personnel manager once told me resignedly, "It goes with the territory." Sometimes, programmers' irregular conduct is caused by the job itself, as when computer response time is significantly faster at night, for example. For this reason, as well as his having fewer disruptions from phone calls and meetings and avoiding rush hours twice a day, a programmer named Ted chose to work in the evenings. But as he worked later and later every night, he appeared at the office later and later the following morning. Eventually, his routine meant that he would regularly arrive around lunchtime and work until after midnight. His productivity doubled, the quality of his programs improved, and his own enthusiasm for the job flourished.

Ted's happy state suddenly ended, though, when the boss of Ted's boss stormed into the office. "What's behind all these rumors that your people wander in and out at all hours of the day and night?" he demanded. "Is this a DP shop or a summer camp?" As a result, Ted's manager issued this edict: "The official company working hours are from 8:30 a.m. to 5:00 p.m. All staff, without exception, are required to be at work during these hours." Ted sullenly accepted this martial law, but his spirit as well as his work deteriorated. Worse still, some of his colleagues blamed Ted for precipitating the crackdown. Three months later, Ted quit "Camp Granada" (as the DP shop became known by other departments).

As a manager, evaluate the productivity and behavior of your staff on an individual basis, and do not assume that unusual ways of working are necessarily bad. However, neither are they necessarily good. Extreme work habits may in fact decrease the individual's productivity, as they may also impair his colleagues' work, or alienate users, or add to your management burden. In Ted's case, strange working hours not only hampered communication with managers and analysts, but they also created problems with the rest of the staff members, some of whom undoubtedly resented the special treatment Ted received. How, for example, were they to know he worked until midnight? For all they knew, he put in a five-hour workday. Your job as manager is to exercise careful judgment in order to decide who really is performing, who of those with their feet on their desks are actually burned-out disgruntled employees, and who are saving you millions of dollars.

Since nobody can be good at every possible job, an employee may well fail because of an inappropriate assignment. So, if you assign a task to a person who has adequate training and if he fails to perform as well as his colleagues, he's probably unsuited to that job. You may want to give him more time in his new position, however, in the hope that what he needs is more experience. But uppermost in your mind should be the thought of moving him to a position more suited to his talents and temperament. An example comes to mind of a programmer trainee who made a poor programmer but an excellent data processing librarian. Alternatively, you might move him to a position having fewer, easier, or less critical demands.

You shouldn't decide on such a transfer unilaterally, however, but you should discuss the matter with the employee concerned. Not only will the decision be better, but he also will feel happier about the resultant transfer if he has a sense of self-determination about it.

A mild case of demoralization is very similar in its symptoms to a lack of motivation, as I discuss in Chapter 13. In more severe cases of demoralization, an employee may be drained of all spirit and confidence. Lacking the energy even to resign his job, he merely waits, daring you to fire him. A demoralized employee has usually been psychologically beaten up in some way. Unless he has personal problems, the most likely psychological thugs are within your own shop or the user community, possibly his staff manager, his project manager, or a user manager.

An example of a demoralized employee is Charlie of the ill-fated screen-formatting task. In another case, I recall a skilled software toolsmith named Bill who was assigned to a project manager named Ben. Ben told Bill that he needed a report generating tool for the users within two weeks. Bill gladly obliged, working sixteen-hour days and weekends in order to deliver the tool and its user manual in the required time. Once Bill delivered the tool to Ben, that was the last anyone ever publicly heard of Bill's report generator. Because of a political dispute between Ben and the user department, the users refused to accept the tool. Only a month later, Ben asked Bill to write a generalized help facility for interactive systems. Just before Bill finished it, Ben told him to stop work on it because he needed another tool more urgently.

At this point, Bill became utterly demoralized, sullen, and uncooperative. His next annual performance review was so poor that he became even further demoralized. Soon afterward, he was fired for unmanageability and for having attitude problems.

Demoralization is a serious malaise, which requires a deep-reaching remedy. Merely soothing the troubled employee is rarely enough. It's best to remove the demoralized employee from his demoralizing environment—or better yet, remove the environment from the employee. In the preceding examples, Charlie and I, as well as Bill and Ben, should be separated in order to allow Charlie and Bill to recover their morale. So that such demoralization is not repeated, it's important that Ben and I learn from our mistakes and, in Ben's case, that the causes of his political problems and debilitatingly shifting priorities be eliminated before they claim more casualties.

A final cause of an employee's failure to perform well is personal, physical, or mental health problems. In *Management: Tasks, Responsibilities, Practices,* Drucker says that no one can hire just a hand; a whole person comes attached to that hand [Drucker, 1973]. Similarly, as a data processing manager, you cannot just hire a brain; you also hire a mind, a body, and a soul. This is an advantage, since the whole person applies all of his own creativity to the job. However, it also is a disadvantage especially if that person is unwell.

Some managers discourage their people from bringing their private lives to work. This is a mistake, because a managerial dictate cannot dissect a person into his components and force some parts to stay at home. If a worker has personal or health-related problems, he brings them along to his job, regardless of whether he should or not. Consequently, for those employees who are open about their personal problems, encourage them to discuss them. For another employee who prefers to keep his private life private but who shows a new or negative or destructive attitude toward you, his job, or his fellow workers, approach the situation with great delicacy. Possibly the source of the worker's low productivity or irascible behavior lies within the shop. You may be able to discover the reason for the employee's difficulties by talking to one of his colleagues. For example, begin the conversation with, "Harold, you've been close to Jim for some time now. I've noticed that Jim is preoccupied and talks to himself in the hallways." If Harold doesn't feel that he's breaching Jim's confidence, he might be able to indicate why Jim seems to be troubled.

If you cannot discover the causes by such means, gently encourage the reticent employee to tell you about any external causes that have contributed to his change in attitude. These may be health problems (including alcoholism), social changes (such as divorce), or financial problems. In such sensitive areas, don't try to address these problems yourself. Seek the advice of your Personnel Department. Suggest that the employee visit either the company's own counselor or an outside one. It's fair to tell him that you'll keep his job open if he attempts to overcome his adversities, but that you make no such guarantees if he makes no attempt. Your primary duty in the end is to preserve the harmony of the shop for everyone, and secondarily to attend to the well-being of each employee.

12.2.2 Possible reasons for firing an employee

Although you should avoid firing an employee, there are times when dismissal is unavoidable. Chief among grounds for dismissal are these four: dishonesty or unethical conduct, insubordination, company reorganization or shrinkage, or extreme incompatibility.

If an employee indulges in criminal or other destructive acts, you have an obvious case for dismissing that employee, and even taking legal action. Examples of such acts are deliberately deleting master files, sabotaging a project, leaking company secrets, or embezzling company funds. Even in these extreme cases, you should try to discover why the employee behaved as he did. Otherwise, how can you be sure that someone else won't commit such an act?

In the case of an employee's insubordination, I concur with Voltaire: "I may disapprove of what you say, but I will defend to the death your right to say it." Unlike many trigger-happy managers, I never fire someone merely for disagreeing with me. In fact, I encourage people to poke holes in my ideas, because I find that to be the best way to check whether I've covered all the bases in my planning. However, when each person has had his say and I've decided on a course of action, everyone had better cooperate as a team. There are times when you're justified as a manager in being dictatorial. If, for example, after an open discussion, I decide that all programming must be done in Pascal, I will not accept a Basic fanatic who insists on programming his modules in Basic.

If an employee refuses to cooperate when decisions do not go his way, you're quite justified in dismissing the employee before he spreads sedition and anarchy among your other staff members. However, it's only fair to give offending employees a harsh warning and the chance to change their attitude before firing them.

If your company or department undergoes a reorganization or shrinks in size, you may have more people than jobs. In this case, you unhappily must dismiss people who have done no wrong. However you carry out this action, it will be traumatic. The best way to decide whom to lay off is similar to how you choose people when hiring. Define each job in the new organization. Place the best-suited person in each job so defined, trying to balance each person's potential and experience. The people who cannot be placed must be laid off or, if possible, transferred to other departments.

Several companies have enlightened policies for handling mass dismissals, which take precedence over anything that you can do. For example, a company may refuse to lay off long-serving employees (or will give them a full pension for early retirement); it may ask for voluntary resignations for some remuneration before beginning dismissals; it may actively assist dismissed people to find new jobs; or, if it can afford to do so, the company may avoid mass dismissals entirely, allowing natural attrition to pare down the work force.

If an employee is extremely incompatible—that is, you cannot find a job that he can do well or find a position where he can get along with others—it's time to consider firing him (although by the time you get around to this decision, he may have gotten the hint and resigned voluntarily). Also if, in your judgment, an employee's personality or personal problems are destroying his performance and appear to be incorrigible, you are justified in dismissing the employee. However, you must be guided more by your own human compassion, conscience, and ethics in such a matter than by any general advice that I can give you.

12.3 Summary

Two of the most important managerial responsibilities are hiring and firing employees. To carry out these closely related tasks effectively, you as a manager must understand exactly what skills you need to carry out the work you are responsible for.

To hire the right person, you go through a six-step process. First, define the job in terms of its roles and the personality, skills, and tasks required for each role. Next, advertise the position, being careful not to demand unnecessarily specialized skills or experience. Select interviewees by carefully reading their resumés and by comparing the "be-know-do" of their resumés with that of the position to be filled.

In the interview, with possibly other staff members to contribute additional viewpoints, ask questions that probe the candidate's "be" and "know" qualities that are essential for the job. At the end of each interview, compare your evaluation of the candidate's "be" and "know" qualities with your fellow interviewers' evaluations; select from all the applicants the one who comes closest to matching the profile for the job. Bear in mind that low "be" ratings are usually harder to correct by training than are low "know" ratings. When the new recruit arrives in the department, be sure to properly orient him to the shop and to the corporation in general.

Not everyone that you hire need be a permanent employee: Contract workers or consultants can supply special skills or additional labor needed only temporarily or intermittently, and they can provide a detached viewpoint. However, they demand increased supervision and can complicate relations with the permanent staff.

Never fire an employee if you can avoid it, because losing an employee represents both a loss of an investment and a loss of continuity to your shop. Before you even consider firing a person, look carefully for the reasons for his poor performance, unmanageability, or recalcitrant attitude. Solicit his help in solving the problem. The solution may lie in improving your management of the employee; in changing his job by enlarging it, by reducing it, or by transferring the employee; in restoring his morale; or by helping him to address his personal troubles. Often, the worst solution, however, is a curt dismissal without any other attempt to solve the problems of the offending employee.

Chapter 12: Exercises

1.   Imagine that you are interviewing a potential recruit to your understaffed shop. The candidate looks good to you, but he demands an assignment on a CICS system within a year; otherwise, he says he won't join your crew. Currently, there is no such project in your shop, but one is planned to begin in about six months' time. What would you do?

2.   Imagine the same situation except that the prospective candidate wants to work on a CICS system today or she won't accept the job. The project for which you want to hire her does not intend to use CICS, but another project in your shop does. What would you do?

3.   Assume that your shop has recently decided to install database technology. However, you're having trouble finding someone with the three years of IDMS experience that the first open slot requires. The probable reason is that your company's pay scale prevents you from offering a competitive salary for the position. At last, however, a reasonable candidate has appeared, but he has only one year of experience in IDMS. What would you do?

4.   Review the dismissals that you've carried out during your career. What was the reason for each one? With hindsight, do you think that you could have usefully avoided any of them?

5.   Look around your shop. Whom would you fire if you had your choice? why? What alternative action short of dismissal could you take in each case that would be more beneficial to the shop?

6.   For each of these eight cases, consider whether the employee is exhibiting an idiosyncrasy of behavior that is deleterious to his or others' performance; behavior that is not harmful to his or others' performance; or a definite problem of attitude. What managerial action, if any, would you take in each case?

    a.   an analyst who openly and continually refers to the ideas of his fellow analysts as "male bovine droppings."

    b.   a programmer who never arrives before 4 p.m. and who works until after 2 a.m.

    c.   an analyst who rarely arrives before 4 p.m. and who works until after 2 a.m.

    d.   an analyst who continually brings you tales of other analysts' poor relationships with the users.

    e.   a well-established employee who suddenly begins to sexually harass other employees.

    f.   an analyst who wears sandals without socks, who never stops talking about science fiction, and who lives (unbeknown to the corporation) in a small orange tent hidden in a copse on the edge of the corporate campus.

    g.   a programmer who calls into question to everyone but you your ability to manage your project.

    h.   a fellow manager who calls into question to everyone but you your ability to manage your project.

7.   What kind of reference should you give to someone whom you fire: a good reference, a bad one, or no reference at all? (Hint: There have recently been lawsuits by people over references from former employers.) What is your company's policy on references?

13

Developing Your Staff

As a DP manager, you have a crucial responsibility to develop your staff. In this chapter, I cover three primary ways of developing people: giving them the ability to contribute to the organization; providing them with the opportunity to contribute; and stimulating them to contribute fully. These three ways are, in short, education, promotion, and motivation.

13.1 Education

In Chapter 12, I recommended that you hire inexperienced people with potential, but potential that's not developed is as useless as a pile of bricks in a snowstorm. Even solid experience can quickly become obsolete in the tempestuous climate of computer technology unless it is continually reinforced by education. Therefore, one of your chief duties is to support your staff members' need for training in their particular discipline.

Education is not cheap, but it is far less expensive than ignorance. However, if you truly believe that you cannot afford to send your employees to conventional commercial classes, try an alternative such as peer-group discussions on topics suggested by data processing books. Or, investigate renting training movies, videotapes, or computer-aided learning. Another choice might be local university or adult education courses.

Whatever course of action you choose for staff training, don't abdicate responsibility for personnel development entirely to the corporate education department or leave the training up to the individual project managers. To be sure, the education department can be of great assistance in your staff's training, and equally surely, project managers benefit from having better qualified staff. But there first must be a plan for continuous training of the DP staff. Your responsibility is to define what training is needed and ensure that it is duly carried out.

If there is no plan, training will be either inadequate or inappropriate, and may result only in confusing your staff. I regret to say that I have seen this happen more often than I care to remember. In one company, for example, there seemed to be no logic whatsoever behind the series of seminars and workshops presented to the DP department. All DP personnel attended courses on three different ways of conducting analysis. Next came a course on structured design, followed two weeks later by a design course from a guru who taught that the structured techniques were no good. "So do it *my* way," he lectured.

There are several advantages in having training carried out as the responsibility of staff managers, rather than its being done by project managers or by a corporate department. First, the training plan can tackle a discipline on a broad front, since it is not confined to satisfying the special needs of an individual project. The training can also be more innovative, for example, by introducing people to new techniques in software productivity, even though no project explicitly calls for such expertise. Furthermore, training can be standardized more readily when it is organized as a staff activity than in random, project-by-project training.

A problem with handing over the training responsibility entirely to project managers is that the only training they can be expected to provide would be directed at some specific project requirement. It is certainly not their responsibility to provide major and continuing training to project members, since the project's main purpose is to enhance the users' business, not to develop the workers' skills, although this is a beneficial side effect. Therefore, any formal on-the-project training suffers from these limitations: It is highly specific and limited to the needs of the project; it has short-term goals, being conservative in nature and unlikely to offer education in avant garde techniques; and it is circumscribed by the relatively small amount of project time and money available for training.

In developing a training plan, staff managers can analyze the needs both of ongoing and future projects and coordinate the training of personnel with the projects' timetables. In this way, people can be trained in groups, thus saving money, and project managers can be assured they will have competent workers when they need them.

I realize that this may sound easy. It isn't. Careful planning requires a commitment of both time and money. Shop managers voice their objections to staff training, for example, "In our shop, we're too busy fighting fires to take time for training." Or, "Our turnover is high, and I'd merely be providing training for the other shops in town." Or, "I don't want training; I want employees who don't need any training." My response to these concerns is that by ignoring training, the managers' respective problems will only increase. Without training, both systems as well as the people working on them are on their way to becoming obsolete. Moreover, turnover may well decrease if employees are given the chance to develop their abilities. Unfortunately, an employee who doesn't need training doesn't exist.

Staff managers often must make difficult compromises both in balancing a project's need for skilled people with people's need for education and in matching various projects' needs for training. As with most compromises, nobody is likely to be entirely pleased, but the alternative is rampant individualism and lost control of staff development. Unplanned, uncontrolled training may be satisfactory in the short term but is detrimental over the long run to the shop and everyone who works in it.

13.2 Promotion

As employees mature and gain experience, some are promoted, often to management positions, in order to expand their contributions to their shops. For a promotion to succeed, careful analysis of both jobs and people by staff managers is required. Also, training programs need to be established to ensure the success of newly promoted people in their new positions. Such a program forms part of the long-term plan for the development of your staff.

Unfortunately, many promotions are not successful, with disastrous results for the shops as well as for the people promoted. When things go awry, contemporary cynics offer the Peter Principle in explanation.[1] Although spouting a well-known maxim might help to mend injured pride with a veneer of worldliness, it undermines any genuine effort to understand the problems and to overcome them.

In order to fight the view that the Peter Principle governs the corporate universe and that promotions must eventually cause every corporation to be staffed by bunglers, I present ways in

---

[1]The Peter Principle states, Within an organization, a person tends to rise to his level of incompetence [Peter and Hull, 1970].

which the Peter Principle can be cheated of any further victims, followed by a look at the reasons that many people do become the prey of the Peter Principle.

13.2.1 Successful promotions

The Peter Principle is not a preordination: Incompetence in new managers is not inevitable, but is a problem that can be solved by carefully planning promotions. There are two related purposes in making promotions: One is to make the best possible use of people's talents, and a second is to fill vacant positions with the best people available. However, these two purposes conflict in that someone who is promoted to a position has, almost by definition, little experience in that position and is thus hardly likely to be the best person for that position. Conversely, if only highly experienced people were appointed to vacant positions (either from outside your company or from elsewhere within it), you would never tap the full potential of your staff.

This conflict is not irreconcilable. Remember that all of us at certain times in our careers find ourselves in positions that we haven't mastered. Merely in changing jobs (never mind in being promoted), we're likely to display incompetence until we acquire experience in the new position. Although a promotee may lack the experience of an outside candidate, he has two tremendous advantages over the outsider. First, he is thoroughly familiar with the company's rules and procedures and thus needs less training in those areas. Second, he is well known to you as the manager doing the hiring; you know his strengths and weaknesses and can fortify the promotee's skills through training.

How do you decide which skills to fortify? You can answer that question simply by treating a promotion in the same way you would treat any hiring of any person. Go through the procedures in Chapter 12 for matching a person to a job: First, determine the roles needed for the vacant position, and describe each role in terms of its "be," "know," and "do" components.[2] Then, evaluate the qualifications and personality of each candidate and determine the differences between the job requirements and the candidate's attributes. The significance of the various differences will determine the best candidate, together with areas that will need to be strengthened with training.

13.2.2 Unsuccessful promotions

There are three major causes for promotions to be unsuccessful: faulty job design; lack of follow-up; and promotion for the wrong reasons. Let me explain each cause in some detail.

The first cause, promoting a person to a job that's almost impossible to do, is seldom recognized as a problem. Unfortunately, as Chapter 5 pointed out, the too-small job, the too-large job, and the job designed for an individual's unique set of skills are not that uncommon. Instead, when the new manager errs, everyone concludes "Aha! Promoted to his level of incompetence at last." What they don't realize is that *anyone* would probably have failed at the job. Only after a stream of successive tenants quickly passes through the position does anyone begin to wonder about the job itself.

The second reason that promotions are unsuccessful is when they are carried out hastily with either no follow-up or little provision for training the employee. Some managers seem to think that the way to effect a promotion is to slap the person on the back, write a congratulatory memo, and say, "Zap, you're a manager." The following conversation is not atypical:

---

[2]Appendix C suggests twelve qualities that are desirable in a manager. However, every management position requires additional specific "be," "know," and "do" qualities. [Albrecht, 1983] describes a technique for developing such a plan and for plotting the possible career paths of a data processing employee.

Boss: Frank, I thought you did a good designing job on the HOSERS project. I'm going to promote you to manager of the NERDS project. Whaddaya say?

Frank: Gee, thanks, Boss! Will I get a raise?

Boss: Of course, about fifteen percent. Do you think you can handle the job?

Frank: Well, yes, I guess I'll manage somehow. When do I start?

Boss: Monday. [Thinks to himself] I wonder if I've made a good decision. Oh, well, if he doesn't work out, I can always fire him.

The problem with this approach is that a person cannot go to bed one night a good designer and wake up the following morning a good manager. To be an effective manager, one needs a panoply of skills. Although no person has all these skills innately, with training he can brace up even the weakest of his managerial talents. Unfortunately, however, a nascent manager who undergoes instant promotion is usually denied the opportunity to make up for his shortcomings. Instead, from his first day in management until his last, many a manager spends all his time and effort on fighting the fires that his own deficiencies helped to ignite.

The third cause of unsuccessful promotions is awarding them for the wrong reason. As I said above, promotions should be made to make the best possible use of your people's talents and to place the best people possible in given positions. However, promotions are sometimes awarded (or denied) for reasons that have little to do with these objectives. Although there are probably as many wrong reasons for promotions as there are promotions that fail, I identify ten of them in the paragraphs below, with the last four actually being wrongful *denials* of promotions.

- Promotion as a reward usually follows this pattern: "Flossie did a good job on the STEPS system. Let's promote her to project manager as a reward." However, if you were Flossie's manager, could you be sure that Flossie is anything more than a good technician? Can she manage more than her own activities? Or, might her reward turn out to be a hell on earth for her future staff as well as for her? Moreover, does Flossie really want to be promoted, or will she feel she has to accept the decision in order to get a raise, increased prestige, and to further her career? Chances are that if Flossie did a good job, she's more likely to become a good manager than someone who did an average or poor job. But her doing a good job does not relieve you of the responsibility for evaluating her specific management potential. Neither does it obviate the need to cultivate those of her management skills that are wanting.

- Promotion in submission to an ultimatum is obviously bad. An example of an ultimatum is if Leopold says, "I'll leave if I don't get a management position right now." In such a case, I'm tempted to say, "Goodbye, Leopold!" On the other hand, since Leopold has stated very clearly one of his immediate personal goals, take the opportunity to try to understand his talents and motivations. If he can be developed into a manager, then all well and good. If not, then try to find another suitable position for him. (Incidentally, think about why he threatened to quit. If that's his style, discourage him from throwing down gauntlets. Or could that be the only way to get through to you?)

- Promotion of the most visible (or audible) person is not often successful. An employee's visibility can be a laudable quality if it signifies, for example, his high reputation, willingness to work hard, and so on. Often, however, a person's being highly visible may be the result of a less admirable quality in his nature (boorishness, perhaps).

Thus, a promotion for Lucian because he always speaks up in meetings is not clearly a good enough reason. Does this mean that Lucian always contributes original and intelligent ideas to the group? Or does he make himself noticed by engaging in hyperbolic oratory worthy of a used car salesman? Being well-known and being prepared to speak out on issues are obviously able indicators of leadership in a potential manager. But by themselves, they are not enough. If they are not backed by more solid characteristics such as talent and proven productivity for the position, they constitute very flimsy justifications for promotion.[3]

- A fourth entirely unjustified reason for promotion is to move an ineffective person from his current position to another where his lack of talent is less likely to be noticed. The problem is that this so-called solution doesn't solve anything. It even makes things worse, as co-workers see how well incompetency is rewarded, and as the ineffective person has new opportunities to foul things up at higher, more critical levels of the organization.

I experienced just this situation firsthand in a shop where I worked: "Peasemold isn't much good as an analyst," the DP department manager commented on the eve of Peasemold's promotion. "He'll do less damage as a project manager." What the manager should have done is first of all to try to find out *why* Peasemold wasn't a good analyst. Could his analytical abilities be improved, or could he be better placed in another, nonmanagement position? If the manager concluded after this evaluation that Peasemold was hopeless as an analyst, the chance of his making a good manager would be tiny. And if he wreaked damage as an analyst, then Peasemold as a manager would behave like a Visigoth enjoying a weekend of pillage in Rome.

The only way to effectively neutralize someone like Peasemold by kicking him upstairs is to make him the manager of nothing. He will thenceforth haunt the organization forever, appearing at meetings, watching silently, and disappearing again. Other employees will see him pacing the hallways, waiting for day's end, and writing meaningless memos in order to look busy. One corporation I know is heavily staffed with Peasemolds and resembles a scene from *The Night of the Living Dead*. Kicking people upstairs is a waste of resources.

- Promotion to satisfy tradition is a fifth bad reason. Some positions are traditionally filled by promoting someone within the organization. If no one inside the organization is suitable, it's clearly unwise to be bound by tradition. Introducing outside people injects beneficial new ideas into DP shops, which can become rigid and static without fresh members joining their tight little families and thus lack what geneticists call "hybrid strength."

- Promotion to fill a quota may not serve the department well, especially if the quota requirements have nothing to do with the position to be filled. Promoting Brunhilde simply because she's female and a Baffin Islander, may be worth two points for the price of one on the quota scale but is both extremely patronizing to Brunhilde and of little value to anyone else. If Brunhilde has management potential, however, the promotion has some validity. If she does not, and if you really need a female Baffin Islander in your management ranks, take a boat to

---

[3]Appendix C suggests some of these characteristics, as does Chapter 1 of [Schoenberg, 1980].

Pangnirtung and hold a week of interviews in a local hotel to find someone who will be a talented manager.

- Just as bad as awarding promotions for the wrong reason is denying promotions for the wrong reason, such as denying a promotion to avoid unbalancing a quota. If for example you want to promote Levesley, who is a Tierra del Fuegan, but the quota of Tierra del Fuegans is filled and your management insists that you promote a Mesopotamian, denying the promotion to Levesley is wrong. If Levesley is the best person for the job in his own right, promote him anyway. But also keep your eyes open for likely Mesopotamians.

- Promotion may be denied an employee for a personal reason, either because the employee is bald or fat or thin or of a different gender or race than the manager. This criterion for determining a promotion is usually applied subconsciously. There is a tendency for management within a corporation to become a sort of select club whose members are all stamped from the same mold. Each member of this club tends to try to preserve the club's homogeneity. However, to exclude people who are different in some way is at once unfair and wasteful of resources that are already scarce enough. In addition, the caste of managers that results— again, lacking in hybrid strength—becomes dull, conservative, and inward-looking.

- Always recruiting an external person, rather than promoting from inside the organization, is as bad as the above reason. Although there are advantages in bringing in outside talent, valuable talent within your shop must be tapped whenever possible. Furthermore, excessive hiring from, external sources can make the culture of a shop so lacking in homogeneity that people cannot work together effectively.

- Finally, refusing a promotion for fear of losing a good worker is unsatisfactory, albeit understandable. You always hate to lose a highly competent technical person to management. But, if he shows good management skills and is himself ready for management, promote him. Then if you're correct about his potential, you'll have a rare gem: a technical artisan who can also manage people.

13.2.3 Achieving success after promotion

Of course, in making promotions, you cannot hope to be one hundred percent successful in your selections. The chemistry of an effective manager is both subtle and powerful, and the only accurate test of a person's management prowess is how well he actually succeeds as a manager. Therefore, you can almost guarantee that every new manager will have some failings.

There is no need for you to allow these failings to give the Peter Principle validity. To minimize their inadequacies, upper-level managers should continue to provide managers with regular management training *after* as well as before their appointments to management. (Don't forget to provide yourself with regular training, too!)

Although such training should be aimed primarily at improving their management skills, managers also need to keep up with the cascade of technological innovations. In no field is this statement more valid than in the field of computers and data processing. One DP project manager once graphically described the difficulty of keeping current in his field: "I feel as though I'm paddling my canoe against a rushing torrent of technology. I devote all my energy just to staying in the same place. I keep paddling out of fear, because if I stop, I know I'll be swept away forever."

To be effective, every data processing manager must be at least familiar with the new hardware and software products and techniques that his staff members either are or should be using (although they can't possibly be as technically expert as the technical staff).[4] Without keeping current, a manager may well drift into premature retirement on the job.

13.3 Motivation

Your staff members will be prepared to develop themselves, to strive for excellence, and to contribute more to your shop if they are motivated to do so. Unmotivated people do only as much as they must in order to get by, and they do not make any extra effort to enhance their performance or the performance of the shop. You cannot even successfully educate unmotivated people, for you cannot force unwilling, uninterested people to learn.[5]

How *do* you motivate your staff? The most obvious place to look for ideas is in the literature on motivational theories. These theories are useful for establishing broad parameters of human behavior, and for predicting in general terms what factors are likely to motivate or demotivate employees. Unfortunately, this body of theory presents some very confusing advice to a manager trying to motivate his people. For example, should you reward and punish people to get them to do what you want (theory X and behaviorism)? Or should you assume that people basically want to work and this gives them the responsibility to get on with it (theory Y)? Or should you try to integrate each person's whole being into the organization and blend into cooperative units to accomplish the project's or department's objectives (theory Z)?[6]

Table 13.1
Maslow's Levels of Human Need

	Levels	Examples
BASIC NEEDS	physiological safety social	being hungry needing job security belonging to a team
GROWTH NEEDS	esteem self-actualization	feeling of having done a good job needing to develop

In the confusing welter of theories to explain a person's drive to do a good job, I think that Maslow's now-classic theory serves as a good starting point for understanding motivation.[7] Maslow indicates five levels of human need, which are listed in Table 13.1 in order of priority.

He proposes that a person first tries to satisfy his most important, physiological needs. Then, a person proceeds to satisfy his next most important needs, and so on down the list. If we apply this theory's implications to a DP employee's motivation, we see that a person's three basic needs must be adequately satisfied for a person simply to function at his job. If those are satisfied, he is not further motivated by any additional provision of these needs. For example, if a person earns

---

[4]But don't take this to the extreme that I observed in one shop. There, managers spent so much time in conferences on the leading edge of technology that they had no time for work!

[5]As the headmaster at my school used to announce ponderously at least once a year, "Education is a drawing out and not a pushing in." The pupil must therefore take an active role in his own education.

[6]Theory X and Theory Y were put forward by [MacGregor, 1967]. Behaviorism is a branch of psychology propounded by [Watson, 1919] and popularized by [Skinner, 1953]. Theory Z is a term coined by [Ouchi, 1981].

[7]For an account of psychologist Walter F. Hubner's expansion on Maslow's work [Maslow, 1954], as well as Hubner's superb checklist of eighty-eight ways to stimulate motivation and remove demotivation, see [Giegold, 1982]. See also Chapter 3 of [Thomsett, 1980] for an excellent account of later developments of Maslow's work.

a reasonable salary, extra pay will not of itself motivate him to work better. On the other hand, a dearth in any of these basic needs demotivates a person very rapidly. A person who believes he may be dismissed at any moment is unlikely to be enthusiastic about his job, for he lacks a feeling of safety.

The two growth needs, by contrast, are indeed motivational. If his job augments a person's self-esteem or his self-actualization, he will feel very positive and enthusiastic about that job. He will also strive to excel at that job so as to increase his self-esteem (and possibly his self-actualization).

Motivational theories notwithstanding, my own conclusion is that everyone has his own particular motivation for wanting to do a job and for doing it as well as possible. When I assign a task, I try to put myself into the recipient's shoes and ask, "Why should I bother to do this job? What's in it for me?" There are as many answers as there are people in the shop, including these:

- "I want to do a good job because my review is coming up soon."
- "I want to do well because I'm looking to be promoted."
- "I just want to do enough to get by without getting fired."
- "I'm a perfectionist and I must do a good job."
- "I want to do the same quality of work as the rest of the team; I don't want to be singled out as being different."
- "I'd like to work hard at the job, but I can't because I don't get along with the rest of the team."
- "I want to be the best analyst in the shop."
- "I don't want to do this job at all; I can't wait to get out of this place."

The motivations of data processing people are as varied as DP people themselves. As the old Yorkshire proverb says, "There's nowt so queer as folk." I amend this proverb for modern times to read: "There's nowt so queer as data processing folk." There was a programmer on one of my projects who loved to type structured programs into the computer so much that he would even type other people's programs for them. "I just get a kick out of seeing that indentation," he explained. The trouble was that he spent more time fiddling with the format of his programs than he did making sure that the programs were correct. I know of no theory that would have predicted that programmer's motivations.

Despite all the books on motivational theory, no theory seems to be very good at predicting exactly what will motivate an individual employee. For example, we know from Maslow that depriving an employee of his need for safety demotivates him. But what exactly does that mean? Project manager Ernie may feel serenely secure even though many of his colleagues are being dismissed. Analyst Bert, on the other hand, may become neurotically insecure merely by having his desk moved to another office.

As another example, we know that people are motivated by their need for self-esteem. But Harold may be able to experience self-esteem only through a well-publicized promotion, whereas Helga may be able to derive self-esteem from seeing a job well done and an array of delighted users.

No theory therefore can answer satisfactorily the question of how to motivate each employee in your shop. In the end, you must try to answer it yourself, based on your understanding of the particular needs that fuel their personal drives. Then, you must decide how to fulfill these individual needs while still pursuing the aims of your shop and its projects.

This is not an easy task because it requires that you develop an intimacy with your staff members that is not traditional—at least not in our culture. If you don't develop such a rapport, however, you continually run the risk of demotivating your staff unintentionally.

13.4 Summary

One of your main objectives as a manager is to develop your staff members through education, promotion, and motivation. Education is best organized as a staff function, rather than as a project function, since it is a long-term effort that must extend beyond the boundaries of individual projects. Furthermore, projects lack sufficient resources to carry out general training. Corporate education departments are highly valuable in providing the actual educational service, but they cannot be expected to develop the educational strategy for the data processing department. This planning must remain the responsibility of DP staff managers.

Promotions are awarded in order to satisfy two distinct objectives: to make the best possible use of your people's talents and to fill a vacant position with the best available candidate. However, promotions have so often failed that they have made famous the Peter Principle. Understanding why they fail gives you a chance to defeat the Peter Principle. Promotions fail as a result of any of three causes: the job itself is not doable; the promoted person receives inadequate training before or after being promoted; or the promotion is made for the wrong reason.

To achieve a successful promotion, first carefully analyze the job to be filled and then evaluate the attributes of the candidate for promotion. The differences between what the job requires and the candidate's skills determine the specific training needed before the promotion.

A new manager should not be left to sink or swim. Instead, his training should continue after his promotion, not only in management skills but also in current DP technology. If training is not continued for all levels of managers, the most innovative people in the shop will be forced to leave from sheer frustration at the disparity between their understanding and that of their managers.

The third task in staff development is motivating employees. Although many theories on human motivation exist, including Maslow's hierarchy of needs, no theory can substitute for your familiarity with your own people. Only through your own efforts can you step down from the generality of theory to the specific idiosyncrasies that motivate each person in your shop in a different way.

Chapter 13: Exercises

1. Assume that training has always been neglected in your DP department. Over the years, there have been many excuses for this. Currently, upper management vetoes any training above the barest minimum, because of the department's high personnel turnover (more than thirty percent per year). As a DP staff manager, how would you react to the situation? How would you react as a DP project manager?

    (Hint: Consider different possible causes of high personnel turnover. How would you find the cause(s) of your department's problem? How would your reactions to the situation depend on the causes of the high turnover?)

2. Some corporate bonus schemes award an employee a percentage of his salary in recognition of his contribution to the corporation. This percentage varies from person to person according to his relative contribution. Other corporate bonuses are in the form of profit sharing, with each employee receiving the same percentage of his salary as his bonus. Suggest a bonus scheme that takes into account an employee's contribution over a given year and reflects the total previous corporate investment in that employee through, for example, training. What would be the effects—both good and bad—of such a scheme?

3. If you were the boss depicted in the conversation earlier in the chapter, and Frank turned out to be a bad manager, what would you do?

4. If sufficient salary is enough to satisfy a person's physiological needs (for example, food and shelter), of what motivational value is a raise?

    (Hint: Consider the symbolic values of a salary. Consider also salary to be a bridge between a person's work life and his personal life. How might salary be a means for a person to move through the hierarchy of needs in his personal life?)

5. Variety of work is often cited as being a strong motivator (or at least a strong stimulator). What are the advantages and disadvantages—both to the shop and to the particular individual—of providing each worker with a varied sequence of tasks? What type of person might be frightened, rather than stimulated, by variety?

14

Establishing a Productive
Working Environment

The productivity of data processing professionals depends greatly upon the quality of their working environment. While they can be educated, promoted, and motivated to the hilt, it will all be in vain if obstacles in their surroundings impair their ability to work.

Of course, I do not suggest that every analyst, designer, and programmer be provided with an oak-paneled office, a plush carpet, and a private secretary. What I do recommend is that every person have a working area that's as free as possible from disruptions, and that everyone have easy access to tools and facilities.

Poor employee performance and job dissatisfaction cost a shop much more than the provision of adequate working conditions. Providing extras often improves workers' abilities; for example, wall-to-ceiling whiteboards in meeting rooms can aid complex planning sessions. As a result, so-called extra resources more than pay for themselves in increased worker productivity.

14.1 Effect of poor conditions on productivity

Although the need for an adequate work place seems obvious, I am continually astonished at how bad the environment in some shops actually is. There are primarily four closely related categories that these poor conditions fall into: overcrowding, disruptive surroundings, communication difficulties, and a lack of facilities. Below I give an example illustrating how wasteful each condition is.

14.1.1 Overcrowding

Without doubt, you can save rent and office overhead by packing as many people as possible into your available square footage. However, such overcrowding is a false economy, since it is bound to ruin your staff's performance. The following story illustrates why: A friend of mine was employed as a programmer in a large industrial company. His office measured about fifteen feet by thirteen feet, and it had a large table in the middle. The bad news was that he shared this office with five other programmers, not all of whom worked on the same project. They had no private storage space, only communal shelves where everything had to be dumped each evening so that the big table could be dusted.

At one end of the table was a single phone. However, its number was incorrectly listed in the company directory, so that the six programmers were continually interrupted by wrong numbers. The newest programmer, as a consequence, was elected to occupy the seat next to the phone to take messages. Occasionally, all six occupants of the "Black Hole" (as the room was known) were ejected at short notice to accommodate an impromptu management meeting; and during lunch time every day, they had to yield the table to the company's bridge club.

Stunned that my friend could put up with such detestable conditions, I asked him, "How can you stand this? How can you get any work done?" He replied, "Oh, it's not so bad when you get used to it. And next week, they're moving in a coffee machine."

Not every programmer was as stoic as my friend, as evidenced by the high rates in turnover and absenteeism in both the Black Hole and the rest of the shop (where conditions weren't much better). As you'd expect, the quality and quantity of software produced was very low. Yet, unbelievably, corporate management refused to lease any more space for the DP department. Small, but well-measured, savings in building costs had resulted in large, but unmeasured, losses in data processing productivity.

14.1.2 Disruptive surroundings

An unfit working environment often results from thoughtlessness, rather than a deliberate attempt to reproduce the offices of Scrooge and Marley. For example, one solution to the problem of accommodating workers in a limited space is the use of cubicles, essentially small offices created by arranging self-standing vertical partitions. Since each cubicle houses a single employee, it's a way to ensure some privacy. However, unless cubicles are carefully chosen and arranged, they actually contribute to a disruptive environment.

Some of the most notorious menaces to privacy and tranquility are cubicles that are open on one or even two sides; those that open on to well-tramped thoroughfares or are located next to a coffee machine or water cooler where everyone gathers; cubicles that are tiny; and those with low sides that can be peered over.

Cubicles are often so poorly arranged that they resemble shantytown housing more than a professional office environment. Such an arrangement is typically a source of continual distraction and interruption. One of the oddest setups I ever encountered was a labyrinth of partitions that required passage through others' cubicles in order to reach one's own lair. Inhabitants of this maze were constantly interrupted by baffled and obviously disoriented strangers asking, "Where does Jane sit?" One frustrated analyst, whose cubicle was located at an especially busy crossroad, sighed, "I get more work done going home on the subway." An even more peculiar feature was their unsystematic coloring in some of the most offensive hues in the visible spectrum. (A wag posted a sign that read, "Welcome to Rubik's Cubicles.")

Data processing work demands long periods of concentration in order to achieve both quality and quantity of output. Even if physical conditions are not conducive to privacy, instill into your staff a tradition of respect for individual privacy. Also, do whatever you can to promote peace and quiet. Several effective techniques include screening the occupant of a cubicle from passersby; providing "Do Not Disturb" signs, with the rule that the signs must be heeded; and allowing the use of stereo headphones to drown out ambient sounds. Let your staff members decide what they feel is best for them, within reason of course.

14.1.3 Communication difficulties

Facilitating communication between people is tough enough without the working environment's adding further hurdles in the path. Nevertheless, some managers seem to go out of their way to make communication difficult. Even something so simple as where project team members sit in the shop can make a big difference. Although circumstances may prevent all team members from sitting together in a cozy family unit, I cannot understand why so often the other extreme prevails.

For instance, one project I encountered had its analyst/designers on the sixteenth floor of a building, half its programmers on the eighth floor, and the other half on the ninth floor of a building across the street. The project suffered from communication overhead, with numerous phone calls and formal meetings. Some errors that could have been easily avoided in the design's interpretation were directly attributable to the seating arrangements. The moral of this tale is a team that works together must sit together.[1]

14.1.4 Lack of resources and facilities

The supply of resources and facilities, which include everything from computer test time to pads and pencils, can directly influence worker productivity. But sometimes, the effect can be subtle. For instance, in one shop where I consulted, programmers were not allowed to enter the line printer room to tear off their printouts personally. Fair enough, you say, since most shops have similar restrictions to prevent a free-for-all in the operations area. However, this shop's only alternative was to deliver listings on a large cart every four hours. So, if you printed your program listing, say, at noon, you could have it in your hands at either 12:10 p.m. (if you were astoundingly lucky) or 4:10 p.m. (if you weren't).

This practice tended to decrease productivity by forcing programmers to work with outdated listings for longer than they should have, but it also discouraged them from listing as much as possible as often as possible and to waste time continually trudging off to see if "anything's back yet."

Management finally ordered a large hole knocked through the wall between the printer room and the terminal room and installed racks of mail boxes, one per account number. Then, the operators simply stuffed any output for a given account into its corresponding mailbox, whence its proud owner could pull it out whenever he wished. Both programmers and operators agreed that this new scheme was a big improvement and that with it, they could get their work done faster and more accurately.

14.2 A radical alternative

A possible solution to these problems is emerging with the advent of personal computers. The alternative to merely improving the workplace is replacing it with an entirely new one: the home. By telecommuting, the programmer stays home but his program goes to work.[2]

The following story illustrates how a lack of programming facilities could be overcome by a radically new way of working. Some DP departments are notorious for having more programmers than computer terminals for them to use. Lack of crucial equipment for them to do their jobs is disruptive, costly, and frustrating for all concerned. In one shop that I visited, programmers waiting for vacant CRTs milled around as aimlessly as teenagers in a shopping mall. The department manager told me that they'd tried different ways to share the scarce resources, such as having programmers take next-to-be-served numbers; limiting sessions to one hour; signing up in advance for sessions; and instituting various odd/even day schemes and shift work. Unfortunately, none of the attempted solutions was satisfactory.

With my famous devastating ability to solve at a stroke a seemingly intractable problem, I suggested, "Why don't you install more terminals?" The manager gave me a withering glance that

---

[1]Melcher, for one, disagrees with this rule, observing that personal conflicts within a team may increase if team members sit in close proximity [Melcher, 1976]. However, I feel that if a team is more disposed to fighting than cooperating, it can hardly be called a team in the first place.

[2]The term *telecommuting* was coined by [Nilles et al., 1976].

said "wise guy!" and opened the door to a store room. Inside was a stack of unused CRTs. "If we hook up any more of these," he explained, "our response time would go through the roof." I thought it politic not to pursue this conversation further with any talk of leasing a more powerful CPU or extra memory.

Telecommuting offers two possibilities to this shop's problem. First, using a home computer to simulate an online shop terminal solves one problem (the lack of physical terminals), but it doesn't solve the problem of a too-large computing load on the host mainframe. Moreover, it may require the use of slow communication lines between the smaller computer and the host. So, a second, better possibility is to use a home computer with communication software to transmit data in "batch" mode. This not only creates an extra terminal, but also removes a large amount of drudgery from the mainframe computer. The programmer can transmit his data either over communication lines in the evening or on floppy disks transported to the office.

Working at home may bring benefits in its own right, quite apart from the addition of terminals.[3] A difficulty with the traditional workplace is that its conditions are often detrimental to the high-precision tasks of data processing. Software design and programming in particular require periods of deep concentration followed by times of more relaxed, creative thought. The office environment, however, is rife with involuntary distractions (such as phone calls, reminders that it's lunchtime, and queries of the type "do you know where the YOBS folder is?").

In a DP department, in which people were allowed to work at home for two days per week, I carried out a straw poll of the programmers who had worked at home. These programmers reported that their productivity changed from an increase of one hundred percent in the best case to a decrease of twenty-five percent in the worst case. The programmers whose productivity improved gave the following reasons: time saved with no commuting; a more relaxed environment at home ("I like to pace around when I'm thinking"); easier to concentrate with fewer interruptions and without endless meetings; and convenience in working odd hours ("I'm a night person and it's more convenient to work until 2 a.m. at home").

For those programmers whose output worsened, their reasons included being disrupted even more at home than at work ("My wife doesn't believe that I'm supposed to be working; she keeps trying to get me to paint the garage"); and being easily distracted ("I'm so bored and lonely at home; I just can't seem to get motivated" and "At home, I do anything but work. I clean up; I go out; I watch television . . . anything!").

Clearly, since working at home isn't for everyone, it must be evaluated case by case. You must also consider its possible negative effects on those who work at the office. One difficulty, for example, may be scheduling meetings when some necessary participants can't be there. Also, there may be resentment by fellow workers who want to work at home, too. The situation may destroy the communal spirit of the shop, not to mention the chances for communication, if only about twenty percent of its members are present at any one time.

Nevertheless, with the cost and strain of commuting increasing all the time, telecommuting appears to have a firm place in our DP future. Despite its drawbacks, it offers the ability to move the working environment out of the traditional workplace and let the bytes, rather than the people, do the traveling.

14.3 Summary

As a staff manager, you are responsible for the working conditions that let your staff members perform to the best of their ability. You need not transform the office into a haven of luxury, for you are not on a spree of philanthropy; neither are you angling for the eternal gratitude of your

---

[3]For an in-depth treatment of this topic, see [Olson, 1983] or [Deken, 1981].

staff—there will be none. But for sound business reasons alone, you must remove all the obstacles that you can from the working lives of your employees. This includes exploring such radical alternatives to the traditional workplace as telecommuting.

Chapter 14: Exercises

1. An open-plan office is a large room with many workers but with no partitions between them. What drawbacks are there to the working conditions provided by an open-plan DP shop? Are there any benefits?

2. Have the members of your staff form a group to (a) list the various ways in which their productive time is sapped by unproductive activities, and (b) suggest ways to reduce this wastage. What problems would the suggested ways to improve productivity cause you as a manager?

15

Working in a Mediocracy

A "mediocracy" is an organization in which the mediocre prevails. Most people in a mediocracy are mediocre in both mind and soul, and most products of a mediocracy lack merit. Although a few individuals in a mediocracy may strive to rise above the second rate, their attempts are likely to be doomed by the prevailing ethos of their surroundings.

Sad to say, many data processing departments are mediocracies. These shops hug a narrow brow of dullness, being unable to scale the slope of high quality but also just avoiding the chasm of complete extinction. Such shops deliver systems that are barely passable and retain personnel who are virtuosos of the banal. Yet, they produce just enough that works in order to survive.

In this chapter, I first examine the causes of a DP mediocracy and describe its negative effects. I then offer ways to change the mediocracy, depending upon your level in the organization.

15.1 Causes of a mediocracy

From my description, you might conclude that a mediocracy is just another department suffering from poor hiring practices or some other ill that I described in previous chapters. In fact, all the problems that are generally and unthinkingly lumped under the Peter Principle contribute notably to the development of a mediocracy. However, the full explanation for its genesis and for its differences from a department that simply has problems is both subtle and complex.

To help identify the underlying causes of a mediocracy, I use a cause-effect diagram. This tool, which is explained in more detail in Appendix B, is shown in Figure 15.1. To the immediate left of the problem I'm investigating (the mediocracy), I identify two prominent, closely related causes: the formation of employee cliques who work for their own good, rather than for the corporate good; and the tendency of employees to gain self-advancement through denigrating others' work and reputations. These each have their own causes, as shown in the diagram. If you follow Figure 15.1 all the way to the left in each branch, you will arrive at the five primary causes of a mediocracy: absence of well-defined objectives for projects and the department; weakness of the formal organization; employees' desire for self-advancement through competition rather than cooperation with fellow employees; departmental problems that limit employees' ability to perform well; and chronic self-perpetuation of a mediocracy.

15.1.1 Absence of well-defined objectives

With well-defined objectives for tasks, there is a kind of absolute scale against which to measure people's performance. Hence, it's possible to gauge reasonably objectively people's true

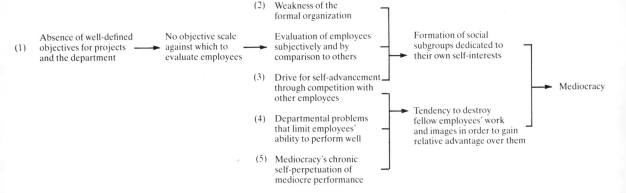

Figure 15.1. Cause-effect diagram.

contributions to the aims of their department. It's also possible, again with at least reasonable objectivity, to decide whom to reward for their efforts and achievements.

Without well-defined objectives, however, managers have little by which to measure people's performance objectively and little basis for deciding how to reward people. Instead, people's contributions are judged subjectively according to the whims of the evaluator and relative to the contributions of other people. This, in turn, tempts workers to advance themselves by discrediting others, rather than by making substantial improvements to their own performance. It also encourages people to behave sycophantically, rather than honestly, toward their bosses and results in unproductive image-building efforts rather than productive work.

15.1.2 Weakness of the formal organization

As explained in Chapter 5, the formal organization is basically the organization depicted on the company's official charts with positions defined by job descriptions and objectives. The informal organization is the formal organization adapted to fit real circumstances and the actual personalities of the members of the organization. Without the framework of a sound formal organization to give it a fundamental structure, the informal organization must do the duty of the formal organization as well. As a result, the organization is subjected to the random forces of the organization's various strong personalities, which coalesce into groups united in bending the organization to serve their own social and business aims. These often unstated aims do not necessarily benefit the organization as a whole. For example, a group of people unites behind a pet project that interests them, such as the development of a robot that is technically fascinating but that has no market.

Some employees may not belong to any subgroup and so, denied an opportunity to contribute to departmental society, they feel alienated from the department. They thus form a loose subgroup of outcasts who snipe at the deeds of others. They become the bitter, antisocial employees who are found in almost every mediocracy.

15.1.3 Desire for advancement through divisive competition

Competitiveness and individualism are two of the cornerstones of our Western culture. Competitiveness in moderation is a healthy quality, since it tends to stimulate people's innate creativity and their desire for improvement. In the business world, this quality means, for example, that each of two competing airlines continually works to improve service to its customers. A single monopolistic airline, on the other hand, may well stagnate in complacency for lack of any incentive to improve.

Unchecked competitiveness, however, can be downright harmful. For example, nobody benefits if Hogwash Airlines sets its schedules so that passengers miss connecting flights on Codswallop Airlines. Furthermore, if Codswallop Airlines starts a rumor that Hogwash's pilots all are dropouts from the West Fredonia Air Force Academy, again the cause of commercial air service is not furthered.

This unethical and unproductive type of competitiveness is akin to rats in a rat race, an attitude that is totally unacceptable when it is shared by professed colleagues within an organization. Unfortunately, it is exactly this internecine destructiveness that reigns supreme in a mediocracy.

The achievements of a department are the achievements of its people. In an effective department, each person works toward his allocated subset of the department's goals. In the malignant competitiveness of a mediocracy, however, people expend much of their energy on their own self-advancement, largely to the neglect of the department's needs. They may do this by frenzied attempts to look good to their bosses and to be the star.

The cult of the individual superstar is another aspect of our culture that has grown out of all proportion to its true value. Though uplifting, the saga of the brilliant innovator who ran with an idea to become the hero of the hour has little relevance to a modern corporation. The spirit of independent and individual success is not a realistic spirit in today's complex organizations, for the simple reason that one person cannot singlehandedly take on the problems of a whole department and hope to solve them. It fails, too, because it leads to disharmony, rather than coherence in the contributions of a department's workers. Contributions thus tend to cancel one another. Just as farmers know that plowing is faster when the horses in the team all pull in the same direction, so too all the "horses" in a DP department must pull together, especially since the many technical intricacies involved call for full cooperation by many skilled people, rather than for random and uncoordinated solo efforts.

Not only does unbridled competitiveness lead to the poor integration of people's efforts, but it also leads to divisive contests to prove who is the best. No one can truly win such damaging struggles. Unfortunately, members of mediocracies often spend more time engaged in contests than they do in genuine work. Often, they seek to win out over fellow employees not by dint of their own efforts, but by sabotaging or belittling their colleagues' efforts. Thus, an archvillain in a mediocracy not only wastes his own time but also wastes the time of many other people. His motto is, Get ahead at all costs, even if it means climbing over the corpses of colleagues. Of course, if everyone goes by this motto, there will be a great deal of carnage and very little advancement. (I once asked a DP manager in a mediocracy how many people worked in her department. "About half of them!" she replied with a grin.) Ultimately, the mediocracy reaches the point at which no one is prepared to do anything significant for fear of having any ostensible failure held against him.

One veteran of a mediocracy graphically described the situation: "The best way to stay alive and live in peace here is just to go through the motions of working, but to avoid at all costs producing anything visible. Otherwise, everybody criticizes it and delights in pointing out its flaws and your own patent incompetence. Ironically, the better your contribution actually is, the more uncomfortable your colleagues become and the more likely they are to attack it.

"Right now, for instance," he went on, "Eldridge is broadcasting to everyone that Walter's project should have been completed by June, and Walter is retaliating by advertising that Eldridge's project is way over budget. Theodore is trying to ward off criticism by discrediting me with my users, but I'm better at discrediting *him* with *his* users. By now, none of our users trusts any of us."

In short, then, the ruinous effects of uninhibited rivalry in a shop are these: Individuals' efforts are uncoordinated with one another; people spend too much time in competing rather than contributing; people engage in destroying others' contributions; and people become conditioned to do nothing visible, innovative, worthwhile, or controversial so as to avoid the criticism of their colleagues.

15.1.4 Problems that limit employees' ability to perform well

A department's decline into a mediocracy is accelerated if that department has problems that constrain employees' performance in some way. For instance, a lack of training limits a worker's ability to perform well. This not only reduces the quality and quantity of the department's achievement, but also frustrates the employees themselves. These frustrations fuel the fires of competition, since the easiest way to advance oneself when one's own performance is circumscribed by factors beyond one's control is by demeaning others' performance in some way.

Departmental problems, therefore, often act as catalysts for a decline into mediocracy. However, the removal of these problems does not necessarily allow the department to recover from mediocracy, as we shall see below.

15.1.5 Chronic self-perpetuation of mediocracy

In an oddly recursive way, a mediocracy is one of its own causes and is thus self-perpetuating. Specifically, there are three ways in which a mediocracy constantly suppresses the overall level of performance of its staff: First, a manager in a mediocracy usually hires new employees who are especially insipid in order to reduce the risk of his being usurped by someone who is more competent than he is. This results in the well-known mediocratic phenomenon of the bland leading the bland. (Some recruiting firms contribute to this effect by referring only mediocre candidates to a shop that has a reputation itself for being mediocre.)

Second, employees who are truly competent and are eager to make a genuine contribution to the department soon resign from a mediocracy, leaving behind them the dross of nonproducers and internecine warriors. I term this effect the Inverse Gresham's Law: A mediocracy hoards mediocre people and drives good people into general circulation.[1]

Third, a chronic mediocracy incorporates mediocrity within its basic culture. Such mediocracies are thus extremely difficult to redeem, as I discuss in Section 15.2.

One particular incident comes to mind as an archetypal example of the counterproductive shenanigans in a mediocracy. Alison was a project manager in a large mediocratic DP department. Igor worked on Alison's project. Igor wasn't the most talented or well-liked person, but Alison was stuck with him. She couldn't fire Igor solely for disliking him and no other manager would take him.

Then, Alison had a brain wave: Roland was a new project manager who needed a database designer for his project. Alison could solve her problem with Igor by passing him off as an IMS expert, even though Igor's knowledge was limited to writing database calls in COBOL programs. Although every other manager knew this, Roland was grateful for getting Igor. Alison was overjoyed. In one stroke, she had rid herself of Igor and slipped him into Roland's project as a sort of Trojan Horse. Oh, perfidious Alison!

Sure enough, with Igor on the critical path, Roland's project slipped further and further behind, with only a woefully inadequate database to show for the time spent. Eventually, Roland relieved Igor of any database responsibility, but it was too late. Roland's boss relieved Roland of

---

[1]Gresham's Law is a tenet of monetary theory that states when two units of currency are equal in debt-paying value but unequal in intrinsic value, people will tend to hoard the one having the higher intrinsic value and force the other into general circulation.

responsibility for the project. Who looked good in comparison to Roland? Everyone, especially Alison. Unfortunately, she had used her resourcefulness not to help the department, but rather to destroy one of its contributors. And that's typical of how a mediocracy operates.

15.2 Responses to a mediocracy

Your ability to bring about change in a mediocracy depends upon your position in the organization. If you're close to the bottom of the hierarchy, there's very little you can do. Any individual's effort at that level, by the very nature of a mediocracy, is likely to get neutralized. The best you can hope for is to form a grassroots coterie and, either by diplomacy or revolution, work together to rid your shop of the oppressive yoke of mediocracy. Unfortunately, however, your efforts may be misinterpreted as political maneuverings and subverted by the usual mediocratic machinery. Your best bet is to subscribe to the Inverse Gresham's Law and to find a shop that will truly appreciate your talents.

If, on the other hand, you're at the middle level of the organization, you do have a chance to make inroads into the mediocracy. Start by offering your colleagues help and encouragement without any strings attached. Once they overcome their bewilderment and accept that your cooperation is genuine, your colleagues may begin to follow your example and help one another.

Set a similar example to inspire the people who report to you. By training and grooming them as I described in Chapter 13, you encourage them to excel and thus liberate them from their lackluster limbo so that they can realize their full potential. But remember one constant, brutal fact: You're still in a mediocracy, and all your good intentions may very well come to naught. The mean-souled multitudes may defile your good examples and seek to destroy you. Even your boss may become nervous of being usurped and do his utmost to suppress you. If such attitudes persist, I think that the Inverse Gresham's Law deserves another recruit: Vote with your feet.

If your position is high in the mediocratic organization (for example, you head the DP department), you have the best chance of all to exorcise the mediocratic hobgoblins. Your first lines of attack are at three of the primary causes of a mediocracy: absence of well-defined objectives, weakness of the formal organization, and departmental problems that limit employees' ability to perform well. As a top manager, you are in a position to establish an effective formal organization, such as a matrix structure, and valid shop objectives to defeat the first two weaknesses. As a high official in the mediocracy, you are also obviously in the best position to tackle any problem that limits employees' performance.

Your greatest impact in a mediocracy, however, is that you alone can deal potently with the two most troublesome causes of a mediocracy: people's drive for self-advancement through pathological competitiveness, and the mediocracy's tendency toward chronic self-perpetuation. The reason is that both of these causes are cultural in nature and the culture of an organization is difficult to change. An organization's culture is established by the people at the top levels of the organization, through unwritten laws, powerful personalities, and precedents; and the culture is disseminated through the organization by role models and examples. Therefore, it is only the top-level people who can change the culture.

In order to rid your shop of mediocracy, therefore, you must explicitly end the cultural patterns that give rise to and perpetuate the mediocracy. What specific steps should you take then? First, outlaw all political infighting within your shop, reminding everyone that playing politics is the first resort of the incompetent. Set a good example yourself by not indulging in such activities, and punish anyone who persists in Machiavellian machinations—even going so far as to fire him for more than one serious offense.

Encourage cooperation and a team spirit among your people. Foster the attitude that what counts is contribution to the shop and not the acquisition of individual kudos. (A slogan I once saw on a DP shop's wall was borrowed from President John F. Kennedy: "Ask not what your company can do for you. Ask what you can do for your company.") Encourage egolessness by instituting such practices as walkthroughs. Further the cause of excellence by setting up quality circles in which people can convene to improve the shop as a whole. Again, show that you're serious by setting a good example yourself. Demonstrate that you're not afraid of talent by hiring skilled people into the shop and by thoroughly developing the talents of your current staff members.

Explain to everybody that interdependent, cooperating employees form a much stronger and more powerful department than do independent, naturally competitive employees. Point out that you all have similar big problems, but they are not necessarily bigger than all of you together can solve.

Communicate that your new ethical code is to cooperate with your fellow employees in order to best serve the overall goals of your department and your company. If the whole company benefits, so also does everyone in the company. Conversely, if the company suffers, so do all its employees, and being a pack of squabbling rats on a sinking ship is hardly an ideal employment situation.

Of course, you won't be able to transform your mediocratic department overnight. The longer the mediocracy has persisted, the longer it will take you to change it. Even when you have conquered the mediocracy, a modicum of politics will remain. There will always be politics so long as there is more than one human being in your shop. If your department has a sound formal organization, firm objectives and a cooperative, meritocratic culture, your shop will no longer fall easy prey to as many plots, cabals, and conspiracies as in 19th century Europe. Politics will be constrained by your new manifesto of excellence and good service.

As a footnote to this section, let me present two warnings about what not to do about a mediocracy. My first warning is, Do not spend vast sums of money on schemes to improve appalling employee relations. Such schemes as lavish Christmas parties and boondoggles to industry conferences held in tropical climates do nothing for improving professional employee relations over the long term. They cannot solve the problem of a poor formal organization.

My second warning is, Do not introduce detailed policies, standards, and procedures into the shop without understanding their impact upon the organization. By introducing policies and procedures, you may intend that everything will be rigorously defined and that therefore everyone will turn out excellent products in a cookbook manner. Unfortunately, introducing such rigor into a mediocracy usually spells disaster for two reasons. The first reason is that if the procedures are developed or tailored inhouse, they are themselves a product of the mediocracy and are likely to reflect the mediocre qualities of the host organization.

The second reason is that when the bureaucracy mandated by the detailed policies, standards, and procedures is superimposed on the mediocracy, the resulting structure is even more stifling. The mediocracy becomes enshrined forever in a probably mediocre set of painstakingly elaborate procedures. The effect of this is that the procedures become religious dogma to be followed without question. As soon as anyone tries to escape the prescribed path, his deviance will be exposed in a type of religious inquisition by his colleagues. Everyone will become trapped like flies in amber by the new bureaucracy. Eventually, obeying the procedures will become an end in itself, and a more important end than producing products. The mediocracy will reach a new depth of vapidity.

Therefore, before introducing policies, standards, and procedures into your organization, consult a text such as [Mintzberg, 1979] for a discussion of the good and bad aspects of a bureaucratic structure and its relevance to creative technical work. Then, if you decide to establish procedures, make sure you first expunge any mediocratic problems from your organization. If, for example, you set up a shop with policies, standards, and procedures, but without any objectives and rationales, you will have created an environment fit only for lifeless automata: an ultra-mediocracy.

15.3 Summary

A mediocracy, examples of which are unfortunately provided by many DP departments, is an organization in which the mediocre prevails. Mediocracies are typically composed of overly competitive, undisciplined employee factions, which war with one another in attempts to gain relative advantages. The primary causes of a mediocracy are fivefold: absence of well-defined objectives for the organization; weakness of the formal organization; employees' drive for self-advancement through competition with other employees; departmental problems that limit employees' ability to perform well; and the mediocracy's tendency to self-perpetuate.

Your ability to rectify a mediocracy depends greatly on your place in the organization. If you are at a low level, you unfortunately have little chance to affect anything and your best response may be to resign. At the middle levels, you have the chance to set a good example and to spread forth excellence in a middle-out approach. However, without strong allies to your cause, your attempts may also be doomed.

At the top of the organization, however, you are in a good position to make an all-out assault on the primary causes of the mediocracy, including the pervasive mediocratic culture itself. Break down the mediocracy forcefully and set good examples yourself. Avoid, however, the traditional superficial remedies of spending large sums on employee relations and establishing stultifying bureaucratic procedures intended to enforce quality. These will only bury you more deeply in mediocrity.

Chapter 15: Exercises

1. What characteristics of a mediocracy, if any, does your shop possess? Which of the causes of a mediocracy do you think are predominantly responsible? What do you recommend to nullify these causes in your shop?

2. In this chapter, I emphasize the value of cooperation and teamwork. However, some DP people tend to be loners by choice or by their difficulty in communicating or for a variety of other reasons. How should you handle a loner? Should you assign him to a team anyway? dismiss him? find one-person tasks for him to handle? provide him with remedial therapy?

3. Would Alison's ploy with Igor work in your shop? If so, why? If not, why not? What could you do to prevent such tricks in the future?

16

Respecting Reality

In the early 11th century, there reigned over England a good and powerful king named Canute the Dane, whose navies ruled the seas from Greenland to the Baltic. Canute's power was reputed to be so great that when it was said he commanded the seas, his obsequious courtiers believed the sea itself would obey him.

Canute set out to demonstrate how foolish were these beliefs. He ordered his throne be moved to the shore of the English Channel. There, in regal splendor, he and his courtiers awaited the tide to come in. With all the pomp and majesty befitting his position, he commanded, "O tide, cease thy flow!" The tide, however, continued to flow in, and Canute and his lackeys got rather damp. The moral that Canute thus bequeathed to us is, Pompous human dictates are powerless to stem the inexorable tides of reality.

16.1 Three stages of shunning unpleasant reality

Reality, when it is unquestionably benign, is welcomed by everyone. But often (especially in data processing), reality bears down with a grim visage, bringing cost overruns, missed deadlines, and technical errors. All are part of the reality that is most feared and hated by DP managers. Indeed, many managers, emulating Canute, try to quell such savage swells of reality simply by declaring that they don't exist. Such repudiation normally has three stages: denial, anger, and delusion. Not all managers, however, go through all three stages, nor do they necessarily pass through them in the order listed. I describe each of the stages in the sections below.

16.1.1 Denial of unpleasant reality

The first stage in trying to escape an unwelcome reality is to pretend it doesn't exist. This stage typically takes one of three forms, depending upon the personality of the manager concerned: ignoring reality; seeking out a fellow disbeliever in reality; or simply telling reality to go away.

Ignoring reality and trusting that it will somehow go away of its own accord is a spectacular ploy that some managers adopt in order to avoid reality. In Canute's terms, that's like burying your head in the sand and hoping that for once, the tide won't come in. But a manager who tries this ploy will drown just as surely as will the manager who tries to command reality to stay away. In project terms, burying your head in the sand means abandoning all planning and control of the project and hoping for the best. This laissez-faire approach works only for the manager who has a friendly angel to ensure that his toast always falls butter-side up, that he's always dealt a royal flush, and that his projects are always resoundingly successful. Unfortunately, friendly project angels are in short supply. Recklessly casting the fate of a project to the elements of chance usually ends in catastrophe.

Some managers go even further than blissful oblivion in their denial of reality. These managers adopt a Micawber-like pathological optimism of "Something is bound to turn up" or "It will all work out in the end; don't worry." I remember one project manager whose project fell behind schedule early in the analysis phase and whose astonishingly sanguine reaction was, "I'm glad we fell behind so soon because now we'll have plenty of time to catch up." But, as we know, however bad a project becomes, it will get much worse unless its manager takes firm action to correct the project's problems, rather than hope that the problems will somehow cure themselves.

A manager adrift on an ocean of tempestuous tidings will actively seek out good news from any source that he can. If he can find just one person who will tell him that the project is going fine, he can justifiably (in his own mind, at least) cancel the counsel of a hundred others who believe that the project is heading for the rocks. Consequently, a harried manager may ally himself with the most junior coder who says that everything's great and reject his most experienced analysts' advice if they say that the project is in trouble.

A common variant on this attempt to find a haven of succor is pointless browbeating of colleagues and subordinates until someone finally admits, "You're right; reality doesn't exist." In the following dramatized conversation between a project manager and a senior project member, the manager has an uneasy suspicion that up to a year's more work is left on the current phase of his project:

Project Manager:	Cassie, you know we need to deliver the next phase of the BRUTUS system to the users by March 15. Here it is, almost November, and I need a realistic estimate of the completion date. Give it your best shot.
Cassandra:	Well, Boss, you know that Florence has just quit, Dougal's still sick, and we won't have Brian on board until Doris gets phase 1 of the OATS project delivered. I would say sometime around the end of June, but I'll need some time to make a more accurate est—
Project Manager:	[Flustered] June? I promised the users that I'd have this system installed by March 15. Let me see the breakdown of your figures. Why is programming going to take four whole months?
Cassandra:	Because each program takes an average of four person-days to write, and we have 55 programs left. I assume we have three programmers and 19 working days per calendar month.
Project Manager:	Wait a minute! That was on the earlier part of the project. Now, the programmers are a lot smarter, we have that new debugging aid, and Personnel is advertising Florence's spot; we'll have an extra programmer in no time. I'd say two months for programming. What do you think?
Cassandra:	Boss, you said I should give it my best shot and I still say four months.
Project Manager:	Cassie, I'm disappointed in you. I thought you were enthusiastic about this project. Why do you want to drag it out past the deadline?
Cassandra:	[With a sigh] Okay, Boss, two months for programming, then.
Project Manager:	You've got another two months here for testing and integration, but we can't afford that luxury on a time-critical project like this one. We'll save a lot of time by waiting until all the programs are coded and then testing them all together. I'll allow two weeks for testing.

Cassandra:	But that way, we'll have to face the bugs all at once. It will be chaos.
Project Manager:	Come on, Cassie, there is such a thing as overdoing testing. You said yourself that we didn't have many problems in the previous phase. I'm sure we won't have many bugs from our high-quality programmers. Heaven knows, I don't pay them to create bugs. So, what do you say to March 15?
Cassandra:	[Resignedly] Oh, I guess so.
Project Manager:	Great! I'll tell the users that you estimate delivery on March 15. By the way, is there any chance we can get it done before March 15 so that we won't have a last minute scramble?
Cassandra:	[Silently] Aaargh!

The purpose of this manager's negotiation is to recruit an ostensible ally to his unrealistic views. He may have done this in order to convince himself of the validity of his position or in order to have a scapegoat to blame when everything falls apart ("But you told me we could deliver the system by March 15th.") or merely in order to feel better in the crisis. Of course, even if this boss gets everyone in the shop to deny that reality is approaching, he too will surely drown as the tides of March sweep over him.

Some aggressive managers try to deny reality by simply demanding that it go away. This technique, of course, works about as well for a data processing manager as it did for Canute. I recall a project some years ago that was in severe difficulty, owing chiefly to the abysmal quality of the technical work that had been done in the project's early stages. The result was that by the time programming was under way, the project seemed to be moving through cycles of one step forward and two steps back. The users, not surprisingly, were becoming impatient with the continual delays and the excuses from the DP department. Dinsdale, the quick-tempered user manager of the project, eventually decreed that the system must be delivered on September 1, which was less than a month away.

Doug, the project manager on the DP side, had a similar personality to that of the user manager (and hence the pair went by the secret sobriquet of the "Piranha Brothers"). He declared that, pursuant to Dinsdale's ultimatum, every project member was a coder and was to work late and on weekends in order to get the system completed by September 1. Anyone who disagreed with that policy or was seen not to be pulling his weight would be instantly dismissed. The catch phrases for the project were to be "ruthless efficiency" and "crush all resistance to progress."

But this wonderland of malice turned out to be a fantasy world, far removed from the realities of project management. The two Piranha Brothers, despite their impressive dictates, failed to conquer the might of reality; the end of this saga is revealed in the next section.

16.1.2 Anger

When a manager can no longer sustain his denial of a bleak and ever-encroaching reality, he often passes into the second stage of his repudiation of reality: anger. Managers who deny reality by means of arbitrary decrees, like Dinsdale and Doug, are often those who later indulge most heavily in anger. In this stage, an unrealistic manager tries to shake off responsibility by striking out at people around him and by nominating victims to bear the blame for his own misdeeds. (Possibly Cassandra will be cast in this role on the BRUTUS project.)

To resume the tale of the Piranha Brothers, they both exhibited anger shortly after programming had begun. As the system testers discovered literally dozens of bugs per day, everyone realized that fixing the bugs would cause the project to become months late in completion. Doug became so incensed that he fired the entire testing team for disloyalty to the project.

By September 1, the system was far from complete. Nevertheless, Doug insisted on installing what there was (bugs and all), while complaining bitterly about the users' patent inability to understand the system and their all-round ingratitude for his mammoth effort. Condemning them loudly for their incompetence, he also attacked his own programmers, rolling heads faster than during the Terrors of the French Revolution. His rage, however, was but a brief madness: Dinsdale snapped his jaws and Doug was gone, dismissed by his department manager after a terse meeting with the users.

16.1.3 The delusion of instant salvation

In the third stage, which may follow, precede, or replace the stage of anger, the unrealistic manager deludes himself that he is about to be saved by a miraculous turn of fate. This stage is especially prevalent among those managers who, in stage one, waited for something to turn up. At this later stage, with time running out, they frantically attempt to find a chimerical "something." I call this the search for the *Wunderwaffe*.[1]

The desperate manager expects his sought-after Wunderwaffe to be a miraculous tool or technique that will suddenly turn a languishing project into a stunning success. He also tries to convince others of his belief. A typical melodramatic scene has a penitent project manager pleading to a group of stern-faced users. "Just give me one more chance," he begs. "With this Wunderwaffe, I can deliver a perfect system to you in three weeks."

A hard-pressed project manager has a legion of Wunderwaffen from which to choose. Currently, there are more data processing productivity aids on the market than diets in magazines. These tools and techniques include, for example, structured techniques of various kinds, methodologies, prototyping tools, quasi-relational databases, and fourth-generation languages. Although most vendors of such products are honest and would never sell their wares as Wunderwaffen, some vendors are not so scrupulous. A rather shady vendor I once encountered told me, "There's a wealth of gullibility out there. Many managers," he continued, "are waiting for an instant mindless solution to all their troubles at once. Some managers are drowning deep in problems and will grasp hysterically at any product I throw to them."

This, in fact, was what happened in the next episode of the Piranha Brothers' project. So far, Doug's project, having passed through low-quality analysis and design phases, fell completely apart during programming, and Doug was fired. Dinsdale, from the user department, inherited the project.

What Dinsdale inherited hardly gladdened his heart. The deadline for delivery of the system had long passed by; half of the programming staff had left; most of the code that existed seemed unusable; and he had had no prior experience in DP project management. But this hour of crisis brought forth a man of salvation, in the shape of a gentleman who stepped off a plane with the latest thing in application generators. "The Norman I application generator," the vendor promised Dinsdale, "will cut your programming time by up to seventy percent and reduce your testing time to almost zero. But wait, there's more!" he went on. "If you order now, we will provide this fine product to you at a fifty percent discount as a special inaugural deal to our first customer ever."

Dinsdale was euphoric. Just when it appeared his newly acquired project would bed down with the fishes, here came a smiling vendor in a three-piece suit to throw him a life saver, and at

---

[1] *Wunderwaffe* is German for *miracle weapon*. When the Third Reich was almost in ruins, many Germans believed that such a weapon was already in production and would deliver them out of defeat and into world domination.

half-price yet! "This indeed is a sign of salvation," thought Dinsdale. Unfortunately, as it turned out, the Norman I application generator was not all that it purported to be. The so-called complete application generator turned out to be just a high-level database manipulation language, together with a rudimentary screen handling facility. It also used extremely naive transaction rollback and file locking algorithms, which simply did not work. Several other bugs in this product led to the generation of incorrect code. But the still ecstatic Dinsdale ignored these flaws. He chose to observe only how fast his team was producing lines of application generating statements and how close he seemed to be coming to delivering a working system.

In all this frenzy, no one noticed that the analysis work done on the project was shoddy. For example, the deletion of a customer from the database was permitted even when the customer had a nonzero account balance and outstanding orders. The combined result of all the problems was that by the panicked use of this unproved tool, the project team merely turned out garbage faster than ever. Dinsdale needed that application generator as much as a drowning man needs a glass of beer.

As you might guess, the project ended unhappily. The users again flatly refused to accept the delivered system and Dinsdale was removed as project manager (and, incidentally, from the company as well). The project had to be restarted from the beginning.

The moral of this incident is not to eschew labor-saving tools. Rather, the moral is, A manager of a project that is in severe difficulties must still accept the reality of the situation. Of course, if you're holed up in your managerial bunker, being shelled by volleys of problems, it's wonderfully comforting to be able to believe in a speedy salvation by means of a secret weapon. But if this Wunderwaffe doesn't arrive—or if it fails to solve your problems when it does—your managerial position may be obliterated before you have time to tune in to reality.

16.2 Whose reality is it, anyway?

In discussing the imprudence of not respecting reality, I begged the important question of how to determine what reality is. In talking glibly of an unqualified reality, I tacitly assume that reality is an objective, absolute notion. But in fact, reality is both subjective and relative. Reality, you might say, exists only in the mind of its perceiver. Therefore, how can you follow my rather trite admonition to respect reality if every person in your shop has a different perception of what is real?

The answer lies in integration. As I mentioned in Chapter 6, one of the primary functions of an effective manager, albeit the most neglected one, is to integrate the manifold realities, the personal viewpoints, of the people around him into a common viewpoint: a group consciousness. Furthermore, the manager is responsible for melding the group's view of reality with the views of other projects or departments, as well as with the view of upper management. All this requires great time and effort and, because we live in an imperfect world, can rarely be fully achieved. Moreover, the time and effort invested will be more than returned in the greater productivity of people working as true teams, rather than as motley collections of loners.

The key to the integration of differing viewpoints into a common viewpoint is effective communication. Communication in organizations is a vast subject, including the topics of effective writing, effective reading, effective speaking and presentation, effective listening, and holding effective meetings (the topic of Chapter 10). Other factors include the direction of communication, such as upward from subordinate to boss and laterally among peers. Since I cannot cover every facet of effective communication here and since [Giegold, 1982] provides an excellent list of references on effective communication, I concentrate on the most important means that a manager has to synthesize the realities of his subordinates: effective listening in the upward direction.

The upward channel of communication tends to become blocked more often than do other channels. How often have you felt "I'm just not getting through to him" when you present an idea to your boss? Either party of a communication might be responsible for the clogging of the channel, but it's the duty of the senior-level party to try to remove the obstruction. Here are some hints for clearing the communication line by concentrating on listening to the message that your subordinate is trying to put across:

First, let it be known that you're genuinely interested in your subordinate's point of view. Set aside time to talk, rather than postponing discussions indefinitely. Avoid the situation that I observed recently of a project member's reluctance to state her views to her boss because, she explained, "He's out of touch with reality." (If no one on the team speaks to him, I'm not surprised that he's out of touch! He's in a vicious cycle of isolation breeding more isolation.)

Relegate your own view of reality to the back of your mind for the duration of the conversation, and focus your attention on your subordinate's message. Try to distill the central ideas of your subordinate's statements while he's talking and, at regular intervals, compare realities with the speaker by repeating to him his central ideas, as you've understood them.

Take action on your subordinate's ideas, even if the only action can be informing him, "No action is possible at this time." Share your feelings as well as words, and watch for facial expressions that reveal how your subordinate feels. Never punish anyone for bringing an unpalatable message to you. Instead, thank him, for bearing an unwelcome message is an unpleasant task. Never attack anyone or impugn his motives for talking to you.

To some managers, my exhortations to listen effectively appear tantamount to bolshevism. I hear shrieks of "I can't run my department by committee"; "Sitting back and listening is an obvious sign of weakness and indecisiveness—I'll lose the respect of my people"; and "If you take away my power, I'll be overrun by my subordinates." I'm not implying any of those things. Obviously, as a manager, you must retain the authority to enact a decision and the responsibility for the effects of that decision. What I do propose is that before you make a decision, gain the benefit of others' perceptions of reality. Otherwise, you are more likely to lose the respect and cooperation of your people than if you do consider their views. (The examples of the previous section demonstrate this point convincingly.)

Furthermore, if you ponder reality from a solitary executive bastion, make a lone decision, and then issue an imperious dictate, you risk, first, selecting the wrong solution to the right problem; or, second, selecting the right solution to the wrong problem; or, third, causing anger, fear, resentment, confusion, antagonism, nausea, or a variety of other emotions in your subordinates. You will thus demotivate them from executing your decision willingly.

I recall a manager who believed that the way to achieve a common view of reality was to impose his own view on everyone else. On one occasion, he decided to install new word processing equipment in his office. But the way in which he made his decision caused him to fall into the first and third traps above. He chose the word processors in a methodical way, bringing in several vendors to give demonstrations and selecting the brand that he found to be best.

Unfortunately, he didn't ask the people who'd be using the word processors for their opinions on the new equipment, since that would presumably detract from his managerial dignity. The human engineering of the machines that he purchased was appalling, reducing secretaries to tears of frustration by the perversity of their new electronic tools. Perceiving their difficulties to be due to their own inadequacy and inability to rise to the age of automation, they desperately persevered, since the word processors were there by the edict of the boss. They feared that any resistance would be interpreted as disloyalty and that they would be dismissed.

However, the manager's decision was shown for what it was by one of those lunchroom scenarios that periodically make a swaggering manager look foolish. One of the manager's secretaries met a secretary from another department, and they compared notes. It transpired that the manager had bought obsolete equipment and that good, modern word processors were much easier to use. When the word got back to the department, the other secretaries felt relieved, but gradually, with reduced respect for their manager, they transferred to other departments and even to other companies.

16.3 Summary

Some DP managers do not behave realistically when reality is other than what they desire. Typically, such managers pass through one or more of three stages in their attempts to stave off unpleasant truth: denial of reality; anger against others; and the deluded belief in a forthcoming miraculous salvation. Each of these forms of behavior is detrimental to the manager's project or department.

Respecting reality depends first of all on determining what actually is real. You can do this only by soliciting other people's, especially your subordinate's, perceptions of reality. The key to this is effective communication and, in particular, effective listening, which requires not only hearing but also active comprehension of what's being said.

The result of consolidating your perception of reality with other people's perceptions may be dire news. Your project may not be in the state that you'd fondly wish it to be in. Grim situations are a test of your mettle at making hard decisions and taking effective managerial actions, because reality won't go away, either at your bidding, or of its own volition. Although respecting reality will be tough in times of adversity, you must nevertheless always keep your head and never try to refute Canute.

Chapter 16: Exercises

1.   Review your career. What types of reality have you most avoided? What were the consequences of these avoidances? What do you do differently today in order to respect these realities?

2.   How does lack of respect of reality afflict your shop? Does each person have his own pattern of aberrant behavior, or is there a common style of behavior for the whole shop? What fiascoes have recently resulted from someone's not respecting reality?

17

Minimizing the Human Toll

Is your project late or overbudget? Do your users constantly harry you with unreasonable demands? Does every demand that you satisfy spawn two more demands that you then must satisfy?

Is your staff turnover too high? Do your best people continually quit? Do your worst people demand ridiculous raises? Are your staff members refusing to work any more unpaid overtime to meet impossible deadlines?

Do you waste much of each day in playing politics? Do your colleagues stab you in the back when you try to do something worthwhile? Are you developing paranoia and an ulcer?

Did you take this job because it was the only way to get a raise and a promotion? Do you crave the technical work that you joined your profession to do? Do you worry about becoming technically stale?

Does your boss make your life hell by assigning you to all manner of unrelated tasks? Does he change their priorities daily? Do you spend so much time in meetings that you have no time to get anything useful done? Does your schedule force you to alternate between starvation and overeating? Do you have to work until midnight every day just to keep pace with your bulging in-tray? Was your last vacation during the Bicentennial?

Is there a picture of you on the wall at home so that your kids will remember who you are? Do you dream of lying on the white beach of a South Pacific island, being massaged by gentle natives? Would you settle for a Sunday off to mow the lawn?

These questions represent a summary of the exasperation of thousands of innocent souls in DP mediocracies who are consumed by torment within infernos of hopelessness. If you answered yes to more than half of these questions, you too are probably a victim of mediocratic stress. The effects of such stress on a person are both tragic and costly. They include poor performance, lethargy, absenteeism, changes in personality, mental or physical breakdown, alcoholism, premature resignation, and such vexation of colleagues and subordinates that they too are driven to quit. Stress is undesirable not only on humane and moral grounds, but also on purely economic grounds.

Mediocracies cause stress by imposing an unhealthy workload on people and by creating an unhealthy psychological environment in which to work. Both these sources of stress can be compounded by a person's own psychological traits.

In this chapter, I look first at the sources of mediocratic stress and the ways in which personal traits may add to this stress. I conclude the chapter with suggestions for ways to avoid or minimize the stress.

17.1 An unhealthy workload

Throughout this book, there are examples of the unhealthy workload that mediocracies create: the too-large job that no one person can realistically handle; the job composed of disparate, unrelated pieces; intolerable working conditions; senseless deadlines; absurd, time-consuming reporting requirements; interminable, meaningless meetings; and so on.

I recall consulting at a large mediocracy, whose recruiters blared, "With the Nil Desperandum Company, you will have the chance to grow in a challenging and rewarding position and to live in the most beautiful state in the nation." Unfortunately, the truth was that in the Nil Desperandum DP department, you would be crushed under an impossible workload and would never get to see "the most beautiful state in the nation" by daylight.

On the first day of my consultation at this company, my client, Pete, was unable to meet me until 8 p.m. "Too many fires to put out," he explained. When he finally tore himself away from his fire-fighting duties, he grabbed me by the shoulder and we headed for the local hostelry for a drink. Pete, it turned out, was the manager in charge of three fairly large projects, any one of which would be enough to fill an average project manager's day. The reason for Pete's workload was a personnel shortage, which was in turn caused by budgetary constraints.

After his fourth drink, Pete confessed, "This is the first time in a month that I've gotten out of the shop before eleven. Mine's the worst job in the world. Sometimes, my job gets so bad that I feel like everything's crowding in on me, squeezing me till I can't breathe. I always have this feeling that I've overlooked something crucial and that the whole mess is about to come crashing down on me. I literally lose sleep at night thinking about that.

"What makes it worse is that every day, my management stacks more work on my desk. As if I hadn't got enough to worry about already." Pete rambled on some more about the vagaries of his bosses and life in general. However, at 6:30 the next morning, Pete was back at his desk, finishing the status report that he'd put aside in order to talk to me the night before.

Pete was handling his onerous workload with superhuman dedication, but I wondered when something would snap. Perhaps he would have a nervous breakdown or a heart attack, or he would develop an ulcer from irregular eating habits. Perhaps his wife would leave him or his children would land in jail to get his attention. Perhaps the Nil Desperandum Company would kill the goose that had laid so many golden eggs for it.

Pete had gotten into that vicious cycle wherein management assigns a disproportionate number of tasks to the department's designated beast of burden, who can be relied upon to get them done, rather than to the departmental loafers, whose tardiness or unreliability makes them unattractive targets for assignments. In Section 17.4, I offer ways to minimize stress and recap my recommendations to Pete for the good of both him and his shop.

17.2 An unhealthy psychological environment

Because of the main characteristics of mediocracies described in Chapter 15, employees in such organizations suffer under tremendous psychological pressures. For example, a weak formal organization or one that continually fluctuates causes feelings of insecurity. As employees vie for the best positions in the mediocracy's informal organization, political maneuvering and cutthroat competitiveness determine the organization's survivors: the most political animals, who are probably mediocre workers, at the expense of the less political, who may be superior performers. This latter group, being unable to excel at intradepartmental warfare, suffer considerable stress in trying to carry out their everyday duties while under constant fire.

Communication among colleagues is low in a mediocracy. This creates high tension, suspicion, and isolation. When the loneliness becomes severe, it may transform the assurance of "it's hard to soar with eagles when you work with turkeys" into the self-doubt of "maybe I'm a turkey, too." This self-doubt compounds the stress of professional loneliness with a loss of self-esteem.

Mediocracies that result from misorganization often exhibit tangled, rather than simply nonexistent, lines of communication. Such mediocracies cause severe frustration to build because in order to gain approval for a simple action, people may have to write numerous memos, make dozens of phone calls, and hold several meetings. This overhead may require an order of magnitude more effort than the action itself.

Another cause of a mediocracy—absence of well-defined objectives—can result in responsibility without authority. In the extreme, this problem causes both frustration and anger, because employees feel they are judged by factors over which they have no control. In chronic cases, it causes complete apathy toward one's job.

When autocratic managerial decisions are handed down, such managerial aloofness results in stress for the employee who feels, "The boss makes the decisions. I don't matter." If the boss's decisions are misguided, the attitude worsens into contempt for the boss and an unwillingness to follow his decisions.

When employees feel threatened that they could be fired for showing dissent, they become insecure, as no one can be certain about what will be perceived as dissent. The fear also leads to psychological conflicts within themselves as they have to choose, in effect, between feeding their families and maintaining their personal integrity. This problem results, too, in the suppression of reality, as people decide not to tell a boss an unpleasant truth for fear that he will confuse the messenger with the message.

Finally, being insufficiently trained or being in the wrong job leads invariably to lowered self-esteem, demotivation, and a pathological defensiveness that also isolates people from one another. (In Section 17.3, I talk specifically about being in an unwanted job.)

17.3 Personal traits and stress

Different people, each with a different psychological makeup, react to the stresses of the workplace in different ways. Therefore, a mediocracy's psychological environment can affect its workers differently. There are four factors in particular that can be used to predict how a worker interacts with a mediocracy's psychological environment.

The first factor is a person's self-confidence. Every member of a mediocracy is an impersonal body battered by the impersonal forces of mediocratic dynamics; yet some people interpret each blow of a mediocratic battle as a personal attack against which they must vehemently defend themselves. This, of course, leads to poor, unproductive relationships between co-workers, since they cannot constructively criticize their peers without their taking it personally. As a result, every activity becomes stressful to those who place their egos in the firing line.

The second factor is the amount of genuine interest in the job. When a person takes a job that he doesn't really want, either for a raise or for added prestige, he soon may become unhappy and subject to stress. Of course, this problem may occur in any shop, not necessarily a mediocracy. When it occurs in a mediocracy, however, no one is likely to be concerned about the person's lack of interest. Furthermore, the uninterested worker is likely to waste his time on the political games of the mediocracy, which probably affords him more fun than his job ever does. The shop thus gains a willing and enthusiastic exponent of mediocracy. His stress at being in the wrong job thus adds to everybody else's stress, too.

The third factor is personal problems, which by themselves cause stress. Despite some managers' beliefs, no one leaves his personal problems at home when he comes to work. Therefore, these problems compound any stress caused by work pressures. I remember a project manager who was under considerable strain from financial and other worries. Irritable and short-tempered, he blamed his project team for being imbeciles and for ruining the project. Naturally, the entire team avoided him as much as possible until one day, first one team member and then others quit the project, citing their irascible manager as the reason. Eventually, he was fired, which did little good for his stress, financial troubles, or the shop as a whole except in the short term. Of course, the mediocracy didn't worry about that.

A fourth factor in the interaction between a worker and his work environment is his addiction to work. A work addict—the usual term is *workaholic*—has several telltale characteristics: He works excessively long hours, far more hours than his job truly requires (which differentiates him from Pete, who worked long hours in an attempt to keep up with the tasks), and generally takes no vacation time. If he does, he finds excuses to call the office or to return early. He continually seeks additional chores and becomes edgy if he runs low on things to do. He tends to judge others by the length of time that they work, rather than by what they produce. For example, he might make careful note of who arrives after 7 a.m. or leaves before 10 p.m.

I'm not sure whether this is a characteristic of the breed, but most of the workaholics I've met are mediocre workers. Their productivity is low; if they produce more than others do, it is only because they work so many hours. They leap from task to task, generating a lot of motion but very little progress. Some workaholics are loathe to complete a task, since once it's completed, it's gone.

Workaholic managers create stress in themselves (on which they seem to depend, as if it were a drug), in their families, and worst of all, in their subordinates. I once worked for a workaholic manager, who was also highly neurotic. Steve had the annoying habit of calling people "for a chat" in the middle of the night and of dragging them into his office on a Sunday evening merely to announce that he was uneasy about some matter or other. During normal hours, he would twitch and fidget around the shop infecting everyone with his nervousness.

Everything made him uneasy. He once told me, "I'm uneasy about Zeb. He's coding so slowly that he'll never get the reconciliation program done on time." Somewhat later, he said, "I'm uneasy about the reconciliation program. Zeb coded it far too fast. It's really critical, as you know, and we can't have any bugs in it." Then, he took the reconciliation program and spent most of one night going through it, line by line, looking for bugs. He didn't find any, but he marked several lines of code that he was "uneasy about."

Steve was also uneasy about delegating. He wanted to do most of the jobs of the project himself, and he certainly tried to, meddling in almost everyone's work. Perversely enough, however, although he tried to take work away from the team, he still expected us to work all hours of the day and night. We became extremely angry at Steve's senseless waste of our most limited resource—our time—and many of us transferred from his project at our earliest opportunity.

17.4 How to minimize stress

A plan to deal with the stress of working in a mediocracy, as well as in other shops, has two parts: The first part is to repulse or minimize the chief agents of stress, and the second is to learn to cope with the stress that remains.

17.4.1 Saying no

When, like Pete, you have more work piled on your desk than you can possibly do competently without working all night, you must simply say no. Say no to the unreasonable demands of your job, of your boss, and even of your subordinates.

When I gave this advice to Pete, he retorted, "How can I say no? I can't let my people down. If I say no to my boss, he'd fire me like a shot. I don't know what you mean by saying no to my job, but I can't take time off; there's too much to do as it is."

Saying no is tough, and seems almost impossible to do when you're experiencing intolerable pressures, guilt, and feelings of inadequacy and inability to cope. However, consider the alternatives. If you continue to accept too many assignments or those that are unachievable just to please your boss, the very thing you fear is most likely to happen: failure on a grand scale. I doubt that your boss would be very pleased with that. If his response to your telling him "enough already" is to fire you, thank him. He's a bad manager and you'd be much better off working for someone else. (This certainly isn't easy, for making a decision between an unbearable present and an unknown future may itself be a source of anxiety and stress.)

Unfortunately, saying no so forthrightly may of itself add to your burden of stress. However, there are more diplomatic ways to say no than to provoke a confrontation. For instance, take a list of your current tasks with estimates of their duration to your boss, and ask him for help. Although this may start a wrangle about your estimates similar to Cassandra's conversation with her boss in Chapter 16, be prepared with evidence to support your estimates. Your boss may not be aware of your problem and bringing it to his attention may be enough for him to lighten your backbreaking load.

If he belittles your problem, withdraw to reflect on the following possibilities: One, he's right, and you're making a mountain out of a hillock. Two, he's a louse and he doesn't care about your problems. Three, he appreciates your problem but fears saying no to the people who are overburdening *him*. Fourth, he appreciates your problem but constraints, such as budgetary ones, prevent him from doing anything, such as adding more staff or providing tools to increase productivity.

In the second, third, and fourth cases, return to your boss armed with the record of the hours that you've worked during the past few months. Tell him that if his current demands continue, you will be forced to resign. State this as calmly as you can, and don't make it sound like a threat or an ultimatum, because it isn't. You, in fact, are reasonably and unemotionally discussing your problem with your boss in order to try to find a mutually beneficial solution. You aren't reacting by simply quitting when the stresses become unbearable. That does no good at all for anyone—not you, your boss, nor those left in the shop.

17.4.2 Relax

There is little point in working long hours for the sake of working long hours, except perhaps to satisfy workaholic needs or to escape an unhappy home life. Even working hard, as Pete did, may not be productive if the strain of the job ruins the quality of your work. Sometimes, the most efficient way to work is to say yes to yourself and to turn off your job when it becomes ridiculously intrusive.

Even when you've reduced the workload to a feasible level, your work may still be stressful at times. On those occasions, don't let the job or other people in the shop get you down. Accept that you're not a machine, and take the time to look after yourself; otherwise, bad eating, sleeping, and exercise habits will harm you physically. If you become obsessed with your job, the lack of cerebral variety in your life will hurt you mentally. With too little stimulation, you will become dull in all senses of the word, and your project will suffer from having the deadened mind of a fractious, jittery captain at the helm.

Certainly, just as there are times during a project when you must work both long and hard, there also are opportunities during the project to relax. Be smart: Take them. Working smart often bears better fruit than does working long or working hard. When you escape the tensions of the shop, with the noisy telephone and huge pile of work assignments, memos, and meeting invitations, both you and your project will benefit. You will be able to calmly mull over the problems that seemed so harassing at the office. (Somehow, the unhurried unconscious mind often succeeds in solving problems that paralyze the conscious mind.) Rather than spin your wheels in frustration, take the chance to put your job, your staff, your colleagues, your bosses, and yourself into quiet perspective.

How should you relax? That's obviously up to you. Some people like to sit quietly and stare into space or watch a movie or listen to a symphony. Others prefer more physical exercise, such as tennis or golf. It is said that yet others relax by reading books on data processing, thereby assuaging their guilt, perhaps, over not working; they also can share in the experiences of other DP professionals and realize they're not alone in their troubles.

Opportunities for longer periods of relaxation arise from time to time. Don't forgo your annual vacation. Not only will it give you a break, but it will also give others a break as well. If you feel the twinge of a workaholic conscience, attend a data processing seminar if you must. But go to one in Hawaii.

17.5 Summary

Stress in workers is unhealthy, both for themselves and for their organizations. Mediocracies create stress in people by imposing an unhealthy workload upon them or by forcing them to work in an unhealthy psychological environment. Psychological stresses may be due, for example, to tangled lines of communication, responsibility without authority, autocratic managerial decisions, a rapidly fluctuating or weak formal organization, the threat of being fired for showing dissent, being insufficiently trained or being in the wrong job, cutthroat competitiveness, and loneliness.

Compounding these stresses are a worker's personality, four critical factors being the worker's self-confidence, his interest in the job, personal problems, and an addiction to work for its own sake. You do have some control over the amount of stress in your environment. You do not have to choose between meekly accepting a crushing, ever-growing workload and resigning from the shop. Instead, you can say no to the load that is placed upon you and calmly and rationally discuss possible solutions with your boss.

To counter the harmful effects of stress in your environment, take every chance you can to relax and recharge your brain cells. Create opportunities to relax if none present themselves. You and everyone around you will benefit by your relaxation. You will even perform your job more effectively. Occasional relaxation is not only more enjoyable to most people than to work nonstop, but it's also smarter.

Chapter 17: Exercises

1.   What are the most stressful aspects of your job? What symptoms of stress do they bring out in you? Have you or anyone else in your shop ever tried to do anything about these aspects?

2.   Who in your shop causes you the most stress? Why? Imagine that you are that person. How would you as that person behave toward yourself?

3.   What tasks of your job do you enjoy the most? Which do you hate the most? (I identify the most hateful tasks by noting which ones I postpone for as long as possible.) Could your job be redesigned to be more fulfilling? Is there another job with a better blend of enjoyable tasks that might be available to you?

4.   If your job was created fairly recently, find out why it was created and what were its original objectives, activities, communications, decisions, and lines of authority and responsibility. Are they the same or is the job different today? How is it different? If your job is a well-established one, describe the performance of your predecessors. What were their qualifications? What did they do in the job? How well did they execute the job? Why did they leave? Where did they go? Are they happier now?

5.   If you were to leave your job, for example, through promotion, lateral shift, or resignation from the company, who do you think would be your successor? How do you feel about that?

6.   Do you enjoy weekends more or less than weekdays?

7.   Assume that your salary, vacation time, and other benefits would not markedly change by a change in your position, and identify which of the following statements apply to you:

   a.   I would prefer my former technical job.

   b.   I would prefer to stay where I am now, but I want more management training.

   c.   I enjoy technical work most; I want to be allowed to use my seniority and experience by becoming an inhouse technical consultant.

   d.   I don't want to cause trouble; I'll put up with anything until my retirement.

   e.   My skills would be better employed at this level of the organization but in a different job.

   f.   I would be more valuable to the company if I were higher in the organization.

   g.   I don't like data processing, but
   - it's all I'm qualified to do.
   - it pays well.
   - I'm too old to change.
   - computers are the way of the future.

h.   I'm frustrated in my career by lack of mobility in the ranks above me.

i.   I'm worried that younger, more up-to-date people beneath me are about to usurp me.

j.   I enjoy/hate/fear dealing with my users/subordinates/peers/managers.

k.   I acquired this job through
     ■ my own active pursuit.
     ■ an unsolicited offer I was pleased to accept.
     ■ an unsolicited offer I was afraid to turn down.
     ■ involuntary causes (for example, through a
       demotion or after being laid off from another company).

l.   I expect to leave this job in _____ years. I hope my next job will be
     _____. I expect that my next job will be _____.

Afterword

This afterword was related to me by a long-time acquaintance, Sid Martin. It tells not only of the shocking universality of the problems in our industry, but also of the need for constant vigilance, no matter where we are, to ensure high quality both in our management and in the systems that we produce.

The life of a programmer is not the glamorous life that some people envision. It's certainly not what I expected when I entered this business twenty years ago. I was lured to data processing by movie images of computers, with their flashing lights and spinning tape drives. Somehow, I classed computers with jet planes and sports cars. I thought that by becoming a programmer, I'd be pulling over into life's fast lane. The white heat of technology burned in my soul.

But things just haven't worked out. Twenty years later, as I've watched my former colleagues becoming analysts, managers, and database consultants, I'm still nowhere. Although officially I'm called a senior systems specialist, my only assignments are the dregs that no one else in the shop will accept.

Take last Wednesday, for example. I worked until midnight debugging a program that had to be delivered the following morning. Scarcely had I gotten home than the phone rang. The nightly customer accounts system had broken down again and the regular maintenance programmer was on vacation. So, once again, dogsbody's name had appeared at the top of the call-out list. But I was so used to that, I'd even stopped asking, "Why me?"

I managed to fix the problem and returned home by six that morning, time enough to grab a few hours' sleep before a mandatory one o'clock project meeting. I knew I'd probably have to work until midnight again in order to make some urgent changes to the receivables system. This was the wrong morning to get a 9 a.m. call from Gulliver Watson.

I hadn't seen or heard anything from Gulliver in five years or more. He had been my boss for a time and then he had been my boss's boss. Suddenly and inexplicably, he had vanished. Rumors of his whereabouts abounded for a while, with sightings of him in a sail boat near Maui and reports of post cards mailed from Sumatra or Bhutan. Yet others reported he'd become a wind surfing instructor in the Endive Islands. Interest in his fate eventually waned, and I was one of the few in the shop who even remembered Gulliver Watson.

Not that my memories of him were pleasant. He was a short, stocky man with a grey beard shaped like a spade; he resembled one of those stone gnomes that grace certain people's lawns. With an intense and caustic personality, he embraced various bizarre crusades and regarded anyone who didn't share his views to be beneath contempt. Once, for example, he ate only bread and water for a week as a protest against the "cruel treatment" of mass-produced vegetables. Still, he always carried out his job diligently, and was a rising star in the shop when he disappeared.

Here was a call from him after all these years. To me, of all people! And in the middle of the night (to me, anyway). Did he want his old job back? If he did, he'd called the wrong guy. I certainly had no pull with upper management. I couldn't even get my own brother a job as a janitor at the company.

"Sidney?" he shouted over the background din. (Apparently, he was calling from a subway station or airport runway.) "How about dinner tonight?"

I explained my work schedule. He was sympathetic but persistent. "Lunch, then. I know a great sushi bar. Meet me there at 11:30 so we can beat the crowd." Resignedly, I agreed, got directions, and hung up.

Sushi Gizmo was an interesting little restaurant, which contrived to combine the Japanese love of raw fish with their devotion to gadgetry. Covering every wall were robotic dolls, costumed I imagined from scenes in Kabuki plays. Tucked away in a corner was the sushi bar, where I found Gulliver. Ignoring my outstretched hand, he gave me a bear hug that left me speechless.

"Sidney, good of you to come. Have a seat right here." I sat down, gave my order, and asked, "So, Gulliver, what have you been up to these past five years? I've heard some pretty weird stories about you."

He smiled. "All of them true, I'm sure, all true. To begin, I've spent some time in the Pacific area."

"Japan?"

"No, an entirely different part of the Pacific," he replied enigmatically. "The Inscitian Islands."

"I've never heard of them."

"Few people have. They were opened to tourists about twenty years ago, but tourists are admitted only by personal invitation of King Zoot. That way, the islanders reap tourist revenue, but they avoid their small country's being ravaged by mindless, shutter-happy hordes."

"How did you hear of them?"

"Serendipity of the most unfortunate kind," he replied. "It all started after I traveled around Europe and was just about broke. I needed a job, but I wanted to continue traveling. Then, opportunity fell into my lap.

"A small European computer company needed someone to oversee the exporting of its computers to Australia. The job included supervising the loading of the machines at the dock to their installation at the client's site. I was ideal for the job, and it suited my goals. But, fate intervened to change my plans.

"The first shipment of computers was loaded on board, and I settled in for the journey to Australia. Our voyage passed uneventfully until, a few days from our destination, a fearful storm came up. Our captain's efforts to control the ship were useless, and we landed on the reefs around the Inscitian Islands. We had to abandon ship in lifeboats.

"Many of the crew were lost. The lifeboats with the survivors drifted ashore at various of the Inscitian Islands, but I was the only one to be cast ashore on the island of Toog.

"When I'd recovered and the storm had abated, I spotted some native fishermen. Using hand signals, I persuaded them to salvage the cargo from the wreck. They hauled what they could of the computers ashore and, miraculously, some of them still worked."

I interrupted at this point. "But where on earth did you find power for the machines?"

"Ah, you see, electricity was one of the benefits that tourism had brought, and the island of Toog had become a curious mix of witch doctors, grass huts, and television sets. Now, with some clever rigging on my part, it also had computers. The electronic and the paleolithic sat side by side.

"It wasn't long, of course, before King Zoot heard of the unexpected bounty brought to his shores. He ordered it all be carried to the main island of Great Inscitia, to be used by the state airline, Garusum Airways. However, to appease the Toogans, he consented to leave them one small but complete computer system, which had become a cult object. I thought this more than generous, as I couldn't see how the Toogans could use even a fraction of the computer's capacity. But it turned out I was wrong."

I had to interrupt again. "Why didn't the European company claim its equipment?"

"It did. Or, rather, its insurance company did, and most vociferously, too. But, King Zoot was too canny for them; he insisted that the claim be heard in Inscitian courts. When the case came before the judge, who coincidentally was King Zoot's brother-in-law, he dismissed it out of hand. So, the Inscitians kept their machines.

"They also kept me. King Zoot issued a—how shall I put it?—very firm invitation to me to remain there until I had written some software for the airline and had trained some natives to take over from me. I well remember the King's phone call. Though his voice was barely audible over the crackles of the primitive telephone line, I heard his command in the halting English that he spoke: 'Mr. Watson, stay here. I need you.'

"It took me about eighteen months to get some basic accounting applications running and to train people in operating the machine. Just as I was about to leave, King Zoot invited me again in his own special way to help the Toogans."

We were almost out of beer, so I ordered more. "Two large drafts, please." Gulliver resumed his tale.

"Surprisingly, the Toogans had many ideal applications for computerization. For one, their priests were keen astronomers, with heaps of data to record and predictive algorithms to implement. Their existing methods were, so to speak, cast in stone: The priests had elaborate assemblies of rock pillars whose various alignments and shadows were used both to record and to predict astrological events. Unfortunately, subtle slippages of the ground beneath these pillars meant they needed constant maintenance. Also, the high priests' requirements for astronomical data kept changing because no one had assessed what they really needed. So, teams of Toogans had to regularly uproot the giant pillars and move them to new locations. A truly monumental effort!"

As our beers arrived, Gulliver continued. "It didn't take long to transfer their stone and papyrus astronomical systems to the computer. But then we ran into a difficult problem. Toog, you see, really has two halves: east of the mountains, where I was, is East Toog, which is inhabited by a large, powerful tribe. West of the mountains, in West Toog, there live a dozen or so small, but ferociously independent tribes, which don't see eye to eye with the East Toogans on most issues.

"For example, the East and West Toogans use different alphabets. The East Toogan's alphabet is large, rather complex, and not always logical; the West Toogans have a simpler, more streamlined alphabet. I used the East Toogan alphabet to write the systems for the computer, but the West Toogans were so upset with my choice they refused to use any of the computer output and actually prepared to go to war with the East Toogans over the issue.

"King Zoot, when he heard of the war plans, was outraged. The last thing he needed was a civil war in his kingdom. So, he slapped a court order on the East Toogans that prohibited them from imposing their alphabet as a de facto standard. The East Toogans, in turn, hired lawyers on Great Inscitia to fight the injunction, and the court battle is going on to this day. I shouldn't be surprised if it's never resolved to everyone's satisfaction.

"That problem was nothing compared to those we had with the Toogan fishermen, however. They're a close-knit, suspicious, cantankerous group; no Toogan can become a fisherman unless his father was a fisherman. To safeguard their monopoly on fishing, they jealously guard their trade secrets."

"Why did you have to get mixed up with the fishermen anyway?" I asked.

"They asked me to help them with fish migrations. You see, many factors affect the patterns of fish movements, and the relationships between the various factors are complex. Just as the fishermen would figure out where the fish would be, then the fish would migrate somewhere else. So, since the fishermen rescued the machine in the first place, they felt they deserved its help in predicting where the fish would be.

"Unfortunately, they behaved petulantly; they refused, for instance, to use the tide predictions worked out by the priests because they hated and distrusted the priests. So, the fishermen insisted on using their own inaccurate tide predictions. We thus had to keep two inconsistent sets of tide data in our database. The problems worsened when we added all the other seasonal data that the fishermen needed.

"Nevertheless, we triumphed in the end, and the GHOTI project was a success. We called it GHOTI because that is the Toogan word for 'fish.' As we turned out beautifully accurate fish flow diagrams on a color plotter, the fish catches burgeoned, as did the fishermen's profits. My story doesn't end, though, on this happy note.

"A priest was operating the computer during 'ancestor shift' (the time we call the 'graveyard shift'). He purloined extra copies of the fish flow diagrams and gave them to his brother-in-law. This person, along with some of his buddies, set up a major fish-poaching ring. Since the poachers operated in the same areas with the legitimate fishermen, they continually risked being caught.

"To help his brother-in-law, the priest who stole the diagrams began altering a few numbers in the database to steer the fishermen away from the best fishing areas and away from the poachers, as well.

"Rumors of this poaching gang eventually reached the Toogan Police. To catch the poachers, the police set up a sting operation, called Operation Goldfish Bowl. With officers posing as black marketeers, they lured the poaching fishermen into a room by offers of extravagant payments for their catches. Other officers watched the dealings from another room, and then they carted all the poachers off to jail.

"The poachers, after initial refusals to reveal their methods, eventually confessed all. Soon, the police weren't the only Toogans to know of the glaring holes in our data security. As soon as the fishermen heard the news, their distrust of the priests confirmed anew, they returned to their traditional pre-computerized fishing methods. Practically overnight, our success turned into failure, and all because of our lax data security."

Something puzzled me during Gulliver's account. "Gulliver," I asked, "it seems to me that none of the Toogan projects was small . . . "

"True."

" . . . so how could you possibly have done all that work singlehandedly? I mean, you must have had some help, right?"

"Oh, for sure. Every project involved a dozen or so Toogans."

"So, how did you manage this motley group of would-be DPers?"

"A very good question, Sidney, which I can begin to answer by describing our organization. The priests had total control. They believed in a structure that you might call 'dynamic.' Every month, on the first appearance of the new moon, the priests reorganized: They assigned the workers new jobs and new responsibilities; analysts became programmers, programmers became operators, and so on. These reorganizations were accompanied by elaborate tribal ceremonies, with much dancing, shouting, and human sacrifice that lasted a full day and a night."

"But that must have been terribly disruptive."

"Oh, yes, work stopped completely during the ceremonies, while the Toogans waited and wondered at their new assignments."

"No, I meant the continual reorganizations must have been disruptive."

"Well, they were, but not as much as you would think. The Toogan priests didn't reassign the most productive people. They only reorganized the workers who didn't do much anyway. In fact, the reorganizations were beneficial in one way: The troublemakers had hardly any time to make mischief before they were shifted to another position."

Since I'd just been working on some programming estimates, I asked Gulliver about the estimating techniques he'd used.

"The Toogans used a simple but effective project estimating technique. Two teams were formed, one team of analysts, programmers, and other workers; and one team of managers. Each team estimated the time required to complete the project. The teams then grabbed opposite ends of a long rope and pulled as hard as they could. The team that pulled harder got to use its estimate for the project.

"To motivate the contestants, they placed a pile of hot coals between the teams. Because most of the managers were better fed and stronger than the programmers, the team with the managers almost invariably won, and so it was the analysts and programmers who got burned."

This so-called estimating technique, I thought to myself, was at once barbaric and absurd. I was glad we didn't practice such things in our shop. Gulliver broke into my thoughts: "If you think that's strange, quality control was even more amazing. Every new program has bugs, and ours were no exception, even after the programmers had supposedly debugged them. So, the witch doctor was assigned the task of exorcising the bugs. Going into a trance, he whooped and danced in a frenzy around the computer. Next, he poured coconut milk over the program listing and ended by sticking long pins into an effigy of the coder."

"Did that work?" I asked in disbelief.

"No, but it sure looked good. The witch doctor eventually came to grief, however, after he released a faulty astronomical program into production and the chief astronomer waited all night in vain for an occultation of Feles Minor by Jupiter."

"What happened to him?"

"The priests sold him to some headhunters from the north side of the island. I dread to think of the ghastly things they did to him. Life on Toog can be brutal."

This didn't seem brutal to me. Quite fair, in fact. I could think of several people in our shop whom I'd be very happy to pack off to the north side of Toog. At that point, I glanced at my watch and realized in horror that I was already ten minutes late for my project meeting. "Gulliver, I have to run."

"But don't you want to hear how I escaped from Toog?"

"I'm sorry, Gulliver, but it's later than you think. Some other time, perhaps." We paid the check and left. I assessed the relative speeds of taxis and trains, and I decided to treat myself to a taxi. I grabbed a cab that had just deposited its fare. Gulliver gave me a farewell bear hug, and I bade him to call me again soon.

As we drove through Manhattan, the familiar sights of Macy's and Times Square seemed wildly inappropriate. Where were the mangrove swamps and dense jungles? My mind was still on the island of Toog.

When I got back to the shop, Debbie (the chief analyst on our project) was waiting for me. She wasn't pleased. "Sid, you should have been here at one o'clock."

"Why, what happened?" I asked.

She gave me a poisonous stare. I began telling her about my lunch with Gulliver, but I could see I was getting nowhere. "I think that working nights has finally gotten to you," she said. "Come on, Sid. Pete is already in the meeting room."

Pete, our project manager, didn't look very pleased with me either. "Sid," he said, "I've just been reviewing your programming estimates for the PISCES project with some of the user management. We all agree that your figures are much too high. It would be better for all concerned if you reduced them to a more realistic level."

I looked at Debbie for some support for my estimates, but she offered none. So, alone and facing the massed strength of these management heavyweights, I had no other option but to give in. "Okay, Pete, I'll cut the flab out of my estimates and revise them downward."

Pete looked satisfied, but his next words chilled my blood: "Now let me tell you all about our forthcoming departmental reorganization. . . ."

Appendix A

Derivation of a Project's CPM Chart

A critical path method (CPM) chart is a kind of network diagram that has as its purpose to schedule and coordinate the various activities and events of a project [Gallagher and Watson, 1980]. Another example of a network diagram is a program evaluation and review technique (PERT) chart. The most common graphic convention to construct CPM charts uses the four symbols shown in Figure A.1.

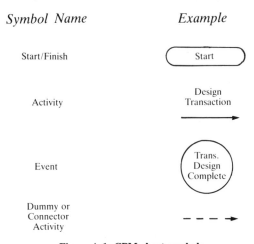

Symbol Name	*Example*
Start/Finish	Start
Activity	Design Transaction
Event	Trans. Design Complete
Dummy or Connector Activity	

Figure A.1. CPM chart symbols.

In Figure A.2 is an example of a CPM chart for the simple project of making a cup of instant coffee with cream. Notice the chronological scale at the bottom of the chart. The project is begun at time 0, event A is reached after two minutes, B is reached after three minutes, and so on, until the project is completed after a total of eight minutes. Observe also the three-minute slack time between events B and C. This implies that even if we were three minutes late in measuring the coffee, the project would not be delayed. Hence, measuring the coffee is not in the critical path of the project, the path START/A/C/D/FINISH, as indicated. If the completion of any one of the activities on the critical path were delayed, however, the whole project would be delayed by an equal amount.

In addition to describing each of the events in the CPM chart, I usually find it worthwhile to list the assumptions upon which the validity of the CPM chart depends. In this example, I assume that the following are available: water, kettle, source of heat, measuring device (spoon, for example), cup, cream, and coffee. If any of these assumptions were not true, the CPM chart would have to be modified to include, for example, the activity, "Run to store to buy coffee."

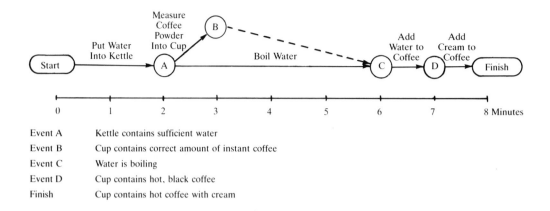

Event A	Kettle contains sufficient water
Event B	Cup contains correct amount of instant coffee
Event C	Water is boiling
Event D	Cup contains hot, black coffee
Finish	Cup contains hot coffee with cream

Figure A.2. CPM chart for the coffee making project.

A.1 Deriving a CPM chart from a DFD

How do you derive a CPM chart for a project? A good method is to convert a data flow diagram of the project into a CPM chart. This conversion is basically straightforward:

1.   Convert the DFD bubbles into CPM activity arrows.

2.   Convert the DFD arrows between bubbles into events that link the completion of one activity to the inception of the next.

However, be aware of a number of subtleties in the transition from the DFD to the CPM chart. As an example, let's convert the DFD in Figure A.3 for the coffee making project into a CPM chart. If the procedure is exactly as I described above, we should get the CPM chart in Figure A.2.

To begin, we draw an event named START. Next, we look for activities or bubbles on the DFD that can begin immediately. These are bubbles numbered 1 and 3, whose inputs rely only on the first assumption of the project (that is, the availability of the kettle and a measuring device such as a spoon). These steps give us the partial CPM charts of Figure A.4.

Now, we look for activities that can begin as soon as either event A or B has been reached. "Boil water" can begin once the kettle contains sufficient water (event A), giving us Figure A.5. Continuing this way gives us Figure A.6. The dotted line in the figure is needed from B to C to show that C depends upon B's completion, but that no activity is required between B and C. In order to complete the CPM chart for the coffee making project, we need only estimate the time required to derive each activity on the chart (a process that, of course, usually requires a great deal of effort). Then, the CPM chart should be exactly like Figure A.2.

However, Figures A.2 and A.6 don't look the same at all. For one thing, measuring the coffee into the cup begins at different times in the two charts. The reason is that the measuring coffee activity and the filling kettle activity go on in parallel. That's fine, since neither activity depends on the other. But (and this is a big "but") Figure A.6 assumes that two people are available to carry out these two activities at the same time. However, this is pointless extravagance. Since event B is not on the critical path, there is no hurry to get it done. Thus, we can get rid of a pair of hands by moving "measure coffee" back to its position in Figure A.2. Then, the person who is free after

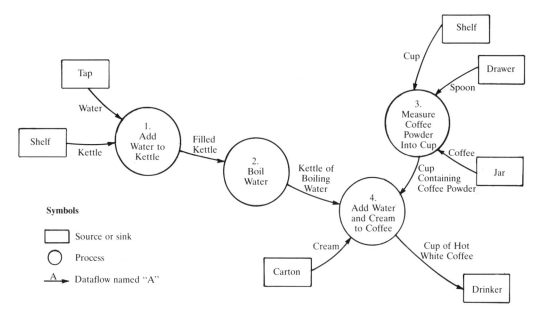

Figure A.3. DFD for the coffee making project.

Figure A.4. Partial CPM charts.

event A can measure the coffee while the water is being boiled. (We can assume that the stove will boil the water without further human effort.)

Note that the final activity in the chart of Figure A.6, "add water and cream to coffee," is really two activities. I should probably have drawn it as two bubbles on the DFD, but I did this purposely to show you the kind of thing that is typical in practice. This activity can be broken into its components in two different ways: serially or in parallel. As shown in Figure A.7, the serial decomposition of the activity produces the CPM chart of Figure A.2. The parallel decomposition, however, has a definite advantage over the serial decomposition. Since adding the water and the cream is on the critical path of the project, anything that we can do to speed it up will speed up the whole project. On the other hand, to implement this parallel decomposition, we'll need to hire an extra worker. Furthermore, adding the water and the cream at the same time may produce an inferior cup of coffee. Check bubble 4's specification that accompanies the DFD in Figure A.3 to determine such effects.

A.2 Benefits of the CPM chart and the DFD

If a CPM chart can be derived from a DFD, why then do you as project manager need a CPM chart as well as a DFD? There are two reasons, both of which stem from the difference

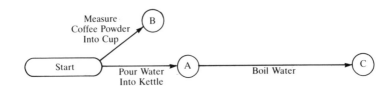

Figure A.5. Partial CPM chart.

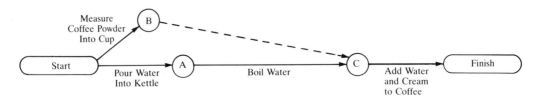

Figure A.6. CPM chart for the coffee making project.

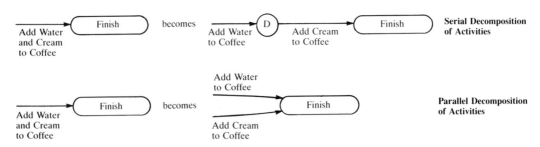

Figure A.7. Serial and parallel decomposition of activities in the coffee making project.

between the two tools: A DFD shows what is to be done, while the CPM chart shows how it is to be done.

The first reason for having both tools is that you can create a large variety of CPM charts from a single DFD. Which CPM chart you choose depends on your strategy as the marshal of the project's resources. For example, as we saw above, you have many options in selecting the serial or parallel arrangement of activities as you decide how you wish to deploy your resources.

The second reason is that a CPM chart shows explicit timings of activities, which a DFD does not. This is important in determining the critical path of your project, whose activities demand the most meticulous management. However, many managers do not draw their CPM chart to chronological scale as I did in, for instance, Figure A.2. This is because of the tedium of updating the chart if schedules slip. Nevertheless, you must always indicate on the CPM chart in some way the duration of each activity so that you can compute the critical path. A computer will help you greatly in evaluating and maintaining a CPM chart.

Another question might have occurred to you: Why do I need a DFD of my project if I'm going to be using CPM charts? The answer is that it's difficult to plan your project's strategy if you don't have a clear idea of the project activities and their interrelationships. Specifically, you need to know which activities depend for their input on the output of which other activities, as depicted by the DFD. Your job as project manager is to decide how best to work within your constraints to best serve the users' business. The CPM chart you produce will reflect your decisions in the form of a definite plan and organization for activities.

Appendix B

Problem Solving

Investigation may be likened to the long months of pregnancy, and solving a problem to the day of birth. To investigate a problem is, indeed, to solve it.

—Mao Tse-tung, 1930

A problem is the cause, or set of causes, of one or more undesirable effects. Problem diagnosis is the determination of the cause or causes, usually by working backward from the undesirable effects. Problem solving is the removal of the undesirable effects by eliminating one or more of their causes. For example, an undesirable effect might be poor terminal response time on a multiuser mainframe computer. What is the problem, the cause of this effect? There may be many causes, acting either together or separately. For instance, the computer may not have a powerful enough CPU, or the system may be overloaded with users, or the priority parameters for jobs in the operating system may be wrongly set.

In order to solve the problem of poor response time, it is necessary to remove or minimize one or more of the causes contributing to that undesirable effect. But those causes may themselves be the effects of deeper causes. In order to solve the original problem, then, it may be necessary to go through several levels of causes to find the cause that can be removed or reduced.

For example, a problem may be that my car is too expensive to operate. The specific cause of that undesirable effect is that it gets poor gas mileage, which may be caused by dirty spark plugs. To state this situation graphically, we have Figure B.1.

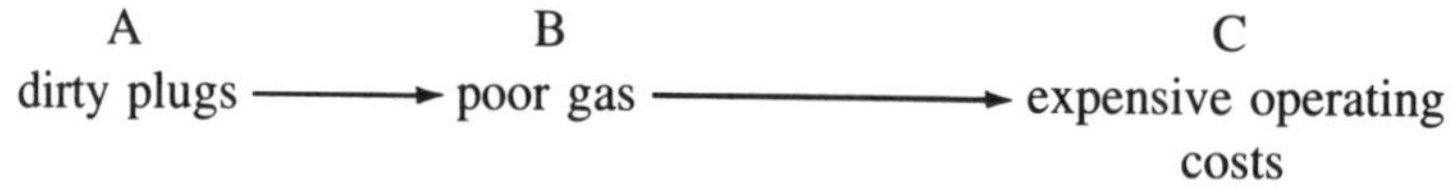

A   B   C

dirty plugs ⟶ poor gas ⟶ expensive operating costs

Figure B.1. Simple cause-effect diagram.

Notice what this diagram means: A is the cause of B (or B is the effect of A) and B is the cause of C (or C is the effect of B). So, is B a cause or an effect? Of course, it's both: the effect of A and the cause of C. Thus, causes and effects are interrelated and there is no such thing as an absolute cause or an absolute effect.

Thus, to solve problem C, I could tackle its direct cause by trading in my car, for example, or tackle the cause of B by changing the spark plugs. Figure B.1 is a simple example of a cause-effect diagram whose purpose is to determine the possibly complex relationship between causes and effects, with an eye to solving the particular problem. Below is a more complex example of a cause-effect diagram, with an explanation of its symbols. Figure B.2 means A is caused by B or C, or D and E acting together; B is caused by F and G together; C is caused by G or H; D is caused by I; and E is caused by J.

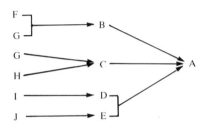

Figure B.2. Symbols in a cause-effect diagram.

The way to construct a cause-effect diagram is to write down the undesirable effect (the problem) to be solved on the right side of the page. To its left, write down all the causes that you can think of, noting whether the causes are linked by ANDs or by ORs. Then, consider each of those causes as problems (that is, as undesirable effects of something), and identify their causes to the left side of the page.

If you create a cause-effect diagram for the problem of terminal response time, you might get Figure B.3. Obviously, you could pursue this network indefinitely, but you must cut your network construction off somewhere. Two guidelines to help limit the scope of study are, first, Concentrate on the piece of the network that you find experimentally to hold the predominant causes of your problem. For example, if you find that the major cause of poor response time is "system is compute-bound," there is little point in your developing a sophisticated network of causes for "disk access is slow or inefficient." You should instead concentrate on "CPU is not powerful enough" and "too heavy a load of computing is being done."

A second guideline is, Concentrate on causes that you can eliminate rather than those that are beyond your ken, budget, or means. For example, your computer might speed up if the velocity of light were increased, but don't work too hard on that cause. Move back to earth, and if you find that the cause of your poor response time is a compute-bound system, you can either increase your CPU power or decrease your computing load. However, if you currently lease a Crayfish Megathinker ZX/168 CPU, which is already straining your budget, you'd be wise to consider ways to reduce your computing load instead (unless, that is, you care to tackle the causes of the strained budget).

B.1 The problem solving procedure

To sum up this appendix, I show the problem solving procedure broken into its eight component steps. These steps form a general strategy, rather than a rigorous algorithm for solving a problem.

1. Write down the undesirable effect you wish to eliminate. Mark it with an asterisk.

2. Build a cause-effect diagram, working one or two levels to the left of the asterisk.

3. Determine experimentally and/or by discussion with experts, consultants, and colleagues the major cause of the effect marked with an asterisk.

4. Mark the cause with an asterisk and delete the previous asterisk.

5. If this cause is not directly removable, return to step 2.

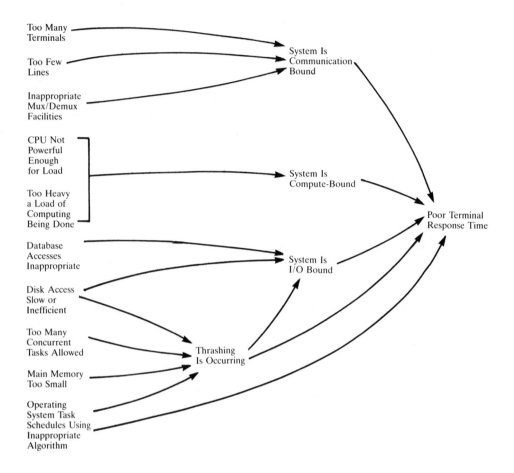

Figure B.3. Cause-effect diagram for terminal response time.

6. If the cause can be directly removed, establish a plan to eliminate or greatly reduce the asterisked cause. (Note that removing this cause may not only solve the intended problem but also produce other effects. If these side effects are collectively bad, the cure for the problem might be worse than the disease.)

7. Execute the plan.

8. Determine how well the problem was solved.

Appendix C

Qualities of a Good Manager

It seems as hard to pin down the qualities of a fine manager as it is to describe those of a fine wine. Giegold, for example, lists more than two hundred desirable characteristics of a good manager, while Sinetar analyzes managerial qualities into three broad, somewhat overlapping categories: leadership, parental, and administrative skills [Giegold, 1982; Sinetar, 1984]. Sinetar then divides each category into personality traits and communication skills. Into each of these six subcategories, she places an average of eight skills and traits important to an effective manager, to yield a total of almost fifty vital managerial attributes—another daunting inventory.

I don't claim that my list of twelve desirable qualities is the result of a thorough scientific study. However, they are the qualities possessed by the most effective managers whom I've observed over the years. If you are already a manager or intend to become one, these are the qualities for you to nurture in yourself. If you are scouting for people to elevate to managership, carefully assess a candidate's strength in each of these characteristics: personal integrity, sensitivity, ability to set objectives, ability to plan, tenacity, inspirational ability, willingness to serve, courage to delegate, technical competence, communication ability, ability to be innovative, and courage to make decisions.

C.1 Personal integrity

Personal integrity is an essential quality in a manager, who must stand up for what he believes is right, rejecting both invidious politics and copycat behavior. Sometimes, he needs to translate personal integrity into righteous anger in order to have the strength of commitment to stand alone from the crowd.

A manager cannot be a pusillanimous, hand-wringing puppet who is manipulated by various special interest groups. A strong manager has a hard-headed dedication to his job, his users, and his staff. He does not have the qualities of bone-headed arrogance, treachery, and lust for power.

But he must also be able to admit an error and to put aside personal pride for the good of the whole organization. He must not allow himself to be bamboozled into knowingly making wrong decisions for the sake of personal expediency, for to do so is to risk betraying both his company and his subordinates. Being an effective manager who does a good job is more important than looking good.

C.2 Sensitivity

A good manager is sensitive to people and is to some degree a psychotherapist in his ability to respond to his subordinate's needs and foibles. Although this quality is not universal to all

217

managers, sensitivity is necessary for a team and DP shop to benefit from its major resource: the human one.

An effective way in which to show sensitivity to subordinates is to schedule an hour or so per week or per month simply to allow each employee to discuss openly and off the record any subject that he wishes.

C.3 Ability to set objectives

A manager must be able to set objectives that are consistent with the objectives of the corporation, always retaining a sense of proportion. Some objectives may be worth achieving, but not worth what it takes to achieve them. Keep in mind that the end must always justify the means.

Furthermore, the effective manager must never be afraid to abandon objectives that are no longer valid. For example, if an objective is to optimize the flow of materials in the manufacture of sealing wax but the market for sealing wax disappears, the objective must be changed.

C.4 Ability to meet objectives

Setting an objective is, of itself, not enough. The true test of the manager's resolve is the ability to plan to meet and to achieve that objective. A good manager must be able to figure out how to translate the current situation into the situation called for by his objectives. The most important tasks in preparing to meet an objective are planning, organizing, integrating, measuring, and revising, all covered in Chapter 6.

C.5 Tenacity

To get the job done, a manager needs more than objectives and plans. He needs action. He not only has to know how to get from here to there, but he must also actually make the journey, persevering through setbacks until he reaches his destination.

Thomsett points out that a vital component of managerial tenacity is the ability to negotiate [Thomsett, 1980]. Much of a manager's time is spent in negotiation: negotiating with users over deadlines, with other managers to obtain workers, with vendors over prices and delivery, with team members over weekend work, and so on. A good manager, therefore, is not daunted by roadblocks. Of course, he doesn't drive straight into them, nor does he stop in his tracks, but he negotiates adroitly around them. Also, if the project strays from the route, he must be able to get it back on track and to even rescue it from the ditch, if necessary, and get it going again.

C.6 Ability to inspire

A manager's staff amplifies his efforts, so that feats many times larger in scope and ambition can be accomplished than the manager could perform by himself. This amplifying effect depends upon a vital proviso: the manager's ability to inspire his staff members to act to the fullest of their abilities.

A manager can inspire his staff members in several ways. One way is to eliminate as much mediocrity as possible from their working lives in order to give them every chance to perform well. Another important way for a manager to inspire his staff is for him to set a good example.

The most effective inspirer, however, is a manager who shows qualities of leadership. It is almost as difficult to define the attributes of a good leader as it is to define those of a good manager. But I think that Sinetar comes as close as anyone in encapsulating those attributes. The words and actions of a leader, she says, bring security, solidarity, and cohesion to his people. Using positive words and tone, he speaks with personal vision. His demeanor radiates vigor, energy, and drive.

To these attributes, I add that a leader inspires his people to strive for success and to overcome difficulties. He also communicates clearly his goals, their justification, and his plan to reach those goals. In doing this, he does not make light of problems, but communicates reality. Then, he rallies his staff to move forward in unison.

C.7 Willingness to serve

A marvelous stereotype of the decision-making executive is a middle-aged man, grim-faced as a granite cliff, sitting behind a gigantic, polished oak desk. On the desk is an intercom, a telephone, a blotter, a small, neat pile of papers, and a pen stand. To his side is the latest desktop computer, displaying some colorful graphics on its screen. Behind the executive is a breathtaking view of a city skyline.

The man exudes power. He presses the intercom and speaks: "Miss Sims, have Johnson from Sales come up to my office at once, and tell Smith from Manufacturing I want to see him at 10:30." Within seconds, Johnson appears.

"Johnson, I've decided to open up the People's Republic of China. I want to see your marketing plan for that country on my desk by 8 a.m. Friday. That's all."

"Very good, J.P."

Later, a crestfallen Smith is shown in. "J.P., I—"

"No excuses, Smith. I've just seen last month's production report. You're fired."

And so it continues: a stream of instant one-man decisions and dramatic actions. For such a go-getting, no-nonsense, decision-making corporate executive, no problem is so large that he cannot think of a solution by himself in minutes and immediately bark orders to his cowering underlings, sending them into a frenzy of activity.

This image that has so captured the popular mind is not only how many managers want others to see them, but also how they want to see themselves. These managers equate management with power and they feel that to be good managers, they must exert their power to the utmost. As a none-too-successful DP manager once expressed it to me, "Power is delightful; absolute power is absolutely delightful."

In contrast to such movie stereotypes of powerful managers, good managership is achieved through dedicated service to worthwhile objectives and through the fulfillment of managerial obligations. The motto "Nobless oblige" ("Rank brings obligations") and the motto of the Prince of Wales "Ich dien" ("I serve") apply especially to managers. Whom does a manager serve and what are his obligations? Obviously, there are obligations to his superordinates and to the whole corporation. He also needs to serve the objectives of his job. Other obligations of the rank include serving the users of the DP facilities and the people working under his direction.

Many managers refuse to view their role in this unassuming way. After all, the manager is higher on the organizational chart than his subordinates. How can he possibly be the servant of his people? The problem is that the organizational chart is a distorted picture of an organization because it emphasizes lines of authority at the expense of lines of contribution. I prefer to turn every organizational chart upside down and to redraw it slightly, as I've done to Figure C.1 to produce Figure C.2.

I see Figure C.2 as a map showing rivers that carry not water, but contributions to the department's objectives. Workers provide the rivers' source with their talents and their efforts. Managers provide confluences for several streams and create broader, faster rivers of contribution from all flows in their catchment area. Many managers thus prefer to think of themselves as being the confluence of talents, rather than the servant of the people. A good manager, therefore, is someone who devotes himself to the users and their needs, his department and its needs, and his project team members and their needs.

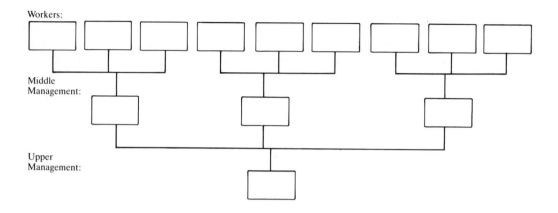

Figure C.1. Upside-down organizational chart.

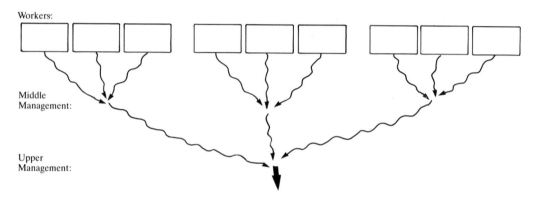

Figure C.2. Chart redrawn to show rivers of contribution.

C.8 Courage to delegate

An effective manager has the wisdom and courage to delegate not only tasks, but also decisions directly related to those tasks. He knows to first break an objective into discrete subobjectives and to assign workers to each subobjective in accordance with their ability and experience. Although he retains responsibility for the overall objective and authority over all its subobjectives, the manager allows the workers themselves to plan the execution of each sub- objective. He also decentralizes the decision making related to each plan in order for the executor of each subobjective to be largely (but not necessarily completely) autonomous. The manager does not intervene in the execution of a subobjective so long as it follows closely to its plan, and intervenes only judiciously in a subobjective's execution that diverges from its plan.

An ineffective manager fails to delegate for a variety of reasons. He may distrust his subordinates' competence, believing that it's always quicker and safer to do the job himself. He may fear that delegation is the first step of being usurped or that a subordinate will discover a weakness in the manager's performance. He may also resent losing credit for work done by a subordinate.

C.9 Technical competence

An effective DP project manager does not become technically obsolete or ignorant of the techniques used on his project. Similarly, a DP staff manager keeps technically current with the technology of his area. Therefore, a competent manager cannot be created from a technically incompetent worker, any more than frog's eggs can become caviar.

C.10 Ability to communicate reality

The ability to communicate reality has three components: discovering reality, respecting it, and communicating it to others. The most important channel for communicating reality, as Drucker points out, is the upward channel [Drucker, 1973]. This means for the manager to listen effectively to the views and ideas of subordinates and to present carefully his own views and ideas to them. Diplomacy and tact are also central features of good communication and the ability to inspire people is a tremendous bonus. Look for these qualities in a potential managerial candidate and encourage their development by providing opportunities to gather information and make presentations.

C.11 Ability to think and be innovative

The ability to think creatively is indispensable in a manager. IBM's founder, Thomas J. Watson, Sr., believed it so vital in an employee that he ordered "THINK" signs posted throughout the corporation. How effective managers think is in many ways similar to how chess grandmasters select their next moves. Like grandmasters, good managers seem not to rely on pure logic alone, but fuse logic, intuition, creativity, experience, pattern recognition, intellectual daring, and who knows what else into their own style of thinking.

In considering someone for promotion, look for somebody who not only thinks in order to do his job, but also thinks about his job. A good candidate is someone who suggests ways to improve his job, ways to make it more interesting, and ways to better fit it with his colleagues' jobs. Better yet, he sees his job from a higher perspective—that of the position to which he wants to be promoted. Best of all, he thinks *above* his potential new position. In other words, if he can think at two levels about his current position, he is almost certainly ready for promotion.

C.12 Courage to make decisions

An effective manager possesses courage to make tough decisions. There are managers who fear making a decision because they don't want the responsibility for having made the wrong decision. All decisions involve risk and, over his management career, no manager can hope to have a perfect success rate.

In principle, selecting one course of action from many alternatives is easy: Choose the option with the greatest yield and least cost. In practice, unfortunately, making a decision is never that simple. One reason is that the various options under consideration typically have benefits or costs that are hard to compare. How do you decide, for example, between one option that costs three chickens and an apple and yields a camel and two oranges, and another choice that costs a goat and five lemons and yields two ducks and a sheep?

A second difficulty in making decisions is that a manager rarely gets full and precise information on each option. Therefore, he usually must make assumptions and/or evaluate probabilities in order to make comparisons. To minimize these two difficulties, a good manager seeks other people's advice. He is not afraid to solicit information from several different sources and advice in comparing different options.

Comparing different options requires experience and good judgment, without making wild assumptions. For example, a DP manager who chooses to decrease the users' costs by $20,000 rather than to increase their revenues by $200,000 (assuming roughly equal project costs) is probably misguided. Or, if person A makes a decision assuming a die will land on six and person B makes a decision assuming the die will not land on six, person B's decision is better, all other things being equal, even if the die does land on six.

To illustrate how disastrous a manager's assumptions can be, let me give an example. A DP project manager decided to implement a semiautomated factory control system, but to save time and money, he decided against developing any manual backup system. In reaching this decision, he assumed that the computer hardware and software would work perfectly from the moment they were installed. However, not only was the system completely new, but so also was the factory, and thus the potential for disaster was very high. However, everything worked as planned, and the manager was promoted for his heroic efforts. Two months later, this same manager undertook a similar gamble in another factory—and lost. Before a backup system could be hastily lashed together, the company sacrificed a great deal of production time and several important orders were delayed as a result.

In making a decision, a good manager doesn't expend disproportionate energy on it. Clearly, something is wrong with managers who spend time in meeting after meeting to discuss the installation of a soft drink machine, but who take only a few minutes to decide on the purchase of a new software package. (Perhaps the reason is that such managers prefer to chat about soft drink machines, rather than software, because they understand soft drinks better than software!)

Making a decision prematurely can be a problem. A decision that can be delayed without jeopardizing anything is best postponed to enable a manager to glean more and better information. However, this should never be used as an excuse for not making a necessary decision. Failing to make a decision is in fact a decision itself: It's a choice to allow the default course of action to occur with the hope that, if things go wrong, no one will notice the manager's responsibility. Usually, this is the worst decision to make.

Vacillating between two possible actions is probably worse than picking one at random. However, if the objective is crucial enough and if an action must be started immediately and if both actions involve a high degree of risk, a good decision might be to do both action A and action B in parallel, if resources are available.

A superior decision maker is not afraid to amend a decision in the light of better information. Of course, making a decision means sticking to it, but if later information reveals that a different decision would be better and if it makes sense to change the decision, then do so. Although it is annoying to all concerned, changing a decision is better than pursuing the wrong course of action.

Bibliography

Ackoff, R.L. *The Art of Problem Solving: Accompanied by Ackoff's Fables.* New York: Wiley-Interscience, 1978.

Albrecht, A. *Measuring Application Development Productivity.* Proceedings of the SHARE/GUIDE Application Development Conference, 1979.

Albrecht, M., Jr. "Managing Careers." *Computerworld,* Vol. 17, No. 33 (August 15, 1983).

Beizer, B. *Software Testing Techniques.* New York: Van Nostrand Reinhold, 1983.

Block, R. *The Politics of Projects.* New York: Yourdon Press, 1983.

Boar, B.H. *Application Prototyping: A Requirements Definition Strategy for the 80's.* New York: Wiley-Interscience, 1984.

Boehm, B.W. *Software Engineering Economics.* Englewood Cliffs, N.J.: Prentice-Hall, 1981.

Brooks, F.P., Jr. *The Mythical Man-Month.* Reading, Mass.: Addison-Wesley, 1975.

Cortada, J.W. *Strategic Data Processing: Considerations for Management.* Englewood Cliffs, N.J.: Prentice-Hall, 1984.

DeBono, E. *Lateral Thinking.* New York: Harper & Row, 1970.

Deken, J. *The Electronic Cottage.* New York: William Morrow & Co., 1981.

DeMarco, T. *Structured Analysis and System Specification.* New York: Yourdon Press, 1978.

_____. *Controlling Software Projects: Management, Measurement & Estimation.* New York: Yourdon Press, 1982.

Dickinson, B. *Developing Structured Systems: A Methodology Using Structured Techniques.* New York: Yourdon Press, 1981.

Donaldson, H. *A Guide to the Successful Management of Computer Projects.* New York: John Wiley & Sons, 1978.

Doyle, M., and D. Straus. *How to Make Meetings Work.* New York: Harper & Row, 1977.

Drucker, P.F. *Management: Tasks, Responsibilities, Practices.* New York: Harper & Row, 1973.

Flavin, M. *Fundamental Concepts of Information Modeling.* New York: Yourdon Press, 1981.

Freedman, D.P., and G.M. Weinberg. *Handbook of Walkthroughs, Inspections, and Technical Reviews,* 3rd ed. Boston: Little, Brown & Co., 1982.

Gallagher, C.A., and H.J. Watson. *Quantitative Methods for Business Decisions.* New York: McGraw-Hill, 1980.

Gane, C., and T. Sarson. *Structured Systems Analysis: Tools & Techniques*. New York: Improved System Technologies, 1977.

Giegold, W.C. *Practical Management Skills for Engineers and Scientists*. Belmont, Calif.: Lifetime Learning Publications, 1982.

Gotlieb, C.C. *The Economics of Computers: Costs, Benefits, Policies & Strategies*. Englewood Cliffs, N.J.: Prentice-Hall, 1985.

Hackman, J.R., and G. Oldham. "Development of the Job Diagnostic Survey." *Journal of Applied Psychology*, Vol. 60 (1975), pp. 159-70.

Lief, R.E., R.D. Dodge, and R.L. Ogden. "Adapting DP Strategy to Management Style." *Computerworld*, Vol. 17, No. 49 (December 5, 1983).

MacGregor, D. *The Professional Manager*. New York: McGraw-Hill, 1967.

Mao Tse-Tung. *Oppose Book Worship*. Peking: Foreign Language Press, 1930.

Martin, J. *Application Development Without Programmers*. Englewood Cliffs, N.J.: Prentice-Hall, 1982a.

_____. *Strategic Data Planning Methodologies*. Englewood Cliffs, N.J.: Prentice-Hall, 1982b.

Maslow, A. *Motivation and Personality*. New York: Harper & Row, 1954.

McMenamin, S.M., and J.F. Palmer. *Essential Systems Analysis*. New York: Yourdon Press, 1984.

Melcher, A.J. *Structure and Process of Organization: A Systems Approach*. Englewood Cliffs, N.J.: Prentice-Hall, 1976.

Metzger, P.W. *Managing a Programming Project*. Englewood Cliffs, N.J.: Prentice-Hall, 1st ed., 1973; 2nd ed., 1981.

Mintzberg, H. *The Structuring of Organizations*. Englewood Cliffs, N.J.: Prentice-Hall, 1979.

Mishan, E.J. *Cost Benefit Analysis*, 3rd ed. Winchester, Mass.: Allen & Unwin, 1982.

Myers, G.J. *The Art of Software Testing*. New York: Wiley-Interscience, 1979.

Nilles, J.M., et al. *Telecommunications/Transportation Tradeoffs for Tomorrow*. New York: Wiley-Interscience, 1976.

Nolan, R.L. "Managing the Crisis in Data Processing." *Harvard Business Review*, Vol. 57, No. 2 (March/April 1979), pp. 115-26.

Olson, M.H. "Remote Office Work: Changing Work Patterns in Space and Time." *Communications of the ACM*, Vol. 26, No. 3 (March 1983).

Ouchi, W.G. *Theory Z: How American Business Can Meet the Japanese Challenge*. Reading, Mass.: Addison-Wesley, 1981.

Page-Jones, M. *The Practical Guide to Structured Systems Design*. New York: Yourdon Press, 1980.

Pascale, R.T., and A.G. Athos. *The Art of Japanese Management: Applications for American Executives*. New York: Simon and Schuster, 1981.

Perry, W.E. *A Structured Approach to Systems Testing*. Wellesley, Mass.: QED Information Sciences, 1983.

Peter, L.J., and R. Hull. *The Peter Principle: Why Things Go Wrong*. New York: Bantam Books, 1970.

Peters, T.J., and R.H. Waterman, Jr. *In Search of Excellence: Lessons from America's Best-Run Companies*. New York: Harper & Row, 1982.

Porter, M.E. *Competitive Strategy: Techniques for Analyzing Industries and Competitors*. New York: Free Press, 1980.

Pressman, R.S. "Software Engineering Targets Future Concerns." *Computerworld*, Vol. 18, No. 22 (May 28, 1984), pp. SR9-12.

Rockart, J.F. "Chief Executives Define Their Own Data Needs." *Harvard Business Review*, Vol. 57, No. 2 (March/April 1979), pp. 81-93.

Rosenau, M.D. *Successful Project Management: A Step-by-Step Approach with Practical Examples*. Belmont, Calif.: Lifetime Learning Publications, 1981.

Sackman, H., W.J. Erikson, and E.E. Grant. "Exploratory Experimental Studies Comparing Online and Offline Programming Performance." *Communications of the ACM*, Vol. 11, No. 1 (January 1968), pp. 3-11.

Sayles, L.R. "Matrix Organization: The Structure with a Future." *Organizational Dynamics*, Autumn 1976, pp. 2-17.

Schoenberg, R.J. *The Art of Being a Boss: Inside Intelligence from Top-Level Business Leaders and Young Executives on the Move*. New York: New American Library, 1980.

Sinetar, M. "Roles Managers Play." *Computerworld*, Vol. 18, No. 8 (February 20, 1984).

Singer, L.M. *The Data Processing Manager's Survival Manual*. New York: Wiley-Interscience, 1982.

Skinner, B.F. *Science and Human Behavior*. New York: Macmillan, 1953.

_____. *About Behaviorism*. New York: Vintage Books, 1976.

Squires, S.L., M. Branstad, and M. Zelkowitz. *ACM Software Engineering Notes: Special Issue on Rapid Prototyping*. New York: Association for Computing Machinery, Vol. 7, No. 5 (December 1982).

Steger, J., G. Manners, A. Bernstein, and R. May. "The Three Dimensions of an R&D Manager's Job." *Research Management*, May 1975, pp. 32-37.

Synnott, W., and W. Gruber. *Information Resource Management: Opportunities and Strategies for the 1980s*. New York: Wiley-Interscience, 1981.

Thomsett, R. *People & Project Management*. New York: Yourdon Press, 1980.

Vroom, V.H., and P.W. Yetton. *Leadership and Decision-Making*. Pittsburgh, Pa.: University of Pittsburgh Press, 1973.

Watson, J.B. *Psychology from the Standpoint of a Behaviorist*. Philadelphia: J.B. Lippincott, 1919.

Weinberg, G.M. *The Psychology of Computer Programming*. New York: Van Nostrand Reinhold, 1971.

_____. *Rethinking Systems Analysis and Design*. Boston: Little, Brown & Co., 1982.

Weinberg, V. *Structured Analysis*. New York: Yourdon Press, 1978.

Wigander, K., A. Svensson, L. Schoug, et al. *Structured Analysis and Design of Information Systems.* New York: McGraw-Hill, 1984.

Yourdon, E. *Structured Walkthroughs,* 2nd ed. New York: Yourdon Press, 1978.

_____. *Managing the Structured Techniques,* 2nd ed. New York: Yourdon Press, 1979.

_____, and L.L. Constantine. *Structured Design: Fundamentals of a Discipline of Computer Program and Systems Design,* 2nd ed. New York: Yourdon Press, 1978.

Index

SUBJECT INDEX

AUTHOR INDEX